BEAT PUNKS

VICTOR BOCKRIS

DA CAPO PRESS

A CIP catalog record for this book is available from the Library of Congress.

ISBN 0-306-80939-7

First Da Capo Press Edition 2000

Published by Da Capo Press
A Member of the Perseus Books Group
http://www.dacapopress.com

1 2 3 4 5 6 7 8 9 10——04 03 02 01 00

When Ted Berrigan, who published one of Burroughs' scrapbooks (*Time*, C Press 1965), took copies of the book to Burroughs in his suite in the Chelsea, he also took a plastic machine gun because he couldn't afford to pay any royalties. 'You looked through the sights of the gun and saw images. "It's an image machine gun," I told him,' Berrigan remembers. 'But he didn't seem impressed, and I got out of there pretty quickly.'

From 'Information about the Operation'
by Victor Bockris

In Australia, you ask about sharks and they glance into their tea: "No mate, no. No worries mate. They only come in January when the water's warm see, otherwise it's perfectly safe to swim, mate."

Excerpt from a news bulletin released March 4 1977: "Next thing I felt it go under our feet again and I said, 'For God's sake Vic, pull your feet up – I think it's a ray or a shark!' I kicked at it, I punched it – it had no effect. I tried to hold Vic with me as he was pulled off the edge of the box. Vic just said: 'It's got me again. Goodbye mates, this is it'."

From 'People of the Dream Time' by "Vic" Bockris. *Traveller's Digest*, 1977.

For Peter Orlovsky and Lydia Lunch
and, in particular, the third mind
Brion Gysin

Contents

Introduction

I have often been asked what the subjects of my books have in common and invariably reply, they were all great talkers. This book celebrates the best of those great talkers. Its theme is the relationship between the Beat Generation and the Punk Rock movement.

The Punks, led by Patti Smith and Richard Hell, adored the Beats and the Beats in turn were grateful to the Punks for drawing fresh, renewed attention to their work. The relationship between the two groups was from the start symbiotic, full of fun and, as Allen Ginsberg once said to me walking down the street with Peter Orlovsky late one night after dinner with Isherwood and Burroughs on his way to CBGB, 'chic'.

This collection of twenty-four pieces represents my favorite and most enduring journalism. It includes as well the best voices of their times from Muhammad Ali through Warhol and Burroughs, Southern, Roeg and Richards, to Hell, Harry and Ramone. Reading it now I can smell and taste the aromas of New York City when it was not only the cultural capitol of the world but the maddest, baddest and most fun place to be. I hope it makes you laugh.

Victor Bockris
New York City 1998

Rosebud Feliu-Pettet, who knew Allen through four decades, was among the twenty people with him when he died; her distinction here is that she was the only one who witnessed in their entirety these final minutes of a great life.

1

The Death Of Allen Ginsberg
By Rosebud Feliu-Pettet

April 4 Friday

Evening – Peter Hale calls and asks me to come quickly, Allen is in a coma, dying. Pull on my sneakers and taxi down, trying to keep calm breathing, trying to arrive in state of peace. 15 minutes after Pete's call he opens the door to the loft and I go in to join those already gathered. I went and embraced big Peter – Orlovsky – and Eugene, Allen's brother. About 20 friends talking in low voices, looking lost, comforting each other.

After being diagnosed with inoperable liver cancer the previous Friday at Beth Israel Hospital, Allen had been told he had maybe 2–5 months to live. When I heard the news, for some reason I felt strongly that it would not be that long – I felt that he would go very soon. He had come back home Wednesday in good spirits, organizing things as ever, making plans for the coming days. But someone (I forget who, perhaps it was Bob) had said Allen personally felt that he had very little time left. A month or two, he thought. So Wednesday he was busy, writing and making phonecalls to his friends all over the world, saying goodbye. Amiri Baraka said Allen called him and said "I'm dying, do you need any money?"

But Thursday he was much weaker, he could hobble from bed to chair only with difficulty. There was a phonecall from Italy, in the middle of it Allen begins to vomit, throws up right there on the phone! "Funny," he says, "never done that before." Said he was very tired and wanted to go to sleep. He fell asleep and later that night had a seizure and slipped into a coma. He was alone.

In the morning Bob Rosenthal discovered him unconscious and called the Hospice doctor who came and told him that Allen had most likely had a stroke and had hours to live. The task of notifying family and friends began.

Everyone had feared that as word spread, there would be a huge throng appearing at the loft, but that wasn't the case. People came and went quietly during the afternoon. Bob, Pete Hale, Bill Morgan and Kaye Wright, the office staff were busy constantly at the phones making and receiving calls. Shelly Rosenthal and Rani Singh helping with everything that needed doing. Eugene and several nieces and nephews of Allen's consoling each other. Larry Rivers down from his apartment upstairs, wandering around forlornly in his pink, white and blue striped pajamas. George and Anna Condo and their little girl. Francesco and Alba Clemente, beloved friends of Allen's. Patti Smith sitting in tears with Oliver Ray and her young daughter. Bob and Shelly's sons Aliah and Isaac. Mark Israel and David Greenberg, two of Allen's young boyfriends. Philip Glass and June Leaf. Robert Frank. Simon Pettet. Andrew Wylie. Roy Lichtenstein. Steven Bornstein, who had flown up from Florida. A few others, I don't remember who all was there. I went to the back of the loft and Raymond Foye stood looking pale and so sad. I told him he must be very blessed, he had spent so much time giving support and love to the dying – Henry Geldzahler, Huncke, Harry Smith. "Yes, but this is the big one, the hardest," he said. Allen lay in a narrow hospital bed beside the windows overlooking 14th Street. There were two almost invisible tubes coming out of his nose, attached to a portable small oxygen tank on the floor. His head was raised up on a couple of big striped pillows and he looked tiny and frail, thin arms with bruised veins from hospital tests sticking out from his Jewel Heart T-shirt. Head to the side, slight shadows under the eyes. I had walked through the loft, people whispering greetings, hugging, telling me all that had happened. But still not really prepared for the sight of him. The windows were open, curtains waving softly. His breathing was deep, slow, very labored, a snoring sound. "Hey, Allen, wake up!"

Joel Gaidemak, his cousin and doctor, was there constantly, and a young lady nurse sat in the corner reading, occasionally getting up to check on heart and pulse, or administer morphine for congestion. Gelek Rinpoche said he thought Allen might last the night. Joel didn't think so.

A few chairs were set up nearby, and there was the big white leather Salvation Army sofa of which he was so proud. People sat, or at intervals went to sit beside the bed and hold his hand or whisper to him and kiss him, his hand or cheek or head. An altar had been set up along one side of the loft and Gelek Rinpoche and the other monks sat chanting and praying, the sound so soothing constantly in the background, bells tinkling. A faint scent of flowers and incense hung in the air.

I had a little throw-away Woolworths camera, and Gregory Corso asked me to take a picture of him with Allen. He knelt beside the cot and placed his arm over Allen "like that picture, or statue, of Adonais, right?"

There was a medical chart, a picture of the human skeleton, hanging over the bed. Bob said Allen had put it there, half as a joke, half as a reminder. And Allen's beautiful picture of Whitman (that had hung in the kitchen on 12th Street) gazing down from the wall at the other dear bearded poet in the bed below. As it got late, many went home to try and catch a little sleep. It was around 11. Bob and Pete were just playing it by ear, deciding that anyone who wanted to stay would find a place, on the floor if necessary. Peter Orlovsky was taking photos and I felt a little uncomfortable, the idea of taking pictures at this time, but I figured, hey, if it was you, Allen'd be the first one through the door camera in hand! Eventually, Eugene leaned over, held Allen's hand, whispered "Goodbye little Allen. Goodbye little Allen. I'll be back later. See you soon." He kissed him and left. And Gregory – Gregorio! – too, telling us to call him at once if there was any change.

Joel had said that there was no way to know how long it would be, minutes or hours, surely not days. I had felt from the minute I saw Allen there that it would be very soon. I sat at the foot of the bed where I had spent the last few hours, holding his feet, rubbing them gently from time to time. An occasional cigarette break – the little guest bedroom by the office area was set up as the smoker's lounge. Bob and Pete and Bill were as strong and remarkable as ever, supporting everyone, keeping a sense of humor, and constantly dealing with the dozens of phonecalls, faxes, and the visitors as they came and went. They'd had a few days for the news to sink in, but they were dealing with – literally – hundreds of people over the phone or in person who had just found out and were in the first stages of stunned, disbelieving grief.

I had remained at the bedside and it was now after midnight. I could not believe he still hung on, the breathing so difficult, the lungs slowly filling with fluid. Labored breathing (gulps for air – like those gulps he'd made when he was singing – almost like he was reciting poetry in his sleep). Those who had been there all day were exhausted. It was down to a few now. Bob and Pete and Bill Morgan. Peter Orlovsky so bravely dealing with his pain, strong Beverly holding his hand. David and Mark. Patti and Oliver, there together all day trying to be brave and sometimes giving way to red-eyed tears. Simon Pettet sitting beside me for hours.

Allen's feet felt cooler than they had been earlier. I sat remembering the 33 years I'd known him, lived with him, my second father.

And still he breathed, but softer now.

Around 2 o'clock, everyone decided to try and get some rest. Bob and Joel lay down in Allen's big bed near the cot where he lay, everyone found a sofa or somewhere to stretch out.

Simon and I sat, just watching his face. Everyone was amazed at how beautiful he looked – all lines of stress and age smoothed – he looked patriarchal and strong. I had never seen him so handsome. The funny looking little boy had grown into this most wonderful looking man. (He would have encouraged photos if he had known how wonderful he looked!) But so tiny! He seemed as fragile as a baby in his little T-shirt.

The loft was very quiet. Most were resting, half-asleep. Suddenly Allen began to shake, a small convulsion wracked his body. I called out, and Joel and Bob sat up and hurried over. I called louder, and everyone else came running. It was about 2:15. Joel examined him, pulse, etc., and said that his vital signs were considerably slower, he had had another seizure. The breathing went on, weaker. His feet were cooler. Everyone sat or stood close to the little bed. The loft was dim and shadowy; only a single low light shining down on him. It lent a surreal, almost theatrical look to the corner of the loft. Peter Orlovsky bent over and kissed his head, saying, "Goodbye *Darling*."

And then suddenly a remarkable thing happened. A tremor went through him, and slowly, impossibly, he began to raise his head. He weakly rose until he was sitting almost upright, and his left arm lifted and extended. Then his eyes opened very slowly and very wide. The pupils were wildly dilated. I thought I saw a look of confusion or bewilderment. His head began to turn very slowly and his eyes seemed to glance around him, gazing on each of us in turn. His eyes were so deep, so dark, but Bob said that they were empty of sight. His mouth opened, and we all heard as he seemed to struggle to say something, but only a soft low sound, a weak "Aaah", came from him. Then his eyes began to close and he sank back onto the pillow. The eyes shut fully. He continued, then, to struggle through a few more gasping breaths, and his mouth fell open in an O. Joel said that these were the final moments, the O of the mouth the sign of approaching death. I still continued to stroke his feet and thin little legs, but the Tibetan Buddhist tradition is to not touch the body after death, so I kissed him one final time and then let go.

At 2:39, Joel checked for vital signs and announced that the heart, so much stronger than anyone knew, had stopped beating. A painless and gentle death. The thin blue sheet was pulled up to his chin, and Peter Hale brought over a tiny cup and spoon, and placed a few drops of a dark liquid between Allen's lips. It was part of the Buddhist ritual – the 'last food'. Bob put his hand over Allen's eyes and said the Sh'ma. We all sat quietly in the dim light, each with our own thoughts, saying goodbye.

© 1997. Rosebud Feliu-Pettet.

I attended this Gold Medal dinner with Burroughs and Grauerholz. I was the only person there who had a tape recorder and taped the after dinner speeches. What follows is the heart of them.

2

National Arts Club Literary Award Dinner
For Allen Ginsberg

On February 22nd 1979 the National Arts Club held a banquet to award their gold medal in literature to Allen Ginsberg. Previous recipients had included: Louis Achincloss, W. H. Auden, S. J. Perelman, Tennessee Williams, Saul Bellow and Norman Mailer. The following remarks are extracts from speeches by participants at the banquet who sat at the table of honor. The evening began with Ted Berrigan, master of ceremonies, reading a telegram sent for Allen.

TED BERRIGAN: "Congratulations. Continue to fearlessly beat the drum and play the harmonium of Dharma. With great affection Vajra Karaya the Venerable Chögyam Trungpa Rinpoche and Ösel Tenzing Vajra Hatu." (Berrigan continues, speaking now for himself) Over the years Allen has continued to be a great inspiration to me. I've seen his generosity not only to me but to many others. His concern, his care, his ability to be interested in you, when speaking to you, most of all his great intelligence in his personal practices. I think that's what impresses me most about Allen. I've taken him as a great moral guide in many ways ... I think I should turn the microphone over to men who can speak to you about Allen perhaps from a more intimate vantage point. The Commissioner of Cultural Affairs for the City of New York – Mr. Henry Geldzahler.

HENRY GELDZAHLER: Allen announced to the world that you can be homosexual and inclusive. He is a poet whose truths are described so feelingly and tellingly that their particularities become universal. A poet of human sexuality. We all feel as we read Allen Ginsberg what Allen Ginsberg feels. It is easier and more palatable for me to be an American and to be a homosexual because Allen has stood and spoken out. His eloquence allows us to share his victory ... In my name, and in the name of the City of New York – Thank you Allen Ginsberg!

BERRIGAN: The next speaker is John Ashbery. My friends and I used to joke that you could take a coin and flip it and it'd come up heads John Ashbery, tails Allen Ginsberg.

JOHN ASHBERY: I think Allen was one of the first poets who was able to make a living from poetry – not from publishing it because he's always published with small presses – but from reading it, which is indeed the only way a poet can make a living these days. And he is definitely the first poet who made a living from his poetry and gave most of what he's made to other people. He has devoted incredible amounts of time to giving himself to the things that he believes in. When I was at Naropa I was amazed that all day long poets would come, knock on his door and ask advice about their poetry – how they should get it published and this and that – and he spent (it seemed to me) almost twenty-four hours a day helping these people. And that is something that not too many people are aware of. It's something I would very much like to do myself, *but I just don't have the time* ... I don't think the establishment is embracing him but I think his embrace has eventually included it. I think he's changed the role of the poet in America and now everybody experiences poetry. I think it's much closer to us now than it was twenty years ago. And I think that is due not only to his poetry but to his truly exemplary way of living, which is a lesson to me, and for many of you here, and for many people in America.

BERRIGAN: I wouldn't want any of you to get the impression that Allen's not (just like the rest of us) subject to incredible fits of rage, tantrums, impatience, desire to merge, other normal feelings that go between people who love one another . . . Allen Ginsberg has been very specific in crediting William Burroughs with being his mentor and teacher in his early years. His long time friend and a man who serves him literally and constantly as an information channel . . .

WILLIAM S. BURROUGHS: To my way of thinking the function of art is to make us aware of what we know and don't know that we know. Now Allen's openness, his writings and his outspoken attitude towards sex and drugs, were once thoroughly disreputable and unacceptable, and now have become acceptable and in fact respectable. And this occasion is an indication of this shift of opinion. You remember that it was once extremely unacceptable to say that the earth is round. I think that this shift whereby original thinkers are accepted is very beneficial both to those who accept them and to the thinkers themselves. Somerset Maugham said the greatest asset any writer can have is longevity, and I think that in another ten or fifteen or twenty years Allen may be a very deserving recipient of the Nobel Prize.

BERRIGAN: Norman Mailer is the only person at the speakers' table who was famous before Allen . . . I think my mother first gave me a copy of *The Naked and the Dead* and said, "I don't know if a good mother would give this to a son to read, but I really liked it Ted, and I think you'll like it too . . ."

NORMAN MAILER: I don't truly have in my own mind credentials of a normal order for introducing Allen Ginsberg.

Except, as I sat here wondering what these prefatory remarks might come to, it occurred to me that mountains tend to be immensely self-centred. They're concerned with their own works. They try to notice how a particular plot, how a particular patch of forest, is going down below them, and how the snow fields are doing this year, and they feel the profound stir of the earth beneath their seat and they're tremendously concerned with themselves. They pay a great deal of attention to themselves. If a mountain can, it takes its pulse. Now weather is quite obviously bad at the summit and mountains rarely have anything to see. Occasionally there is a little clearing and the mountain looks out two hundred miles and "My God!" Anapurna says, "there's old Everest!" and it says, "You know, Everest is really impressive when you get down to it."

Well, I can only say that – I'm famous for my vanity – but I can only say when I pick up a book of Allen's, and I can crack it anywhere, start reading a few lines and I say, "My God, I'm not Everest, I'm Anapurna!"

And Allen took the totality of his experience and said, "I believe there's finally only going to be virtue. And I present it to you – the American people – in that fashion, because I believe that if you can come to understand me, you will come to believe, as I believe, that the totality of my actions will represent virtue, that you'll all be larger and more interesting and more imaginative as a nation, and greater."

MRS. ADRIANA ZAHN (President of the National Arts Club): Mr. Ginsberg, Commissioner Geldzahler and all the distinguished people: since the dawn of time poetry has given a wondrous magic for mankind because it reaches the secret places of the heart. Our literary committee wished to recognise this on this particular year, our 80th anniversary, by designating the name of a poet from our province to receive the medal of honor of the National Arts Club. It is now my very great privilege to present this medal to the poet Allen Ginsberg.

ALLEN GINSBERG: It is my turn to respond and give some sense of my thinking on being the centre of attention upon this occasion . . . and the stamp of the city's approval on cocksucking by the commissioner of Cultural Affairs . . .

Obviously I am Allen Ginsberg. I am the person that these people have been talking about and I am positively everything they have said. I boldly acknowledge with friendliness and accuracy the situation. On the other hand it also is an acknowledged fact that I don't know who I am and nobody here is sure precisely of what they have been saying and I'm not sure of what I'm saying and even the gold is questionable . . . who knows, perhaps the universe itself is an illusion, in fact it really is, so that I am completely empty, as you all are, so we can all relax because nothing depends on our being real.

This is an extract from my forthcoming book *Muhammad Ali in Fighter's Heaven* (Hutchinson, 1998).

3

Muhammad Ali On The Art Of Personality

"I have another lecture called 'The Art of Personality'. And the lecture says: personality's not something you're born with; we're born as individuals. My wife's got four children and all of them have got different individualities. So what I'm saying is, personality is the development of individuality.

"Take me for example. I attract people. Pretty girls from all over the country charter planes to my fights because I say things that attract them: 'I'm beautiful! I'm too pretty to be a fighter! Look at me! I'm the prettiest fighter! There ain't never been a fighter so beautiful!' And they just say 'He's *crazy!*' They know I'm pretty." Ali is beginning to enjoy himself. Grinning broadly, he acts out the role of each person.

"Then I attract the redneck white folks that don't like black people: 'I'm the greatest!' " he yells, rolling his eyes with his fist in front of his face. " 'That nigger's too arrogant, he talks too much!' " Ali says in a tight, angry, dull voice.

"I'm pretty! I can't lose! I'm the greatest!" he yells again. " 'The nigger needs a whoppin'!'

"Then I attract the black militants that don't like the whites: 'Yeah! Tell 'em brother. Tell them honkies, brother!'

"Then I got all the long-haired hippies, because I don't go to war. I ain't goin' to no Vietnam. I say:

Clean out my cell
And take my tail
On the trail
For the jail
Without bail

Because it's better in jail
Watchin' television fed
Than in Vietnam somewhere dead.

"Then I attract the Muslims, because of the name Muhammad Ali. Then the Israeli, who don't get along with the Muslims, might come to see me get whupped, because I'm a Muslim. And the Muslim's gonna root for me, because he don't want the Israeli to get his wishes. So you add it all up, I got a helluva crowd. Personality." He sits back, looking confident and amused.

I remember the day these tapes were made as one remembers a movie. Allen and I shared half a joint. The pot put us into a poetic place via which we connected, and Allen produced some of his most poetic, celebratory speech. This is the kind of human speech, as noted in the introduction, that I think has a poetry of its own.

4

Allen Ginsberg On Heroes

(The following is a conversation edited by Victor Bockris from several hours of tapes. It is not exact to the syntax, breaks, interruptions for questions or divigations of the original taped conversations.)

I visited Allen Ginsberg in 1977 at his Lower East Side apartment on 12th Street at one o'clock on a December afternoon. We sat in a spacious, comfortable kitchen, drinking tea and talking for a couple of hours while a secretary methodically typed a manuscript in another room. A half-dressed blonde girl appeared from a side room, smiling.

I asked Allen a series of direct questions about certain key cultural figures, and he answered, sometimes at length, sometimes briefly. For the sake of clarity, I have omitted my questions and simply present his responses as they were spoken.

What is most impressive about Allen Ginsberg, apart from his constant generosity, is that he is always interesting and one can always 'rediscover' his work. He particularly enjoys talking about people whose work has influenced him, or whom he greatly admires.

Heroes are okay if you learn from them. I've learnt a lot from Kerouac, who was a hero to me, and I learnt a tremendous amount from Burroughs. From Kerouac, spontaneous mind and Buddhism; from Burroughs, blank mind and wiping out the word – unconfusing and disentangling semantic difficulties. I learnt certain kinds of heart straightforwardness and simplicity and practical earthiness from Peter. I learnt a lot of love charms from Neal Cassidy and a variety of association and simultaneity of reference from Cassidy, and I learnt three-chord blues from Dylan, and I learnt from nearly everybody.

But I also learnt from people I never met. I learnt elegance of homosexual romance from Genet before I met him, and I learnt laconism and interruption of thought and oddly wielded human syntax from Louise Ferdinand Celine before I met him. I learned some sense of modern line lengths from William Carlos Williams before I met him, though I never really understood it until I heard him speak. And then I learnt excited heartfelt confrontation soul to soul from Dostoyevsky, who I never met, and then I learnt some blues sense from Leadbelly, whom I never met, and I learnt Titanic inspiration hammering on heaven from Beethoven and Bach. I mean, there are transmissions. I learnt mellowness from Shakespeare and Sir Thomas Wyatt. I learnt cranky humor from Christopher Smart. I learnt visionary apprehension from William Blake. I learnt tolerance of my own vagaries and sexual romances from Whitman. So I'm a media freak myself.

Whatever image of myself or Kerouac or Burroughs was spread in the Sixties began with a smelly inarticulate image passed through the hands of the CIA and transformed to become a sort of bum kick, originally. It was only sub-liminally that any kind of generosity was transmitted, or any sense of reliability. Any negative aspects of my character like aggressiveness, confusion of thought, those were picked up on and exaggerated. And what virtues I had came through just by sheer force of virtue rather than by any kind of transmission through *Time* or *Life* or the *New York Post* or whatever medium there was. And as far as television is concerned, I was never allowed to get up and say what I really felt in my own language. I was never, for instance, allowed to read 'Howl' on television. That would have been against the law. So I think the problem is not heroes, it's the medium.

So the problem then is to make use of the media for transmission of the spark of intelligence, awareness and awakedness. The person who does it has to be very straightforward.

I do believe in teachers, though I would say, if you meet your teacher blocking your path to enlightment, cut him down. That's the old Buddhist terminology. If you meet Buddha on the path to enlightenment, cut him down. But to cut him down, to cut the teacher or the hero or the media star down in a spirit of resentment is a mistake and will lead perhaps to the only permanent hell that does exist. It's called the Vajra hell, the unbreakable Vajra hell, which is refusal of intelligence, refusal of awareness. Any action against the hero or the star system which is taken out of resentment or anxiety or jealousy obviously will only lead to more resentment, anxiety and jealousy, and so can't be of any usefulness.

Bob Dylan

Dylan is one of my heroes, he seems like a mighty, triumphant Beethovenian fist shaking at heaven always, and in his later phase, greater and greater, richer. Also, as an oral poet he's supreme: I think he can pronounce his vowels and consonants better than any other bard.

In conversation, he's subtle, very witty, as in songs, but more subtle, he'll say a thing which sounds very plain and 'disruptive' until five minutes later you realise he was actually saying something absolutely simple and straightforward that takes you by surprise. Like he kept telling me all through the

Rolling Thunder tour that I was a king, but that I hadn't found my kingdom. Which is like terrific, right? [Laughing] Total flattery and at the same time total realism. Also, I always felt that he had very shrewd judgements for me. It very often takes me years to catch up with some very casual remark. Like years ago, way back in the Sixties, he asked me to write songs for him and I disdained the notion thinking that I was some kind of velvet poet. And not that he needed it; he was just encouraging me to do something. But he was being absolutely totally friendly, and I reacted paranoiacally, thinking that he was putting me on, or that he was coming on superior, whereas actually he was being totally friendly and quite humble, totally straightforward, and I didn't take it straightforwardly. And it resulted in me learning music and working with him later and then finally writing my own songs. So at the moment, I'm dying for him to sing one of my songs.

I first met him around '63, '64. When I first came back from India, I met Charlie Plymell in Bolinas. I'd never heard Dylan and Plymell played me one of his first records, including the line *I'll know my song well before I start singing*, and I burst into tears when I heard it, it seemed so clear and so heroic. 'I'll know my song well before I start singing.' It sounded like the best of any great writer, Rimbaud or Shelley – some Shelleyian Promethean statement as to the role of the poet – and it seemed such a miracle that somebody had emerged self-born in the middle of America with so much awareness and such confidence and sense of prophecy, that I started crying. Then I met him by surprise: came back to New York and was staying at Ted Wilentz's house when he was running the 8th Street Bookshop and Wilentz had a welcome home party and Al Aronowitz brought Dylan around. But I didn't know until last year that Dylan had actually read some of the beat poetry and had quote 'his mind blown' unquote. Which he said had happened with Kerouac's 'Mexico City Blues' that somebody had handed to him in Minnesota. He said he didn't know what the words meant then, but it blew his mind; I guess the open form and the American rhythm.

I think there's a natural progression in Dylan's work and I always think of it in terms of Yeats. Of mountain peaks and valleys, mountain peaks and valleys, with succeeding intensification and succeeding reality and succeeding genius. Seasons, you know, like *A Season in Hell*, seasons, different seasons, but they're being *inevitable* and *natural* seasons and so *not* to be criticized from a pop point of view: "Is this going to be a bestseller or not?" I mean not from a crass, commercial point of view.

See, all through the period when he was supposed to have been so dumb, there were a series of very great songs – 'Lay Lady Lay', or 'I'll Be Your Baby Tonight' – which are so mellow and so beautiful to hear now, that one doesn't realize that at the time they were received with disdain, as if he'd lost his power. So after a period of hysterical crescendo in *Blonde on Blonde*, he came down – as was natural and healthy and inevitable – to becoming a family man and re-humanizing himself. And the result of that was some very beautiful, calm, sweet songs. And then he did what really one would have wanted him to do – a large record of all his sources – which is the *Self Portrait*. I'm glad he gave us those footnotes, his sources. Like, you know, what more generous thing could he have done? So he replaced hysteria with generosity and some pop reviewers spit at him.

Then, at a time people were saying he was at the lowest point, he wrote his most divine song, which is 'Knock Knock Knocking On Heaven's Door'. Everybody was yelling at him – for not being 'active'? for I don't know what – but around that time he wrote 'Forever Young', which I think will be as lasting as 'White Christmas'. 'Forever Young' is a fantastic anthem, which some day will be heard sung around campfires in the Sierras. [Sings] 'Forever young, forever youuuuuuuung . . .' It's like a beautiful thing to sing; it's a family song, which is how it was intended. Like 'Way Down Upon the Swanee River' or something. Dylan wrote something that permanently gilds the family twilight Christmas evening.

And then, finally 'Idiot Wind', which is, I think, his greatest crescendo song and, as he's playing it these days, I think his greatest sort of Wagnerian piece of folk rock.

I thought the rhyme of *Idiot wind, blowing there in circles around your skull/From the Grand Coulee Dam to the Capitol* was amazing. Also, as I was doing a lot of yoga, it seemed to me he had, by his own nature, come down to some basic realization of breath (prana), and actually the whole song is about *It's a wonder you can still breathe*. And later, *Feed yourself*.

It seemed to me to be a declaration of independence from what is called, in technical Buddhist terms, 'the Ego of Dharmas'. That is to say, being hypnotized by one's own outside world and past and one's creations in the outside world. Because there's that great line about *Being on the borderline between you and me/Finally free/You never know what pain I rise above*. Which is tremendously Bodhisattva-like. Where is 'Idiot Wind'?

[Looks it up in a beautiful, spiral-bound boxed edition of Dylan's *Songs: 1966–1976*. Allen had just gotten his copy and was very pleased with it.]

When I first heard him sing this – *they ride down the highway, down the tracks, down the road to ecstasy* – I thought he was referring to Kerouac. *I followed you beneath the stars haunted by your memory and all your raging glory.* So I began taking that personally, thinking he was talking about us Beatniks. *I been double-crossed now for the very last time and now I'm finally free.* It sounds like his declaration of independence from his fathers.

So, when I first heard that, I megalomaniacally thought he was declaring his independence from *me*. And then I realized that he was actually declaring his independence from *all* me's. From all me's everywhere in every direction, so that almost anybody could interpret that as being personal, in showing some real separation out into solitude on his own, and the acceptance of solitude and individuality, and actually his emergence above pain of clinging and attachment and mystification, to some kind of almost godless glory, isolate, seeing the complete nothingness in the world, the emptiness of the world.

And you'll never know what pain I rise above/As well as your holiness or your kind of love. He's like disdaining all the daughters of Mara, all the temptations of the world, attachments to the world, fears. And then, *Idiot wind blowing through the buttons of our coats/Blowing through the letters that we wrote/ Blowing through the dust upon our shelves* – it's like a universal energy, empty energy, which he's recognised. So it seemed, psychologically, a great statement of attainment of powers, and also like a national prophecy: *Blowing like a circle around my soul/From the Grand Coulee Dam to the Capitol.* It's all Watergate too, so it's the nation, the ego of the nation.

That's another thing about 'the Ego of Dharmas', which has to be the ego of ideas, the ego of your own creations, the ego of your projections, the attachment to some permanent sense of their reality, realizing that they're actually all 'idiot wind/blowing in the wind'. Also still 'Blowing in the Wind'. Change: the Buddhist's second noble truth; existence is change.

Well, it just seemed a very noble song, like the kind of nobility you don't often see, the nobility of a great bard. Which is what the whole Rolling Thunder tour was about. And also a very strange alchemical thing in the sense that he had to take all this money and all this machinery and all this electricity to create a ten-foot-square spot where he would be completely free to stamp his foot in time to what he hears in his own head as music, and create on the spot a new rhythm each time he played 'Idiot Wind' or any other song, and play each song differently each time with all the musicians completely there in their bodies, alert, listening, sensitive, receptive, and respondent to his changes of time and beat, his elongation of the vowels, so they get up on the stage and howl, in the sense of elongated vowels, with complete self-confidence and authority and solace, solitary loneliness, in the middle of 27,000 people and half a million dollars worth of equipment: in a ten-foot square place where one person can totally express himself freely and actually express a good deal of the emotion of the crowd of people around him, speak for people in a sense, speak for others, speak for himself and others at the same time. So 'Idiot Wind' seems to me like an acme of that.

On the *Hard Rain* album, even in diminished volume, there's still the sense of slowdown of time and the slowdown of the song and even the gaps in the song where there's a moment of silence, and you don't know whether the song is continuing, and all of a sudden it continues with the same logic as before. So he's stepping in and out of time. It's noticeable in the fantasticalness of his pronunciation of consonants. The thing that I kept thinking is that expression on his face which looks like pain and/or disdain, or sneer, is really just a mouth working, his face trying to pull back his teeth to pronounce his 't's clearly enough to be heard into the microphone, to hear a single 't' or an 's' above all the roar of the other electrical instruments, to be heard as a human syllable and be understood by the ear so that music had *word*, it had *word* in there. That's why he's a great poet in the sense of great orator. That's the best oratory I've heard, or the best recitation of poetry. It was a great poetry reading . . .

In between the concerts we made movies, almost every day there was a scene to act in, so that would take up half a day or morning: we worked very hard putting on a concert and making movies simultaneously, no chance to get up and laze around all day and not worry about anything and then jump into another concert. Dylan actually was working on the afternoon of a concert: like going out to Kerouac's grave in a caravan and sitting there, and then having a concert in Lowell that night. Singing all the night before and having to get up at 10 am or something, a lot of energy.

Since the tour, he's just disappeared from my vision. Gone back up to heaven.

Patti Smith

I was surprised by Patti Smith's rise. It's sort of heartening to see how somebody else could get ahead. I wonder how she'll do.

I've been teaching Rimbaud this year – she idolizes Rimbaud – and I've been reading Rimbaud's late, last letters when he was dying, about how miserable life was and "all I am is a motionless stump" and I'm wondering how she's going to deal with that aspect of heroism. How will she deal with suffering? How will she transcend suffering and become a lady of energy, a sky-goddess, singing of egolessness? Because so far her proposition has been the triumph of the stubborn, individualistic, Rimbaud-Whitmanic ego: but then there is going to be the point where her teeth fall out and she's going to become the old hag of mythology that we all become. And I think she'll be equal to dying. [Laughing] We all are.

(There follows a brief excerpt from an August 1972 interview with Patti.)

VICTOR BOCKRIS: Why are your influences mostly European: Rimbaud, Cendrars, Celine, Michaux?
PATTI SMITH: It's because of biographies. I was mostly attracted to lifestyles, and there just wasn't any great biographies of genius American lifestyles except the cowboys. But you can read my book, *Seventh Heaven* (Telegraph Books, Philadelphia, 1972) and who do you get out of it? Edie Sedgwick, Anita Pallenberg, Marianne Faithfull, Joan of Arc,

Frank Sinatra. All people I really like. I'm shrouded in the lives of my heroes.

BOCKRIS: Tony Glover says in his review of *Seventh Heaven* that you are writing a poetry of performance. What does that mean to you?

SMITH: I think part of it is because of Victorian England, how they crucified Oscar Wilde. Poets became simps, sensitive young men in attics. But it wasn't always like that. It used to be that the poet was a performer and I think the energy of Frank O'Hara started to re-inspire that. I mean in the Sixties there was all that happening stuff. Then Frank O'Hara died and it sort of petered out, and then Dylan and Allen Ginsberg revitalized it.*

Arthur Rimbaud

He's a hero to those who know about him because he's a model of life, and he had extraordinary physical beauty and beauty of mind. In a way he succeeded in possessing the truth in one body and one soul. He succeeded in completely entering his life and acting without looking backward, acting without second-guessing himself or without shadow-making gestures that had no shadows in the sense of self-conscious ego-manipulation. So that, despite his suffering, at the end of his life he seems to have been completely immersed in existence 100 percent. And he may have wound up dying in eternity rather than dying in a shadow world of lies and self-deception. Must read his late letters from Africa.

The only thing is, Rimbaud doesn't seem to provide a 'final solution' to ego or ego's aggression. What Rimbaud is, is fantastic aggression and charm and intensity and intelligence, and a

* Like a true Beat Punk Patti's chronology is a little messed up, but she got the spirit right. For a complete account of Patti's visionary role as a leading Beat Punk, see my *Patti Smith: The Biography* (The Fourth Estate, London, 1998).

funny soft-spot kind of sexual humility, and openness to being fucked by life. But his myth seen crudely might lead younger people who don't have some stable meditation into nonsensical suicides.

Jimmy Carter

I was afraid that he, being a deistic- or theistic-minded person, might take his ego seriously enough to start an atomic war on some moral issue connected with divine principles. As a non-theist, I thought it was somewhat dangerous to have a hysterical theist in the White House. But I voted for him, because I heard that Ralph Nader liked him, and that he had a good record on ecological matters in Georgia. And also because he promised amnesty to the soldiers who didn't want to fight Nixon's war.

The story of his success is just an old Burroughs story of a good old boy coming round and talking. He wasn't that new; he was a governor, they've run governors before. How did Wendell Willkie get nominated? How did Stevenson get nominated? I mean they're all relatively unknown people in one way or another, without a power base. How did McGovern do it? I don't think that's so strange. It's just another governor running for government against a representative connected with Watergate corruption stories.

I think what it means is that a significant portion of the population became disillusioned with the government lineage and simply voted for Carter to provide some relief. Not that they expected anything better. That's why the vote was so close. Expecting something better would mean a greater movement toward liberating junkies from the thralls of the police state, medicalizing the junk problem and getting the government and the profiteers out of the junk business – both repressing and peddling – and I suppose it would also mean having total rekindling of energy sources and withdrawal from the addiction to petroleum and petrochemical sources, and a more humorous approach to government as theatre.

There might be a little more theatre under Carter, but again there's a problem, which is he's got a ceiling which is God. And his highest appeal is going to be God all the time, the way he's set himself up, and that's not much of a place to appeal to. It immediately stops all rational consideration of the situation.

His smile was kind of strange for a few days. For a couple of days just before the election, his smile became very sinister.

[Allen suddenly breaks into song:]

> *Stay away from the White House*
> *Stay away I wish you well*
> *Stay away from the White House*
> *Stay away I wish you well*
> *Stay away from the White House*
> *Or you'll go to Vajra Hell!**

Chögyam Trungpa Rinpoche

Another hero of mine is Chögyam Trungpa. He seems to have carried forward a practical, visible, programmatic practice of egolessness, and provided a path for other people to walk on.

He's a Tibetan Lama trained from childhood in meditation practices, and he's translated the esoteric classical meditation practices into Americanese so that it's available to hippies and middle-class people, and has entered into the American scene in a very energetic way founding the Naropa Institute (in Boul?, Colorado) of which the Jack Kerouac School of Disembodied Poetics is a branch. He has made space for the

---

* Vajra Hell is the only permanent, unbreakable hell – total opaque selfhood: refusal of intelligence, refusal of awareness.

nat? perceptions and accomplishments that solidified here already in literature, and he sees some correlations between our own natural intelligence and a kind of spacious wisdom characteristic of Buddhist liberation.

When I first met him I thought he reminded me a lot of Kerouac, partly because of the drinking, partly because the spontaneous shrewdness, partly because of the poetic nature of his talent drinks a lot sake . . . He says he wants to be reborn a Japanese scientist.

John Lennon

Just about half a year ago, before I went to teach the summer at Naropa, I went up to visit John and Yoko, they were in the kitchen with their baby, in very good shape, following a very strict diet. They gave me a copy of *Sugar Blues* and warned me about the imperialistic addictive history of sugar. He said one of the reasons he wouldn't stay in Hollywood was everybody was killing themselves on dope and alcohol, or a lot of musicians, anyway: and he didn't want to have a band unless he could have a band with musicians in good health.

Paul McCartney

I met Paul McCartney in his house in England in '66. Mick Jagger was there, reading a book by Elephas Levi – a French astrologer who supposedly taught Rimbaud in 1870; Rimbaud had met Levi in Paris – a book with some astrological or alchemical design on the cover – and McCartney was painting designs on a red velvet shirt, which he gave me as a present when I left.

I told him a little bit about Blake, and he told me a big long story about how The Beatles had first got high on acid, it was a very funny conversation, some friends had given the acid to them in their coffee, and they went out in their limousine to

45

some nightclub, and they stopped on the pavement and were looking down into the nightclub stairwell, and it was all full of garish neon, and it looked like the big mouth of a monster. They didn't know whether to go in or not. And then there were all these people around when they got out of their limousine, looking at them, so they had to go in. And then once they got in it was alright.

McCartney has a kind of sweetness, a cherubic quality. It's in his music, too.

This interview with Debbie Harry conducted in 1996 is the most recent piece in the book, and is combined with some vintage material from 1980. There is a lot of continuity in my relationship with Debbie. Talking with her on the phone yesterday was no different than talking with her twenty years ago, except that she is more confident and stronger.

5

An Interview With Debbie Harry

I met Debbie Harry in 1977, and experienced a good deal of her success with Blondie first-hand through 1978–1982. During this time, we wrote the text for Making Tracks: The Rise of Blondie, *a book of photographs by Chris Stein, Debbie's live-in collaborator on Blondie. They wrote the band's hits together. After Blondie's break-up in 1982 (under sad circumstances caused largely by a mysterious illness that struck Stein down), I kept in touch with Debbie sporadically. I approached her to do this* High Times *interview with some delight, since she was just reaching a peak in her solo career thanks to the movie* Heavy, *in which she starred opposite Liv Tyler, and* Individually Twisted, *her record with the Jazz Passengers. Harry has been touring with the Jazz Passengers and is finding a cool, new groove to work in.*

The interview was conducted at the apartment of photographer David Croland, and in Harry's own Manhattan apartment. Some of the material, particularly the sidebar conversation with Stein, was recorded but never released during the time we were working on Making Tracks. *The new Debbie Harry is in fact no different from the old Debbie Harry inasmuch as she is Debbie – the singer, songwriter, actress and comedienne who will continue to tie us up in individually twisted stitches throughout the '90s and into the next century.*

VICTOR BOCKRIS: What is the most important thing that's happened to you in the last year?

DEBBIE HARRY: Just this past weekend I had to drive upstate to see my Mom and Dad. I sort of had the same feeling I had at the beginning of Blondie. Then, I had this really wonderful instinctive drive, this guiding momentum, this energy, and I just had to use it. I was so instinctive. Everything was just there, you know?

Then, for a long time I didn't want any kind of energy like that. But all of a sudden, driving upstate, I thought, Gee, I wonder if I could do that again? And I just had this little feeling in the pit of my stomach that went, Yeah, I could, and maybe I would want to. But who focuses all their drive on work at my age? I was thinking, I want to do that, then I was thinking I'm already doing it.

BOCKRIS: With the Jazz Passengers?

HARRY: Yeah. This technical jazz singing with the Jazz Passengers is more emotional, more delicate. The voice is in a different position within the instrumentation. You have an obligation to be creative and responsive. You have to respond to every particular feeling, because being there in the moment is really important. It's not just this section four times, the next section two times, then the last section. The parts are woven together, and what somebody else plays and how you respond to that is more like acting.

BOCKRIS: Is the process of writing jazz songs very different from writing rock songs?

HARRY: With the Jazz Passengers, I stepped into a situation that already existed, and then tried to add something of my own to it. That's different than what I did with Blondie. My Blondie stuff was more personal and direct.

BOCKRIS: How did you get involved with the Jazz Passengers?

HARRY: [Producer] Hal Wilner introduced me to them. Hal called me from London and said, Why don't you come and sing a track on this jazz album I'm doing? So he sent me the track and I thought, Oh, kinda weird, but it's pretty good. So

I did it. And then from there I started working with them. I couldn't for the life of me have picked a better situation than the Jazz Passengers to experiment and to sing in a different way and perform in a different way and to know exactly what I wanted to do. It's very nice for me. It's like a great period of creative discovery.

BOCKRIS: Was *Heavy* a good role for you?

HARRY: Getting a real acting part in *Heavy* was a revelation to me. Being other people is really the best thing for me. Being somebody else. I think the picture turned out well and I think the director, James Mangold, is a brilliant guy. Both of his parents were painters, and he's wonderful to work with. I was surprised when I saw the film. I had no idea what the pacing would be like. I was really moved.

BOCKRIS: Are you addicted to your work?

HARRY: I guess I am, but I just think it's the best thing to be productive and to be creative. What else are you gonna do?

BOCKRIS: What is your daily life like these days? When you're living in New York and you're not touring, do you have any practical schedule?

HARRY: Well, I swim every day. If I'm not working that night, performing or going to a club to see a band, I'll get up at about seven-thirty, eight o'clock. I take my dog for a walk and feed the cat. Then I get the newspaper and read it for an hour. I drink coffee and have a pastry. Then I just do phones or tour plans or clean up the apartment. Try to get jobs. Rearrange traffic. I'm trying to organize doing a book of my own again.

BOCKRIS: You want to do your autobiography?

HARRY: Yeah, but I'd like to have more of a sex life before I write it. I mean, the book should be banned somewhere!

BOCKRIS: How recently did you break up with Penn Gillette?

HARRY: A year ago. Basically, we were in a relationship where we planned to meet in airport lounges, which I thought was cool. But then we had trouble on the sex front because he's kind of big, and it was difficult to find a place to squeeze into, you know?

BOCKRIS: Have you been seeing anybody else?

HARRY: No, not really. Dates here and there. Nothing much.

BOCKRIS: Are you working with Chris?

HARRY: We haven't really done anything lately, but we did do some rock shows at SqueezeBox [at Don Hill's, the New York club] last year. And the last record we did, *Double Vision*, we worked on together. It's sort of an ongoing thing between the two of us, although we're not really super-active right now.

BOCKRIS: What do you remember about your teenage years?

HARRY: At sixteen, I found out about pot, which was unbelievable because nobody did it. I lucked out. I had a girlfriend, Wendy, who was a year older than me and she had an older sister who was a real beatnik painter who lived in New York in a loft on Grand Street on the Lower East Side. She had travelled in Mexico and taken magic mushrooms and smoked pot.

BOCKRIS: What was it like when you first smoked grass?

HARRY: I first smoked grass when I was eighteen. It was like an acid trip. I took about three hits off a joint and it lasted for hours and hours and it was great. My whole life just ran in front of me and I realized a lot of things in a flash. I could see a lot of things very clearly. It didn't answer everything, though. I still had some emotional problems and a lot of pain in my body.

BOCKRIS: Did you go out with a lot of different guys in high school?

HARRY: When I was a freshman, my town had these stifled sexual appetites. It was really awful. No matter who you were, if you went out with a lot of guys you would get talked about and people would say you were a whore. It was this big paradox. So I ended up going out with one guy for a couple of months and then another guy for a couple of months. In my junior and senior years, I pretty much had one boyfriend.

BOCKRIS: Were you attracted to a particular type?

HARRY: No. But I was really oversexed. Really charged, hot to trot. Later on, when I got my driver's license, I used to drive up to this sleazy town near Paterson [New Jersey] and would walk up and down this street there called Cunt Mile. I would get picked up and make out with different guys in back seats of cars to get my rocks off, because I was so horny and I couldn't make out with anybody in my town.

BOCKRIS: Did you always have this idea of going to New York and becoming a star?

HARRY: There was quite a big jazz scene in 1965 on the Lower East Side when I moved there. I was into music more and more even though I was painting then. After taking my first acid trip, I started painting sound and decided I wanted to be in music. I hung out with bands and didn't paint anymore. But I had to learn how to feel good about myself, because I didn't like myself. To break up these patterns, I had to become what I wanted to be and who I wanted to be, and it took a long time. I felt that I was another person inside and that I wanted to come out, that I was in pain and always depressed and feeling terrible. Sometimes I'm uncomfortable within my body. Sometimes I don't like to feel at all. That's why taking drugs had a very strong attraction for me, because it made me bodiless, which is very nice.

BOCKRIS: When did you first get involved in the music scene?

HARRY: In 1967. But I was so depressed and so upset, I knew that I would do it wrong and get so far in one direction that it would make people think of me in another way. This happens to many people, like Lou Reed. I knew I couldn't do it the way I wanted to, so at the end of the Sixties I stopped doing music. I had come to a point that seemed like a tunnel. I was at the entrance, and I could either go down into the tunnel and continue or I could take this little winding road off to the side. So from '69 to '73, I took a sabbatical.

BOCKRIS: When you came back out in '73, what was the first thing you did?

HARRY: That was the early glitter period when I used to hang around the [New York] Dolls. They were put down by the critics, but they were the pets of the New York scene. That period – T Rex, Jonathan Richman, the Dolls – was when I jumped back in mentally. I had a little car and used to drive them around, but I was more on the fringes of everything. When I started performing with The Stilettoes in 1973, my intuition was no one was dancing to rock'n'roll. And that was what The Stilettoes wanted to do – bring back rock dancing.

BOCKRIS: How did you learn to become a singer?

HARRY: In the early '70s, when I was living with a guy who was a musician from when he was four years old, I used to practice all the time with earphones on. I was always going to rehearsals and watching people play, trying to learn about the structure of music. That was my musical training period, and it was really necessary. I knew I had to really learn how to sing more and I had to learn how to sing with all different attitudes. I could only sing in a very soft voice. I could never express a lot of emotion, otherwise I would start to cry, so I could only sing like a nice, sweet girl. I could never really let go, so I would practice shouting and singing as loud as possible whether it sounded good or not.

BOCKRIS: When you started Blondie, what was your motivation?

HARRY: I wanted to be successful, but success was not my goal. That was not my obsession. My obsession was actually to just do it and everything else was secondary. I survived the hard times by not being obsessed. I was afraid of not being good enough musically. Blondie were never touted as being musical innovators, but we really had a terrific amount of feeling for the songs and the lyrics we did. They really meant something to us, and we did them with everything we could put into them. That's what made it happen with the audiences.

BOCKRIS: How do you reconcile carrying around the enormous shadow of the legend of Blondie?

HARRY: That's funny, because to me it's grossly out of proportion. It's ridiculous and preposterous, yet it's totally accurate in relation to what is considered really vital and really valuable in the culture. But it just seems totally out of proportion that I should be considered anything other than another singer. The mythologizing of it is absurd. I was just being a driven, obsessed, star-crazed rock'n'roller, and doing my best to be part of all that, and wanting to say a few things that were relevant at the time, and now it's gone way out of proportion.

The concept of the youth culture has an awfully powerful effect, which is incredibly fucking misleading. It's so boring, so incredibly ridiculous, but it controls many people's lives. They think they better get it done now because when they get to be forty-five they're not going to have anything.

BOCKRIS: Where do you see rock heading?

HARRY: The only place left for rock to go is toward more girl stars. There's nothing left for men to do. There's bound to be more male stars, but they can't express anything new. What girls are saying is: "Don't treat me like that, treat me like this." Which Nancy Sinatra initially did with 'These Boots Were Made For Walking'! That's the sort of predominant attitude. It's not the same as 'Take another little piece of my heart now', or 'Baby love, baby love' – all that kind of gush. It's giving girls a chance to develop, get to the stage where their style of living and thought is the same [as men's], not some clandestine activity.

The rules of the game nowadays are: if you can screw somebody and get away with not paying for something and make somebody else pay the price, that's cool. It's a horrible, rotten status quo, and it's not going to get any better by itself. That's the really bad thing about the downfall of religion. Religion said everybody must be good so that everything would stay in balance. I can look at it like a scientist, but still have respect for the powers that would be gods.

Maybe more ritual would install a sense of order and balance. If the proper ritual is followed it has some kind of electromagnetic implication that further on down the line more and more of your circuits will be completed so that you'll be able to do more of the things you want, and more of the things you want to happen will happen. This is what magic really is. You should always strive to summon up your own magic on a daily basis.

BOCKRIS: I'm confused by the Nineties. Historically, the last five years of any decade are supposed to be a fantastic time. But nothing's happening!

HARRY: There's so much information, Victor. People are too aware of history, too informed. There's going to be a new perception, a new idea of what people are. People will be a different thing. The human race will be a different thing. It will be much more sophisticated and aware of its animal motivation. It'll become more intellectual.

BOCKRIS: That's the greatest non sequitur I've heard in a long time: aware of animal motivations so it will become more intellectual.

HARRY: The human animal is motivated by food and sex, right? And now, because we're so informed about political history – the nature of people going after money, power and sex – everybody's exposed. There's no way you can actually do those things without a secretive, animal, clandestine thing. It's just a different kind of behavior. You're going to have to be very psychic and slinky.

"Will You Shut Up?!"

The following conversation between Debbie Harry, Chris Stein and Victor Bockris was recorded at Harry and Stein's penthouse apartment on West 58th Street in 1980, when Blondie was the No. 1 rock band in the world. As Harry and Stein lay in bed, we discussed the text for Making Tracks: The Rise of Blondie.

CHRIS STEIN [*to Debbie*]: At the beginning here you definitely should say I experimented with drugs. Everybody knows it. If you leave it out it's just a fucking whitewash. You say if you didn't try [drugs] you'd have ended up killing yourself, and yet there's nothing in the first page to suggest why you're miserable enough to want to kill yourself.

DEBBIE HARRY: I was miserable. I just thought that's the way everybody was.

STEIN: If you don't say you took drugs and you were depressed and you couldn't sing and you couldn't talk . . . if you don't put the negative side in, it just comes off like a normal life.

HARRY: It was normal. Why don't you put in the nitty gritty about *your* life then, Chris?

STEIN: [*switching the subject*] This stuff on writing a popular song is a little cheerleadery.

HARRY: The method of writing a hit song is to fucking die and then come alive again. Just experience as much pain as possible, then you could write a hit song right. Get four Stella D'Oro breadsticks and a big jar of Vaseline and wait for the full moon in Cancer on a warm night and go down to the street and ram the breadsticks up your ass and then lie down in front of the taxicab so it runs over your stomach and makes the sticks into crumbs. Then belch, throw them all up, take the breadcrumbs and cook them into a cookie and mail it to Ahmet Ertegun. After he eats the cookie, you bring in your tape. This is the magical formula. Or, get a big jar of peanut butter and plug it into the wall. Spread it all over your face while you're holding onto an electrical wire. Rent a twenty-dollar-per-month one-room apartment without a bathroom, lock yourself in with a year's supply of Dexedrine and just sit there and never sleep and just bang on the guitar. Then, at the end of the year, just take the last three minutes of the session and that'll do it. Guaranteed hit.

VICTOR BOCKRIS: When you started Blondie, did you think it was going to be a big, international sensation?

HARRY: Not at first. Things were picking up gradually, but everything was so burned out at the time I never thought, Wow! A hundred people are coming to see me. I'm making it. At that time, who cared? New York wasn't a place for live entertainment, except in cabarets. At first, we played around sporadically. Our first drummer used to pass out from anxiety. At the most important moment when we really needed him to play he would pass out. He was always lying on the dressing room floor after drinking half a glass of champagne. That's when we played at Brandy's. The biggest song we did was 'Lady Marmalade'. One night, this girl Maud Frank the Third came in and invited us to play at her townhouse for a party for the Equestrian Club. This was more or less Blondie.

STEIN: They offered us two hundred dollars, so we jumped at it.

HARRY: We got more than that!

STEIN: The thing was, we were only supposed to play three sets.

HARRY: We got *FUCKING FIVE HUNDRED DOLLARS* up-front, then we said: For a thousand we'll play all night.

STEIN: You're out of your brain!

HARRY: I am not out of my brain.

STEIN: Are you just making this up? [To Bockris] She doesn't have a real good head for details, believe me.

BOCKRIS: [To Harry] You mean this is just a little fantasy in your mind?

HARRY: We did it for more than two hundred dollars.

STEIN: We got two hundred dollars for fucking three sets is the way I remember it, and then they said, Well, play one more time and we'll give you another hundred dollars. We came out with three hundred or three-fifty. I certainly don't remember getting a thousand dollars – for anything at that period!

HARRY: Well, I guess you're right.

BOCKRIS: You only had a couple of songs. How could you play all night?

HARRY: Victor, what are you talking about? You don't even know what our repertoire was. We did 'Poor Fool'. We did Tina Turner songs. We did 'Narcissima' and . . .

STEIN: We didn't do any of those songs! We never did 'Narcissima'. C'mon, Debbie.

HARRY: I'm beat now.

STEIN: So shut up! Why don't you watch TV? [To Bockris] The thing is, when we played at Brandy's we did cover material like 'The Little Tootsie Roll Song' and 'Honeybee'.

HARRY: The early disco stuff that came out in '73 and '74 more or less overlapped into Blondie. We just jammed out.

BOCKRIS: So you really were drawing an audience that early on?

STEIN: Around this time Patti Smith said to Debbie: I love you, come away with me. We'll live as lesbos. Let's stick our tongues down each others' throats. Shall we put that in?

BOCKRIS: [To Harry] Why can't you just tell the story that Patti Smith came up to you and told you to get out of rock'n'roll?

HARRY: 'Cause it's tacky.

STEIN: Yeah, just leave it out.

HARRY: Just say around this time people came up to me and told me to get out of rock'n'roll. Patti wasn't the only one. I was pretty horrible. I deserved to be told to get out of rock'n'roll. I was pathetic. Horrible and pathetic. I was very shy and stiff.

BOCKRIS: You weren't good enough for rock'n'roll?

STEIN: No, that didn't have anything to do with it. Everybody knew she was too good-looking and she was a threat. Our bass player Fred's last show was Jungle Night when Debbie, Tish and Snooky dressed up as jungle girls.

HARRY: We all wore leather thongs. Fred quit that night.

STEIN: He didn't really quit.

HARRY: He *quit*.

STEIN: He didn't.

HARRY: He stopped playing, didn't he?

STEIN: Well, he ran off the stage.

HARRY: For God's sake, when did he quit?

STEIN: He ran into the street in the middle of a song because the set was so horrible and disgusting.

HARRY: It was always disgusting! To say we were a garage band was a compliment, because we were a gutter band. We were a sewer band. We were disgusting.

STEIN: But all this stuff about us being shattered and blown out wasn't any more than usual.

HARRY: You know that's true, Chris! It's true! It was so, because all we did was lay in bed for a while.

STEIN: What are we doing now?

HARRY: That's all *you* ever do!

STEIN: That's all *we* ever do.

HARRY: Bullshit! It was a new thing to me then. I wasn't into it then. I had a day job.

STEIN: Shut up! [To Bockris] Just say that Fred quitting really ripped the bottom out from underneath us. Period.

HARRY: It ripped the bottom out from underneath *me*!

STEIN: Will you shut up?

HARRY: Because it meant the bass part went out.

STEIN: Stop it! There's not much tape left. *Please!* I don't want to do this if you're going to keep carrying on, Debbie!

HARRY: [In a very small voice] Sorry.

STEIN: You gotta shut up and stop it! If you don't I'll kick your fucking ass! Now shut up. Watch *Meteor* on TV. Look, look!

Marianne Faithfull has an ability to create an immediate intimacy, drawing you into the circumference and atmosphere of her life with a jolt of time travel that is extraordinarily powerful if at first a little unnerving. I enjoy seeing her more everytime I see her.

6

An Interview With Marianne Faithfull

"I had this thing that I wasn't good enough because I'm white."

At her hotel on East Fifty-third Street in New York City, I met Marianne Faithfull. We walked one block east to 11 Nido, an Italian restaurant, where we were given a quiet corner table and served an exquisite meal, although I cannot remember what we ate. Within minutes of sitting down with Marianne, I was completely caught up in the rhythms of her being – her energy, pain, strength, anger; her edges.

A star in 1964 – when she recorded Mick Jagger, Keith Richards, and Andrew Oldham's 'As Tears Go By' – Marianne saw her career crash at the end of that decade as a result of a lethal combination of drink, drugs, and being a woman in The Rolling Stones. She returned in 1979 with the brilliant album Broken English, *and the years that followed culminated with her 1990 album* Blazing Away, *a moving and joyous testament of her life. She has just completed a year-long international tour for that album.*

When we left the restaurant after this interview, appreciative waiters applauded Marianne, who went her own way outside. I had to sit down on a stoop for several minutes to collect myself before proceeding. Marianne Faithfull is a very intense person. She was right there all the time I was with her.

VICTOR BOCKRIS: Do audiences react differently to you now than in the past?

63

MARIANNE FAITHFULL: Yes, they do. I feel very much, especially in America, that they've been with me through everything. People have seen me through these things. Their love and acceptance has worked, and now I'm really able to give it back; I'm capable.

BOCKRIS: Small halls and clubs like the Bottom Line are such good places for you. There are so many people who get stuck in that bigger scene, and then they lose contact with the audience.

FAITHFULL: Well, I'm determined not to do that. I need a place where I can see the people and where they can really see me. It's so important that I never try to compete in any way with the male rock thing – whatever that is. I hate it. I hate those concerts. I don't go to them myself. I want to do things that I would like to see.

BOCKRIS: Changing the subject to songwriting, was 'Why D'Ya Do It?' written with Heathcote Williams?

FAITHFULL: It's a poem, and he wrote it. I went to see him and asked him if he had anything for me. He brought this out and said, "I've got this, but I really would like Tina Turner to do it." And I said, "Will you read it?" And he did. I just laughed. "Are you kidding? You think Tina Turner would do this? You're out of your mind. I'll do it. You won't get anyone else to do this, so let me have it." And he did.

BOCKRIS: You once said that 'Sister Morphine' was the most redeeming song you'd ever performed.

FAITHFULL: God.

BOCKRIS: How was 'Sister Morphine' actually written?

FAITHFULL: Mick Jagger had the tune and was playing it around the house we lived in in London, in Cheyne Walk, in the Sixties. I never would have imposed myself on the tune if he had done anything with it. But it never seemed to happen, and I got to like the tune. Then I got impatient, so I sat down and wrote the words.

BOCKRIS: Did Keith Richards write the music?

Andy Warhol at Muhammad Ali's training camp in Deerlake, Pa., Fighter's Heaven, August 1977. Warhol was there to take polaroids from which he would make six commissioned paintings of 'The Champ'. (Victor Bockris)

Warhol on phone at the Bunker trying to find something to do after Jagger walked out on us. NYC 1980. *(VB)*

Peter Orlovsky, Allen's companion for four decades, cops some zzzzs during a Ginsberg-Burroughs politcal discussion at The Bunker. *(VB)*

Above: Jean Michel Basquiat and Debbie Harry yuk it up, Christmas 1986. *(VB)*

Above: William Burroughs, Laurie Anderson and John Giorno at a Giorno album cover session, 1978. *(Marcia Resnick)*

Above: Dylan teaches Allen a few chords before they go to play over Kerouac's grave in the movie *Renaldo and Clara*. Lowell, Mass., 1975 *(Elsa Dorfman)*

Above: Lou Reed smirks as he makes Burroughs sign his last copy of a rare hardback copy of The Last Words of Dutch Schultz. He had forced Bill to give him the book. Burroughs' soon-to-be biographer, Ted Morgan, sits to Burroughs' left He looks so uptight throughout the visit that Lou put him away with an exclamation of "Ted!" when he heard his name, making it sound like the most ridiculous name in the world. Morgan was so enraged by the visit that he forever after claimed Burroughs thought Reed was a horse's ass. In fact, William thought that Lou was sharp and funny. They were two hispers from the same carny world, a world Morgan could not find if you gave him a map. *(VB)*

Above: Ginsberg, Giorno Burroughs look at first edition of *With William Burroughs* in Italian. *(VB)*

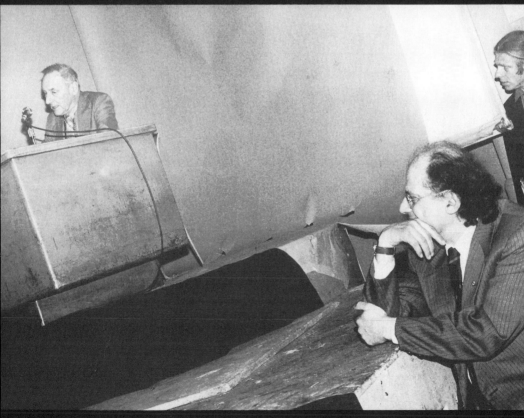

Above: Burroughs reads at Mudd Club. Orlovsky and Ginsberg listen intently. NYC 1979. *(Marcia Resnick)*

Above: The Punks and the Godfather. Victor Bockris, Chris Stein, William Burroughs and Debby Harry. (*Bobby Grossman*)

Above: Terry Southern admires Debbie Harry. NYC, 1978. (*Marcia Resnick*)

Left: The Ramones and Riff Randel (played by PJ Soles) take over *Rock 'n' Roll High School.*

Right: Allen Ginsberg talks to Victor Bockris at a publishing party for Bockris' book on Keith Richards. NY, 1992. (*Bockris Archive*)

Left: The beautiful Liz Derringer snuggles with her husband, the hotter than hell guitarist, Rick. NY, 1973. (*Marcia Resnick*)

ght: Bockris at Groucho Club, publication arty for *Warhol.* London 1989.

RTL présente

8 FÉVRIER 18 h. 30
Théâtre Toursky
22, Bd Ed. Vaillant
MARSEILLE 3ᵉ

BLONDIE

Location : PROCYON
34, rue du Village
(42.37.78)

 Chrysalis DISTRIBUTION PHONOGRAM   UNE PRODUCTION **KCP**

Blondie poster advertising a concert in Marseilles, France, February 8, 1978.
Enough said! (*Chris Stein*)

FAITHFULL: No. Keith Richards didn't have anything to do with it, as such. What he did, which is good, was write to Allen Klein [ex-manager of The Rolling Stones] to tell him that I had written the words; otherwise, I would not have gotten any of the money. But what I want now is the credit.

BOCKRIS: Why didn't you get the credit? Was that just the way things worked in those days? The Stones put only their names on the material?

FAITHFULL: You'd have to ask Mick Jagger that. It's an odd thing. I wrote the words, I did the work; why didn't I get the credit?

BOCKRIS: Did you make formal attempts to get it?

FAITHFULL: Well, I don't know if I did, actually. It's only slowly that I've come to realize that I deserved the credit. I know I wrote the song, but I was in such a lowly place that I was just pleased when I got the money. That pleased me for a long time. Then I realized, This is mad. I should also have the credit. On my record, of course, it says, 'Jagger/ Richards/Faithfull'. I don't know what to do, because I don't want to see Mick Jagger, and I don't want to ask him for anything. I don't think I should. I think I should just get the credit if I did the work. It's crazy.

BOCKRIS: Why did Keith write the letter to Allen Klein? Why didn't Mick Jagger write it?

FAITHFULL: *Are you mad?*

BOCKRIS: It's interesting that Richards did that.

FAITHFULL: Yes, of course. Richards is . . . He didn't go as far as he might have; if he'd done the right thing he'd have said, "Give her the money and the credit." Of course he couldn't do that.

BOCKRIS: Do you feel that when you perform songs by Lennon and 'I'll Keep It With Mine', by Dylan, that you are collaborating with the songwriter?

FAITHFULL: In a way, because I do change it. Just by doing it. I feel very close to the people who wrote these songs. I must admit I feel they wrote them for me. I do feel that they are mine.

BOCKRIS: Well, what about 'I'll Keep It With Mine'?

FAITHFULL: That's definitely mine.

BOCKRIS: Nico's story, of course, is that Dylan wrote that song for her.

FAITHFULL: Well, I expect he did. I don't care. But actually it's mine. I once went to an Otis Redding concert in London. I went with Keith Richards, and it was a wonderful show. It was announced that Redding was going to sing a song that he had written, and he sang 'Satisfaction'. Incredibly brilliant. We went backstage, me and Keith Richards – I don't call these people Keith or Mick anymore, I give them their full names – and I said to Redding, "How could you say that you wrote 'Satisfaction'?" And it was fascinating. Otis Redding insisted, and did not back down, that he wrote it. Now, that's not similar to my situation with 'Sister Morphine', but it is a bit how I feel about all sorts of other things. And I believe that he was right; I understand what he meant.

BOCKRIS: You are compared with Edith Piaf and Lotte Lenya, but neither of them were English.

FAITHFULL: The reason, and it's quite valid, is because of my mother. You see me and you see how my accent is – I'm very English. But actually my mother is Austro-Hungarian and straight from that tradition. My whole cultural background is Europe, not England. My mother danced in Berlin just before the war, saw Max Reinhardt; and my uncle, her brother, knew Brecht and Weill. As a young dancer my mother wasn't great friends with them, but she knew them.

BOCKRIS: Would she tell you about them?

FAITHFULL: Oh, yes. But then I got completely caught up in America. Bessie Smith, Ma Rainey, and Billie Holiday were my goddesses. And it caused me a lot of pain, because I had this thing that I wasn't good enough because I'm white. I didn't know what to do about that. It's terrible, hating yourself for being you. And then I discovered country music, and that helped, because I realized there is white soul. There are white groups, and you can do it if you're white. So I calmed down a bit. Then slowly I began including European things and realizing that they too were white blues and white soul. There is a lineage. And I fit in. And of the English singers, the one that I loved is Ruth Etting.

BOCKRIS. Who would you say are your greatest three or four influences as a vocalist?

FAITHFULL: Billie Holiday, John Lennon, Hank Williams, and Piaf.

BOCKRIS: Does the British culture of the Forties and Fifties explain the brilliant explosion of music that happened in Britain in the early Sixties?

FAITHFULL: It was so repressed; it wasn't like that in America at all. Marilyn Monroe and Lenny Bruce. Charlie Parker. There were a lot of things going on. We didn't have shit.

BOCKRIS: Do you think that the music of the Sixties was predominantly a working-class explosion.

FAITHFULL: It was wonderful. That was the best thing about it. I remember being on tour, my first tour. I was seventeen, a silly little middle-class girl, and so arrogant. I was just so grand you wouldn't believe it, grand as only a beautiful seventeen-year-old can be. I thought I was too good for anything. And there I was in this bus with these guys [Faithfull performed alone but toured with three or four bands, including The Hollies]. They were charming, they were from Manchester – and now they're all great geniuses, Graham Nash and all these people. But they were actually the first human beings I had met, apart from my mum, that is. And my brother was a human being.

BOCKRIS: I remember the grayness of that time, when one could burst into tears spontaneously, just walking around England, particularly on a Sunday.

FAITHFULL: Well, we all experienced that directly, in those times, on those tours. They were really hard work, and of course there were no days off. We worked on Sundays. And there were all these laws – you couldn't do this and you couldn't do that. We couldn't get our work done because these stupid fucks were doing this stuff. [English licensing laws required halls and bars to close early on Sundays, and local police enforced them.] You'd hear the roadies and the band going on about it, in a very normal way, and it was incredible, really.

BOCKRIS: Jonathan Cott quotes you as saying that you are firmly resisting the "long tradition of female singers who immolated themselves on the altar of their art."

FAITHFULL: Well, that's very important; I'm very conscious of that. I've found that when you are in a real state like I was, the question is, can therapy damage your art? It's been a problem ever since therapy began. Mary-Louise von Franz, who was Jung's student, talks about this fear that the artist has of therapy and immature work. Her thing is that the great healing force for this kind of immaturity is work. And this is what people like me, like anyone else in that state, can't take. They can't bear the thought of a disciplined work regime. And yet this is the one thing that will really help you. And then she says that it is very common for neurotics to be writing about their own problems. They get an opportunity to work them out. But what happens is that they never do. There it is, you fuck it up again, and you have to go back to the beginning. Then you keep writing about the same thing again and again, and you never get past that. This is where therapy can help. She says the most interesting thing is that there are enough pseudo-artists in the world. If therapy is going to destroy somebody's art it may not have been such great art anyway. And good therapy will not affect it at all. It won't make it better and it won't make it worse. The artist will work past therapy and go on. I accept that. If what I do could be crushed by therapy, then it wasn't worth doing.

BOCKRIS: There are so many young girls these days who aspire to be pop stars. What advice would you give to a young girl thinking she might go for this?

FAITHFULL: Don't count on fame – that's not the point. It's not important. The celebrity and the glamour come naturally. That part is simple: you just get a make-up artist and a stylist and a publicist. The really important bit is the commitment to life, the commitment to people. And to the work involved. Madonna is a highly disciplined, serious artist. Trust on a very deep level that everything will be O.K. And don't despair. The great tragedies, the big self-destructive tragedies, happen in a split second, when the human being gives up and thinks, I can't do it. It's too much for me, I'm gonna cop, I'm gonna check out. That is an illusion. It's actually a hallucination. It's not true; it's gonna be O.K. Just hang on.

BOCKRIS: The *Blazing Away* album was described as "a form of autobiography as resonant as any literary equivalent."

FAITHFULL: [*Laughs*] It was?

BOCKRIS: That was the press release. Were you consciously putting together a set of songs to make an autobiography?

FAITHFULL: This is hard to talk about without getting very pretentious. The questions for me were, 'Why did all this happen?' 'What is all this about?' 'What have I got here?' 'What is it?' Then suddenly came the question, 'What have I got to give?' And people had been writing to me, asking me to write my autobiography. And I said no. But I knew that there is something in my story – people have told me that it is such a transcendent thing, although I wouldn't call it that myself. I wanted to turn all that into something life-enhancing, because I have quite a bit of offstage guilt about being such a negative role model. I'm forty-four now, my son is twenty-four, and I've had continual criticism from old-guard addicts who feel I've let their side down and all that shit. And I've had to question my responsibility to others and the example I've set.

BOCKRIS: One could say the album is an autobiography of your image, perhaps, more than an autobiography of you, yourself.

FAITHFULL: Yes. And that is what I'd be much more comfortable with, because I'm very aware of that; I remember doing it. I remember making a decision to project a persona for people to have. I'm not saying this was wrong and this was right. I'm not going to judge it myself. That's why I don't want to say that it's transcendent, it's degraded, blah-blah-blah. I am very cautious about saying there is any kind of message. I know, because I've heard it, that there is something in that record. I call it a vibration. In my actual life, personally, there is a lot of grace. There really is. I know that, and that must have spilled over into the work.

BOCKRIS: The way you deliver your material has an edge of joy to it that gives it a positive blast.

FAITHFULL: But you see, that grace has nothing to do with me. I think that as human beings we are just different aspects of God at play. We all have it. All we need to do, really, is clear the channel, that passage, and it shines right through. It's a radiance that all human beings have. All I've done is just clear the channel. And I reflect it back. I'm just giving it back. That's the job.

Susan Sontag revealed a characteristic openness to new experiences and generations by granting me this interview to *High Times*. In going after unexpected subjects for the magazine I was often surprised by how many of them said they had agreed to do the interview because it was for *High Times*. They wanted to reach that generation. Luckily when the piece came out, although the magazine did blow up any quote she made about drugs, making her look like a major user when she hardly ever used them at all, Castro was on the cover. That went some way toward cooling the vibe when I delivered the magazine to her doorman.

7

Susan Sontag:
The Dark Lady of Pop Philosophy

Among American intellectuals, Susan Sontag is probably the only Harvard-educated philosopher who digs punk rock. Sontag became famous in the Sixties when her series of brilliant essays on politics, pornography and art, including the notorious 'Notes on Camp', were collected in Against Interpretation – *a book that defended the intuitive acceptance of art against the superficial, cerebral apprehension of it, then fashionable among a small band of extremely powerful, rigid intellectuals who, for example, dismissed such American classics as* Naked Lunch, 'Howl', On the Road, *Andy Warhol's film* Chelsea Girls, *etc., as trash. With the impact of her concise arguments, Sontag was immediately labeled the 'Queen of the Aesthetes', the philosophical champion of pop art and rock and roll.*

Since then she has written many more essays, a second novel, edited the works of Antonin Artaud (founder of the Theater of Cruelty and an early mescaline user), made two films and undergone radical surgery and two years of chemotherapy for a rare and advanced form of cancer. Thus Susan Sontag continues to live on the edge of life and death, an unusual address for an intellectual essayist but essential for anyone who aspires, as she does, to tell the truth about the present.

Her first book in seven years, On Photography, *was greeted this winter with the familiar violent controversy. Most reviewers treated it as an uncompromising attack on photography itself – everything from photojournalism to baby pictures – and a complete desertion of her Sixties art-for-art's-sake position for the lofty ground of analytical moralism. As Sontag makes clear for the first time in this interview,*

73

On Photography *is not about photography at all, but the way it is put to use by the American system. Thus* On Photography *remains true to Sontag's main idea of her task as a writer: to examine the majority opinion and expose it from the opposite point of view, putting emphasis on her 'responsibility to the truth'. The method has proved explosive.*

Sontag decided to give us an interview instead of attending a Ramones gig at CBGB because she thought it would be fun. She spoke intriguingly for hours about famous dopers she'd known (Jean Paul Sartre, a surprise lifelong speed freak, among them), grass, booze, punk rock, art, the Sixties and – always – truth.

VICTOR BOCKRIS: I've been told that you don't give very many interviews.
SUSAN SONTAG: No, I don't. Sure.
BOCKRIS: Why are you giving this one to *High Times*?
SONTAG: Well, I'm giving this one because I haven't published a proper book in seven years. I'm giving an interview because . . . because it's *High Times*. I was intrigued by that, sure. I thought, well, that's odd. I hadn't thought of that. And also because I'm going away, so it's a little bit hit-and-run. And I suppose in a way I have been hiding.

There is a crisis you go through after a certain amount of work. Some people say after a decade, but when you've done a lot of work and you hear a lot about it and discover that it really does exist out there – you can call it being famous – then you think, "Well, is it any good?" And, "What do I want to go on doing?" And, of course, you can't shut out people's reactions, and to a certain extent you do get labeled, and I hate that.

I find now that I am being described as somebody who has moved away from the positions or ideas that I advocated in the Sixties, as if I've reneged. I just got tired of hearing my ideas in other people's mouths. If some of the things that I said stupidly or accurately in the Sixties, which were then minority positions, have become positions that are much more common, well, then again I would like to say something else.

BOCKRIS: Do you feel you have any responsibility for the effect of what you have to say on other people?

SONTAG: No, I feel I have a responsibility to the truth. I'm not going to say something that I don't think is true, and I think the truth is always valuable. If the truth makes people uncomfortable or is disturbing, that seems to me a good thing.

I suppose unconsciously I'm always making an estimate when I'm starting some kind of project of what people think. And then I say, well, given that people think this, what can be said in addition to this or what can be said in contradiction to that? There's always some sense of where people are, so I do in a way think of my essay writing as adversary writing. The selection of subjects doesn't necessarily represent my most important taste or interests; it has to do with the sense of what's being neglected or what's being viewed in a way that seems to exclude other things which are true.

But I find myself absolutely baffled by the question of the effect or influence of what one is doing. If I think of my own work and I question what effect it is having, I have to throw up my hands. Beyond these baby statements, "I want to tell the truth" or "I want to write well", I really don't know. It's not only that I don't know, I don't know how I would know, I don't know what I would do with it. I'm always amazed at writers who say, "I want to be the conscience of my generation. I want to say the things that'll change what people feel or think." I don't know what that means.

BOCKRIS: Do you think that the Sixties' concept of a new consciousness changing things is rather lightweight?

SONTAG: Yes. In a word.

BOCKRIS: And yet, drugs are now more a part of our society than they were in the Sixties.

SONTAG: Absolutely. There was an article in the *New York Times* the other day about people smoking pot in public in the major cities, and that being absolutely accepted. That's a major change. I have a friend who spent three years in jail in Texas for having two joints in his pocket. As he crossed from Mexico into Texas he was arrested by the border police. So these changes are important.

BOCKRIS: Do you have any feelings about an increasingly widespread use of drugs?

SONTAG: I think marijuana is much better than liquor. I think a society which is addicted to a very destructive and unhealthy drug, namely alcohol, certainly has no right to complain or be sanctimonious or censor the use of a drug which is much less harmful.

If one leaves it on the level of soft drugs, I think the soft drugs are much less harmful. They're much better and more pleasurable and physically less dangerous than alcohol. And above all, less addictive. So as far as that goes, I think *fine.* What bothers me is that a lot of people are drifting back to alcohol. What I rather liked in the Sixties about the drug use was the repudiation of alcohol. That was very healthy. And now alcohol has come back.

BOCKRIS: Do you think drugs encourage consumers?

SONTAG: What I prefer about soft drugs as opposed to alcohol is that it seems to be more pleasurable; maybe it just has to do with my experience. I'm not terribly interested in soft drugs, but I certainly would prefer a joint to a whiskey any day. I think that I rather like the fact that soft drugs tend to make people a little lazier, and they don't, at least in my experience, encourage aggressive or violent impulses. Of course if you've got them, nothing's going to stop you from acting them out.

But I don't feel that drugs are any more connected with consumerism. It's just a historical phenomenon that the drug culture became widespread at a moment when the consumer society was more developed. And, on the contrary, in North Africa, in Morocco, which is a country that I know pretty well, the new thing for the past 20 years among the younger, more Westernized Moroccans, is alcohol. They think of hashish as the drug of their parents, their parents being lazy and not interested in consumption and getting ahead and modernizing the country. So the young doctors and lawyers and movers and groovers in Moroccan society tend to prefer alcohol.

BOCKRIS: I think it's interesting that in this society we take drugs a lot, and in other societies they don't take drugs at all. What's the difference?

SONTAG: I think what interests me now, the little I know about it, is that this is now becoming a mature drug society, in relation to, let's say, Western Europe. This is because we have enough time that people have been taking drugs in different strata of the society; that we're getting different kinds of drug cultures and even a kind of naturalization of the drug thing; that it's not a big deal. Whereas in a country like France or Italy, which I know pretty well, they're about where we were ten years ago. It's still a kind of spooky thing, it's a daring thing, it's a thing that people use in a rather violent or self-destructive way.

BOCKRIS: Do you do any of your writing on grass?

SONTAG: I've tried, but I find it too relaxing. I use speed to write, which is the opposite of grass. Sometimes when I'm really stuck I will take a very mild form of speed to get going again.

BOCKRIS: What does it do?

SONTAG: It eliminates the need to eat, sleep or pee or talk to other people. And one can really sit 20 hours in a room and not feel lonely or tired or bored. It gives you terrific powers of concentration. It also makes you loquacious. So if I do any writing on speed, I try to limit it.

First of all, I take very little at a time, and then I try to actually limit it as far as the amount of time that I'll be working on a given thing on that kind of drug. So that most of the time my mind will be clear, and I can edit down what has perhaps been too easily forthcoming. It makes you a little uncritical and a little too easily satisfied with what you're doing. But sometimes when you're stuck it's very helpful.

I think more writers have worked on speed than have worked on grass. Sartre, for instance, has been on speed all his life, and it really shows. Those endlessly long books are obviously written on speed, a book like *Saint Genet*. He was asked by Gallimard to write a preface to the collected works of Genet. They decided to bring it out in a series of uniform volumes, and they asked him to write a 50-page preface. He wrote an 800-page book. It's obviously speed writing. Malraux used to write on speed. You have to be careful. I think one of the interesting things about the nineteenth century is it seems like that had natural speed. Somebody like Balzac . . . or a Dickens.

BOCKRIS: They must have had something. Perhaps it was alcohol.

SONTAG: Well, you know in the nineteenth century a lot of people took opium, which was available in practically any pharmacy as a painkiller.

BOCKRIS: Would opium be good to write on?

SONTAG: I don't know, but an awful lot of nineteenth-century writers were addicted to opiates of one kind or another.

BOCKRIS: Is that an interesting concept, the relationship between writers and drugs?

SONTAG: I don't think so. I don't think anything comes out that you haven't gotten already.

BOCKRIS: Then why is there this long history of writers and stimulants?

SONTAG: I think it's because it's not natural for people to be alone. I think that there is something basically unnatural about writing in a room by yourself, and that it's quite natural that writers and also painters need something to get through all those hours and hours and hours of being by yourself, digging inside your own intestines. I think it's probably a defense against anxiety that so many writers have been involved in drugs. It's true that they have, and whole generations of writers have been alcoholics.

BOCKRIS: Is it possible to say what it is that makes someone want to write?

SONTAG: I think for me it's first of all an admiration of other writers. That's probably the greatest single motivation that I have had. I've been so overcome by admiration for a number of writers that I wanted to join that army. And even if I thought that I was just going to be a foot soldier in that army and never one of the captains or majors or generals, I still wanted to do that thing which I admired so intensely. But if I'd never read so many books that I really loved, I'm sure I would not have wanted to be a writer.

BOCKRIS: You recently said that artists should be less devoted to creating new forms of hallucination and more devoted to piercing through the hallucinations that nowadays pass for reality. Do you think artists have a responsibility to arrest decay?

SONTAG: Artists are no different than anybody else. They are first of all creatures of the society that they live in. I think one of the great illusions that people had – and that I shared to a certain extent – was that modern art could be in some kind of permanent adversary, critical relationship to the culture. But I can just see more and more of a fit between the values of modern art and the values of a consumer society.

I don't think any of this can be described in the simple way people used to do in the Sixties, talking about being co-opted. It's a much more organic relationship. It's not that things start out being critical and get taken up by the establishment. It's that the values in a great deal of avant-garde or modern art are values that fit perfectly well in a consumer society, where everyone's supposed to have pluralistic taste and standards are subjective and people really don't care about the truth.

BOCKRIS: Do you see punk as a moral movement?

SONTAG: I really don't know how to answer that. One is so suspicious of what one's reactions might be because one is ten years older. I remember when I first heard The Rolling Stones. When I went to their very first concert in New York at the Academy of Music, I was absolutely thrilled. But I was ten or twelve years younger than I am now. I haven't gone to any punk rock concerts, but I have some records. And I find in the lyrics something rather different, a kind of despair that I didn't feel with The Rolling Stones. I mean, I don't feel offended. I don't feel outraged, it's nothing like that, but I feel a sort of bleakness. I agree that the society that is so nihilistic at its core does not deserve a sanctimonious art which simply covers up the inner bleakness of the society, so in that sense, of course I'm not against . . .

BOCKRIS: It releases a lot of energy when someone suddenly puts their finger on the pulse of the time. I know from being in England in '62 when The Beatles broke. It simply made everyone feel good.

SONTAG: I'd like to believe in the comparison you're suggesting, and I try to think that way too because I'm horrified by this kind of sanctimonious moralistic reaction to everything, and I remember exactly what you're describing. I remember saying to myself, to my son and to friends, I've never felt so good. I felt a physical energy, a sensual energy, a sexual energy, but above all a feeling in my body . . .

But you see, I think the Sex Pistols and the other groups would be quite acceptable if they seemed more ironic to people. And I think they are very ironic. But I think they're not perceived as ironic, and once they are perhaps that will be their form of domestication. Then it will be perfectly all right. You see, listen, I didn't want to be labeled the 'Queen of the Aesthetes' in the Sixties, and I don't want to be the

'Queen of the Moralists' in the Seventies. It's not as simple as that at all.

BOCKRIS: I think you're being forced into that position.

SONTAG: Well, I see that now, I see that in everything that I have dared to read about myself that thing comes up. Something that interests me less and less is the narcissism of this society, is the way that people just care about what they're feeling. And it isn't that I think there's something wrong about caring about what you feel, but I think that you have to have some vocabulary or some stretch of the imagination to do it with, and it seems that the means are shrinking.

"How are you feeling?"

"Oh, well, I'm feeling fine. I'm very laid back, er wow, terrific."

What is being said about feelings is less and less. It's awfully primitive. You do your thing and I'll do my thing. That kind of attitude seems very shallow. It seems as if an awful lot of complexity has been lost. If one can keep the debate going between the aesthetic way of looking at things and the moralist way of looking at things, that already gives more structure, more density to the situation.

If I seemed to be championing the aesthete's way of looking at things it's because I thought the moralists really did have it all their way at the time I started writing in the Sixties. If I seem to be championing a moralistic way of looking at things it's because there seems to be a very shallow aestheticism that's taken over. It's certainly not the aestheticism that I was associating myself with.

Oscar Wilde remains one of my idols. I haven't changed. I don't repudiate what I said then, but I hear echoes of a kind of superficial nihilism that seems associated with an aesthetic position that drives me up the wall. It seems that people have become so passive. When you mentioned the word *energy*, of course if I can see punk rock in that way I can feel it, and of course it's not possible to get it by playing a couple of records on this inadequate stereo; you have to be in an audience. I remember the Academy of Music in 1964. What it was like to be in that audience that day was incredible.

BOCKRIS: You should go down to CBGB, that club on the Bowery.

SONTAG: Yeah, I wanted to go down and see the Ramones.

BOCKRIS: You've said that what you're personally looking for is art that would make you behave differently.

SONTAG: Yeah, I'm looking for things that will change my life, right? And that of course will give me energy. And I don't mean moral lessons in this dry sense, but something that would give me energy, that would also not simply provide me with this kind of fantasy alternative but would be an alternative that could be lived out, that would make my way of seeing things perhaps more complicated rather than less complicated.

See, I think a lot of what we get most pleasure out of is essentially simplifying. First of all, most of art in the last hundred years has been saying everything is terrible, and then it says the only thing one can do is resist the temptation of suicide, if that, or forget it, lie back, go with it, enjoy it, it doesn't matter. It seems to me that one should be able to go beyond those alternatives. I don't know how exactly.

BOCKRIS: How do you feel about the future of the planet?

SONTAG: Terrified.

BOCKRIS: But people say that: "Terrified." But I mean do you live in a state of fear?

SONTAG: No, *I* don't live in a state of fear, but I live in a state of desperate concern. I lead a life which is incredibly privileged. We were talking earlier about why I don't make much money, but still just by virtue of being an American, by virtue of doing work that I want to do, that I would do whether I'm paid for it or not, by virtue of being white, I am in a tiny minority of people on this planet. So I don't live in a state of terror; it would be presumptuous of me to be terrified, since I'm always so infinitely privileged just by being:

one, American; two, white; and three, someone who's not a wage slave. But how can one not be full of dread?

Just consider the demographic figure that India is adding 14,000,000 every year. That is to say, a hundred million people every six years. That's when you subtract the deaths from the birth rates. More and more people go to bed hungry every night. More and more people are born than should be born. The environment is becoming more and more polluted, more and more carcinogenic. All kinds of systems of order are breaking down. Lousy as they may be, it's not very likely that one's going to replace them with a better one.

One of the few ideas that I formulated in a very simple way is that however bad things are, they can always get worse. Well, I got very tired in the Sixties with people who were saying that things couldn't be any worse. The repression of the State, fascist America ... Things were terrible, the Vietnam War was an abomination; but all kinds of terrible things have happened in this country, and things can always get worse. It's wrong to say that things can't get any worse. They can.

I think there are long-range ecological and demographic factors that don't seem to be reversible, so that one thinks there will just be a series of catastrophes of one kind or another – worldwide famines or breakdowns of social systems, increasing amounts of political repression. That, I think, is the fate of most people in the world. I think the United States is in a very special position. I don't think the breakdown of this system is imminent at all. But at what a cost to the rest of the world! I mean, the United States has 6 percent of the population of the world, and we're using 60 percent of the resources and creating 60 percent of the garbage.

BOCKRIS: Does it annoy you?

SONTAG: No, it doesn't annoy me, it outrages me.

BOCKRIS: Yeah. I just find it hard to deal with those kind of words, like terror and outrage. Because you're outraged by this and yet, excuse me, but your latest book is – I find it a very interesting book – but it's about photography.

SONTAG: *It's not about photography!*

BOCKRIS: Ah! Fair enough.

SONTAG: (Laughing) Now you've got me. I said it, and I didn't mean to say it. It's not about photography, it's about the consumer society, it's about advanced industrial society. I finally make that clear in the last essay. It's about photography as the exemplary activity of this society. I didn't want to say it's not about photography, but it's true, and I guess this is the interview where that will finally come out. It isn't, it's about photography as this model activity which has everything that's brilliant and ingenious and poetic and pleasureful in the society, and also everything that is destructive and polluting and manipulative in the society. It's not, as some people have already said, against photography; it's not an attack on photography.

BOCKRIS: I think you're a great celebrator of photography.

SONTAG: Well, of course it's been one of the great sources of pleasure in my life, and it seemed to me obvious that that was the origin of the book. It's about what the implications of photography are. I don't want to be a photography critic. I'm not a photography critic. I don't know how to be one.

I have gotten immense pleasure out of photographs. I collect them, cut them out, I'm obsessed by them; to me they're sort of dream images, magical objects. I go to photography shows, I have hundreds of photography books. This is an interest that antedates not only the books, but it's part of my whole life. But I think one can't think about photography. This is a book that's an attempt to *think* about what the presence of photography means, about the history of photography, about the implications of photography.

BOCKRIS: Do you think we're going to see any extreme changes in this country within the next ten or fifteen years?

SONTAG: I ask myself that all the time. A couple of years ago I would have said yes right away. Around '73–'74 it seemed that things were changing very rapidly and for the worse. It seemed to me that there was obviously an immense reactionary current in the country, that things were going to be very depressing. One thing I want to disassociate myself from, although I've said some things that could contribute to it, is this facile repudiation of the Sixties. I mean the Sixties were a terrific time. It was the most important time in my life. If perhaps in the end we were too busy having a good time and thought things were a little simpler than they turned out to be, it doesn't mean that most of what we learned isn't very valuable; and we want to hang onto that and not be seduced by some kind of new simplification or this kind of pervasive demoralization of the Seventies.

I feel very irritated by the way people are so demoralized. What has gotten lost in the past few years is the critical sense. I mean what people finally took from the Sixties was that it was okay to do your own thing, that a lot of what seemed to be political impulse was in fact just some kind of psychotherapeutic effort, and that what one thought or hoped was the growth of some kind of serious critical political atmosphere in the country proved to be an illusion. And so you have the same people who went to Vietnam demonstrations becoming the slaves of gurus and psychiatric quacks a couple of years later. That was disappointing. But it was on the whole a very positive change, I think.

BOCKRIS: Then your answer to the question is that at least at the moment you don't see anything that suggests that we'll see extreme changes here in the near future?

SONTAG: I think the first thing to say is that this society is immensely powerful and that this regime, this system is immensely powerful, immensely successful, immensely entrenched, is very clever, has tremendous capacity for absorbing criticism and using it, not just silencing it but using it.

And that there have to be real structural changes to make a difference, otherwise I think people are going to go on in this consumer way, riding along with things as far as they can, being drugged by consumer goods and averting their eyes to the pending catastrophe.

This country is so rich and so powerful and so privileged. I don't think the present mood is anything other than transition. What I worry about much more is the growing force of reaction. That's why I hate to be labeled as a moralist, because I think that an awful lot of bad things are going to happen in the name of moralism, and one has to be very suspicious.

BOCKRIS: How do you feel at this point about your future?

SONTAG: I want to be a better writer. It seems it would be about getting better. To go on.

BOCKRIS: But you must feel that there are totally undiscovered things in front of you?

SONTAG: If I didn't feel that I could discover things that would be very different from what I'm doing, or if I didn't feel that the work I'm doing is part of an approach to something . . . but I do feel that it's always going somewhere. And yet there must be something wrong with that attitude, too. One could go on and on. Say I beat this rare illness and have a long, long life, would I then just go on forever saying I'm getting there, I'm getting there, I'm getting there, until one day my long life would be over?

This was one of the funniest encounters taped but never used in my book on William Burroughs. We had really wanted to get Keith to talk with Bill, but his legal situation in Toronto regarding the heroin trafficking charges was still not completely solved, and the Stones' organisation was doing everything they could to keep Richards disassociated with drugs in the press. Thus Jagger accepted an invitation to dinner with uncharacteristic alacrity. However, it turned out that his purpose was to block the publishing of anything about the Stones and Burroughs. Trying to get a conversation going between Jagger, Burroughs and Andy Warhol under these circumstances was one of the hardest jobs I have ever done. The hilarious results follow.

8

The Captain's Cocktail Party:
Dinner with Mick Jagger, Andy Warhol
and William Burroughs

*It was a bitter cold night on March 1st of 1980 as I headed towards
William Burroughs' headquarters on the Bowery. His section of the
building had once been the locker room of a gymnasium, and he had
humorously but with a serious subtext named it 'The Bunker'. It was
here in the mid-Seventies that he made a stand against his muse,
hammering away at the typewriter for six years writing the novel*
Cities of the Red Night (1981) *which would signal the commence-
ment of a new blitzkrieg in his career.*

*I was hyper-nervous. The night's agenda was to record during
dinner a conversation between Burroughs, Jagger and Warhol. The
event was to me of monumental significance for it was the first and,
as it would turn out, only occasion on which the three would be
brought together.*

*The meeting had been arranged in part to fulfill an assignment for
Burroughs to write about The Rolling Stones' twentieth anniversary,
for a volume edited by David Dalton. What worried me was whether
Jagger would show up, and if so, when. He was notoriously late
for appointments, including his concerts; Burroughs, a suit-and-tie
gentleman from the old school, aged sixty-three, looked upon late rock
stars as uncouth individuals with no respect for their elders.*

*Within ten minutes of my arrival the doorbell rang. Bounding
down the flight of gray stone steps and opening the series of three iron
gates that separated The Bunker from the outside world, secured by*

89

triple padlocks, I recognized, wrapped in an enormous hooded parka, the skinny, dandyish Andy Warhol. As we entered Bill's domain, I was injected by Andy's enthusiastic energy and lightness of being. He instantly switched on his astonished-by-anything-act, running around the huge white-on-white windowless space like an eight-year-old at a birthday party. Apart from William's battered gray metal detective's desk with an Olympia typewriter atop it, a dining table and chairs were the sole furniture in The Bunker. He admired the Brion Gysin paintings, the pipes that ran across the ceiling, Bill's neatly folded pajamas on his bed. The row of urinals in the toilet gave pause for speculation.

As the doorbell pealed again, I raced down the stairs to find the diminutive photographer, Marcia Resnick, behind a mound of equipment. As she proceeded to set it up, I got Bill and Andy drinks. They sat at the conference table, discussing Professor Shockley's theory on artificially inseminating women of higher than average I.Q.s with men of the same to create a super race.

"Bill, you should sell yours!" I enthused. "Imagine who would want The Sperm of William Burroughs.*"*

"You could do it right now,*" Andy insisted. "All they have to do is put it in the freezer."*

"I'll do it right away!" Bill exclaimed, musing, "I bet Mick Jagger could name his own price!"

Meanwhile, Marcia had arranged an elaborate series of spotlights with which to fry my subjects. Horrified by how Mick Jagger would react on entering the premises to being assaulted by blinding white heat, I ordered her to dismantle her lights, screaming, "How can you expect people to have intellectual conversation while they're being grilled like fish on a barbecue?" She screamed back, but when Bill and Andy agreed, she rapidly stashed her gear in Bill's bedroom.

This disrupted the harmonious scene. In the ensuing silence, Bill's mouth started twitching, Andy stared blankly at his plate as if it were a great painting, I began to sweat, and Marcia cast withering glances at me. Suddenly, the doorbell chimed yet a third time. I leapt from my seat, glided down the stairs, unflicked the triple locks and came face to face with Mick Jagger. Behind him loomed Jerry Hall and Liz Derringer, jumping up and down in the arctic night. As I followed Jagger up the steep flight of stairs, his dragged-out and flat-footed gait signaled that he was not here because he wanted to be.

As the dinner commenced, Bill was at the head of the table with Mick and Jerry Hall to his right, myself and Andy to his left. Marcia and Liz were at the bottom of the table.

I attempted to negotiate an opening, but Jagger would have none of it.

JAGGER: What are we doing here? What is the purpose of this dinner?

BURROUGHS: The purpose of this dinner is very simple. David Dalton is getting together . . . What *is* this about Victor? The twentieth anniversary of The Rolling Stones?

JAGGER: What? What? That's not been going on for twenty years. They're making it up!

BOCKRIS: Bill, maybe we're confusing it with the twentieth anniversary of *Rolling Stone* magazine.

JAGGER: We're talking at cross purposes. The magazine wasn't founded twenty years ago, nor was the group.

BOCKRIS: So this is just a completely mistaken occasion?

BURROUGHS: It seems to be a mistake all round, but I got nothing to do with it. Don't put it on me, man. David Dalton, who you must know very well . . .

JAGGER: I've met him twice.

WARHOL: He's one of my best friends.

BURROUGHS: Listen, what *is* this thing about?

BOCKRIS: Well listen, man, you told *me* about it.

JAGGER: Couldn't it be *your* twentieth anniversary or something Andy? I mean you've been doing something for twenty years.

BURROUGHS: The Twentieth Century, I mean Anniversary Issue uuummm . . . which presumably would be devoted to

The Rolling Stones' music . . .

BOCKRIS: The point is they asked Bill to write something . . .

WARHOL: Maybe this is one of those things that's going to take three or four years to do.

JAGGER: It's off to a racing start.

BOCKRIS: But The Rolling Stones really did form in 1962, isn't that correct?

JAGGER: Yeah, but it isn't 1982.

BOCKRIS: Maybe they're working on it early.

JAGGER: Maybe there won't be a group in 1982 so we won't have to worry about it.

BOCKRIS: There's a scoop, Bill!

JAGGER: They'll all die in a plane crash or something.

BOCKRIS: Are you going to tour China?

JAGGER: We might. They asked us if we could put it together, but I don't think it's going to work out. Go on over and have a look first.

BOCKRIS: What are the problems?

JAGGER: Money. Someone's got to pay for it. No audience. We have to create an audience first. They have to sell it first.

JERRY HALL: I thought the audience was picked, isn't that what you said?

JAGGER: It would be if you did one show in a small place.

BURROUGHS: I think of pop music as being radar, in a sense, that you send it out and something bounces back. It may be good or it may not, but often it is.

JAGGER: It's a long way to go.

BURROUGHS: I am saying in this essay that the whole cultural revolution – and I'm talking about the Stones as heroes of the revolution deserving citation, you understand – is over and we have won. Then who are the 'we' and what have we won exactly?

BOCKRIS: You're saying the dissemination of new language and important messages has gone further through pop music than any other form?

BURROUGHS: Yes, that it's one of the most influential things in the cultural revolution because it reached millions. You see, a book can sell hundreds of thousands of copies, but pop music is immediately reaching millions of people.

WARHOL: A book's very hard because the person who translates it can just make it completely different.

JAGGER: I think TV and movies surely must be more effective.

WARHOL: Did you ever hear anybody translate one of your songs into a different language? Does it come out the same?

JAGGER: No, it changes it, doesn't it?

WARHOL: Really a lot.

BOCKRIS: But if the right brain gets a song playing over and over in your head you can't expel it, whereas you can dismiss a movie image at will.

JAGGER: Not to my experience. I get rid of the songs playing in my head. I used to be like that when I was a kid, I couldn't get rid of movie images.

BURROUGHS: Mick, I was saying that the whole cultural revolution was concerned with confrontation, and wouldn't you say this was exactly what pop music was concerned with? Real confrontation between the performer and the audience – never complete of course?

JAGGER: In live music, yes. Listening to the music at home, I don't think it's like that.

BURROUGHS: I was simply saying that my feeling is that the whole cultural revolution is really about confrontation between disparate groups.

JAGGER: But that all seems to have gone past and become sort of fragmented.

BURROUGHS: The whole bit about minority recognition is nothing new. I mean, I can remember back in the 1920s two guys ran an antique store. Everybody in town knew that they were gay, but they didn't want to confront it. It would seem to me that what is happening in an evolutionary way is total confrontation between disparate groups. They got to get together one way or another. That's the way we're going to leave the planet in one piece, you see. You've got all these groups and it comes to a point where they have to get together in one way or another, maybe at a great disadvantage . . .

BOCKRIS: It's quite possible that people could leave the planet during our lifetime, but somehow it's completely unimaginable to me.

HALL: I think lots of people would like to go.

BURROUGHS: Yes, I'd love to go. I'd go *this second.* But do you feel, as I do, that the whole cultural revolution, and a lot of pop music, is about the whole idea of confrontation? Aren't you actually paid to confront your payants? Isn't that what you're doing?

JAGGER: No, it's not like that really. I don't think so. I wouldn't say that was always true. Sometimes it's true.

BOCKRIS: Why do you say that, Bill?

BURROUGHS: Well I just feel that the whole cultural revolution is going in the direction of confrontation.

BOCKRIS: What cultural revolution?

BURROUGHS: My dear, do you realize that thirty or forty years ago a four-letter word could not appear on a printed page. You're asking about what cultural revolution! Holy shit, man, what'd you think we've been doing all these years?

WARHOL: We never think about it, though. He's young enough that he doesn't think about it. A lot of people don't think about it.

BOCKRIS: It happened, and The Rolling Stones were a very big part of it.

BURROUGHS: Pop music was one of the big things in the whole cultural revolution. See, every time they got busted for drugs we were that much closer to decriminalization of pot all over the world because it's becoming a household word.

JAGGER: But what happened after that?

BOCKRIS: It's different, Bill, it's not the same situation now. There was a thing in the paper recently about Ron Wood getting busted. That's not revolutionary, people don't think about it as some sort of symbol.

BURROUGHS: No, but the point is that revolutions gain certain objectives or they don't, and after the objectives are gained, well, that's . . .

BOCKRIS: That's what I'm saying, *there is no cultural revolution now.* I mean, do you think there's a cultural revolution, Mick?

JAGGER: Not that's immediately observable. There's a slow one.

HALL: I think there's always cultural change.

JAGGER: There's no cultural revolution now, I wouldn't think so.

HALL: It's too tiring.

BOCKRIS: But the intensity of audiences hasn't changed that much?

JAGGER: They're intense about certain cultural ideas. There's the whole question of their being able to do anything about it. There's a sense that they just can't do anything about it, and it's always been like that. There was a certain point where people thought that they could, but I think that time passed years ago.

BOCKRIS: When you're playing to audiences now, they're not looking for some incredibly new thing, right?

JAGGER: I've no idea. I never really think about it. There are a lot of people who like to politicize their art with whatever they're posturing to. Is there a telephone in this joint?

[Jagger goes to the phone, and returns a few minutes later.]

BOCKRIS: You haven't played Italy for a long time, right?

JAGGER: I don't play at the moment.

BURROUGHS: Don't blame you there. This whole business happens for months and months and months where I can't write a word, which is, I think, comparable. It's something called writer's block, where you just can't do it.

JAGGER: I don't really want to play on the road at the moment.
BURROUGHS: I don't know whether that happens in other . . .
BOCKRIS: Are you still inundated with movie scripts?
JAGGER: Yeah, but everything just falls to pieces.
BOCKRIS: Bill's big future is as an actor. Bill's getting into acting now.
BURROUGHS: I wouldn't say that.
WARHOL: He wants to play you in the film *The Mick Jagger Story*, starring William Burroughs. He's trying to study you because he's working on the part!
BURROUGHS: Now wait a minute, I think you're advancing a slightly false position here. I play CIA doctors. I can't see my way to playing Mick Jagger.
WARHOL: You know I've known Liz since she was eleven years old.
JAGGER: You knew her then?
WARHOL: These girls all told me they were twenty and they were eleven!
BURROUGHS: What? You've known her that length of time Andy? I don't mean to be untactful . . .
WARHOL: They were pretending they were adults.
LIZ DERRINGER: Some of us went off to the movies, some of us married rock stars.
WARHOL: You hit the big time.
DERRINGER: Some of us jumped out of windows.
WARHOL: Our best friend Andrea Feldman jumped out of a window for the big time.
DERRINGER: She said she was going to make a smash hit on Park Avenue, and she did. She jumped out the window.
WARHOL: She was a confused kid. We cry over Andrea every time.
DERRINGER: She loved Andy so much she used his name. Her name was Andrea but everyone called her Andy and she

always called herself Mrs. Andy Warhol.

WARHOL: Warhola.

BOCKRIS: Who was this Julian Burroughs who said he was your son, Bill?

BURROUGHS: Some kind of a fraud, I remember. Who is this guy?

WARHOL: He was a guy who was running away from being in the army who said he was your son, named Julian Burroughs. And we starred him in a movie called *Naked Restaurant*.

HALL: Is he really your son?

BURROUGHS: No.

HALL: Daddy!

BOCKRIS: But you know Bill was married twice. Ilse Burroughs was his first wife. Like W. H. Auden, he married a woman to get her out of a Nazi-occupied country. W. H. Auden married Thomas Mann's daughter, Elsa Mann, right?

BURROUGHS: Refuting any imputation of anti-Semitism.

WARHOL: And she lived on the Lower East Side.

BOCKRIS: And Ilse Burroughs is still alive.

WARHOL: No, no, but Mrs. Auden lived on the Lower East Side, St. Marks Place. God!

BURROUGHS: Mrs. Burroughs certainly does not live on the Lower East Side! She lives in some fashionable place in Italy.

BOCKRIS: She's apparently very wealthy.

BURROUGHS: I don't see how the fuck she could be wealthy. Certainly not from me.

BOCKRIS: Did she marry you to get a green card or something?

BURROUGHS: Yes. To get away from the Nazis. She came to America and her first job was to work for Ernst Toller. He was a big scientist in those times who worked on the atom bomb. It was rather an amusing story, really, because she was working as his secretary and she always kept very regular hours, getting back at exactly one o'clock after she'd gone out to lunch. Well, it so happened that this day some guy passed her on the street, some old refugee asking for alms, and she was delayed for about ten minutes. When she got back she started going through pictures or something and she said, "Ooooooohhhh, I left without my hat, it is hanging up somewhere." So she goes and opens the bathroom door and he's on the other side. He'd done this several times before, but he'd always arranged it so that someone would come back and rescue him in time.

BOCKRIS: I don't understand what happened. I lost you in the bathroom. He is hanging on the other side of the bathroom door? *Who* is?

BURROUGHS: ERNST TOLLER! She was his secretary.

BOCKRIS: And he was hanging?

BURROUGHS: My dear, look. She was his secretary. He had tried this other times before, but usually he arranged it so that someone came back.

BOCKRIS: He always tried to hang himself and he always tried to arrange it so that someone would come back?

WARHOL: But nobody came back.

BURROUGHS: She was ten minutes late this particular day, that's all.

BOCKRIS: When did you last see The Rolling Stones?

BURROUGHS: Mick's farewell in England. It was at The Roundhouse, I remember.

JAGGER: And after that we only met twice over the intervening years, but we never spoke to each other.

BURROUGHS: I wouldn't say that Mick!

JAGGER: We did talk to each other.

BOCKRIS: You met and there was very little conversation, so one can conclude that the influence, if any, has been mostly sartorial.

BURROUGHS: WHAT! SARTORIAL?

BOCKRIS: Look how similarly dressed they are!

HALL: That's true.

JAGGER: I think Bill's used to being more formal than I am.

HALL: You do dress kind of alike.

JAGGER: But Andy has that special undervest. What's that thing you've got on?

BOCKRIS: It's a bullet-proof jacket.

BURROUGHS: What the hell is that thing? I didn't even get a look at it.

WARHOL: It's a bullet-proof jacket.

BURROUGHS: Yeah, it really is. Oh well, God knows you need one, Andy!

BOCKRIS: So Mick did you ever shoot anyone, or did anyone ever try to shoot you?

JAGGER: No.

BOCKRIS: Bill shot someone, and Andy got shot, let's see . . .

JAGGER: Who did you shoot, Bill? [There was a static pause. Burroughs' eyes, unbluffed, unreadable, pinned on Jagger's face, looking a little surprised that Mick was not aware that he had accidentally shot his wife in Mexico in 1948.]

BURROUGHS: It's a long story. It's a bad story. But I haven't shot anyone right lately. I assure you of that, Mick. I been on my good behavior.

BOCKRIS: Do you need a gun?

JAGGER: Oh yeah. On the road.

BURROUGHS: I always try to keep a gun around the place in case something really awful happens. It gives you a feeling you got something that you can rely on.

JAGGER: Especially in this society.

BURROUGHS: I guess it's pretty much impossible in England.

JAGGER: It's all right in the country, but you can't carry small arms around.

BURROUGHS: This fucking jerk mayor that we got now, he wants to pass some law about mandatory sentences for possession of firearms.

WARHOL: Well, more cops were *killed* . . .

BURROUGHS: Well, so what! You think that the guys that

killed a cop are gonna be deterred by an extra year they might possibly get for possession of a firearm? Holy God what kind of thinking is this? The only person that's gonna suffer from this is the citizen who has a gun.

BOCKRIS: What else do you have written in your notes, Bill?

BURROUGHS: We talked about cultural revolution.

BOCKRIS: We decided that there wasn't a cultural revolution.

JAGGER: Between you and me.

BURROUGHS: What do you mean there isn't a cultural revolution? There was a great cultural revolution that gained many of its objectives, and now there's no necessity . . .

BOCKRIS: So now we're just hanging around waiting for the next thing?

JAGGER: You tell us, Victor.

WARHOL: There's not going to be any wars.

BOCKRIS: Do you think there'll be a war?

JAGGER: There'll be all kinds of them.

[At this point Mick got up to make another phonecall. I hastily whispered to Bill that the interview hadn't proceeded according to plan: *couldn't he think up some more questions.* "I asked him everything I had written down here," Bill replied, adding dryly, "I don't think there's anything more to be extracted." Mick came back in from the other room and announced that he had to leave. Handshakes and farewells were perfunctory. After Mick, Jerry, and Liz left, Andy, Bill, Marcia and I stood around in a dazed group.]

BOCKRIS: I find with these things that if I feel it was good afterwards it was always terrible, and if I feel it was really terrible it was usually good. So it's probably very good!

WARHOL: You were really terrible.

BOCKRIS: It was terrible. Nothing . . .

WARHOL: Happened.

BURROUGHS: Well, I really didn't expect anything *to happen.*

100

The following week, Bill and I figured out what *had* happened. I had been trying to get Keith Richards to visit Burroughs, and Keith had been keen to comply. But Keith had only just gotten off the 1977 heroin trafficking charge in Toronto that could have effectively, once and for all, destroyed The Rolling Stones. Consequently, we concluded, Jagger did not want Burroughs' name associated with Keith Richards' or, for that matter, the Stones', and that he had come to The Bunker for the sole purpose of nixing the possibility of Burroughs writing anything for the Stones' twentieth anniversary, to turn Burroughs off the whole project – and had succeeded.

It was perhaps a testament to the power of William Burroughs' name in 1980 that Mick Jagger himself had felt it necessary to make sure that Burroughs' name would not publicly be associated with his band. Big Bad Bill still stood for the outlaw-pirate myth Keith Richards alone embodied in the Stones.

When I showed William the transcript of the tape he chuckled vigorously, "It's great, man, it's great. And I've got the perfect title, because it's just like when the captain of the ship has a cocktail party and he has to invite all the notable people aboard, but nobody can find any common ground for conversation. We'll call it 'The Captain's Cocktail Party'."

This interview, conducted in 1977, very much in the shadows of the Toronto bust, was one of Richards' first great interviews. He had shied away from the press in the 1960s, but starting in the early '70s he has given a series of interviews which collected together today would, I believe, remain the most articulate, poetic series of interviews with a rock star ever given.

9

An Interview With Keith Richards

Keith Richards has been the Rolling Stones' lead guitarist for the last 15 years and one of rock's leading crusaders and criminals. His most dangerous brush with the law came in 1977 in Toronto, Canada, when he was arrested for possession of heroin with intent to sell.

I interviewed him at a rented house in Westchester County, 60 minutes outside of Manhattan.

BOCKRIS: Do you feel that it was your destiny to be a musician?

RICHARDS: Well, when I used to pose in front of the mirror at 'ome, I was hopeful. The only thing I was lacking was a bit of bread to buy an instrument. But I got the moves off first, and I got the guitar later.

BOCKRIS: Is music magic to you?

RICHARDS: In the way that *magic* is a word for something that is power that we don't fully understand and can enable things to happen. I mean, nobody really understands about the effect that certain rhythms have on people, but our bodies beat. We're only alive because the heartbeat keeps going all the time. And also certain sounds can kill. It's a speciality of the French for some reason. The French are working with huge great speakers which blow down houses and kill laboratory technicians with one solitary blast. I mean, the trumpets of Jericho and all that.

I've seen people physically throw up from feedback in the

studio. It's so loud it started their stomach walls flapping. That's the most obvious aspect of it. But on another level, if you go to Africa or Jamaica, you see people living to that rhythm. They eat, talk, walk, fuck, sleep, do everything to that rhythm. It's magic in that it's an unexplored area. Why, for instance – zoom in 'ere – should rock and roll music suddenly appear in the mid-Fifties, catch hold and just get bigger and bigger and show no signs of abating?

BOCKRIS: Brian Jones was the leader, then Mick became the leader, but now there's a feeling that, musically, you're the leader of The Rolling Stones.

RICHARDS: I guess it takes a long time... I mean, I'm basically doing the same thing now as I always have done. I run around trying to communicate with the rest of them, because Charlie's sitting down and Bill's over there and I'm more free, and I give them the tempo because early on I evolved a certain style of playing that is fairly basic. I know that I can give what's needed to Charlie and Bill and Ronnie to keep the thing together.

BOCKRIS: And to Mick?

RICHARDS: I hope Mick should get the whole thing. I'm trying to keep all the separate things together so that by the time it gets to the front of the stage and out into the audience, it's jelled together.

BOCKRIS: Is the guitar an instrument you can get further and further into?

RICHARDS: I think most guitar players feel that they're always still learning. Nobody ever feels that they've reached anywhere near covering the whole thing. It's still coming up with surprises. Although that's not *the* most important thing to me.

It's never been a function in our band to do one thing or another. We're all doing all of it, you know. That's what happens and that's what interests me about it, it's not who's playing virtuoso. I'm interested in what people can do in terms of an overall sound and the intensity of it that can be done on that level. I mean, five people produce one thing out of five separate things going on. After all, what's the point of dissecting everything and putting parts under a microscope and ignoring the rest?

BOCKRIS: Do you get very high off the response to your records when they're particularly effective in some way?

RICHARDS: Yeah, sometimes, you try to, but it's not always that immediate. You put a record out, and then you get the feeling everybody's disappointed with it. Then two years later you bring another record out, and you suddenly realize that they're all holding this other record up and saying, "If only it was as good as this one." And I know it's not because we're ahead of our time, because that's not ever what we're trying to do.

It's not avant-garde, no, that's not it. It's just that when you've been around as long as we have, people have got their own fixed idea of what they want from the Stones, and it's never anything new. Even though they do really want it, they still compare it with this big moment in the back seat of a car 15 years ago, and it was never as good as then. There's so much nostalgia connected with it that you can't possibly fight, so you have to sometimes let the record seep into their lives. let them have a good time with it first.

A lot of the time with records it's the experiences that people have been through while that record's been playing that makes it special to them. "It's our song, darling." That sort of shit. And the longer you've been around the harder it is to fight that one, 'cos you got so much other stuff which is somebody else's song, darling. And although they're interested and they'll buy the new record, it doesn't mean as much to them as the one they heard that magical night when they screwed 15 chicks.

BOCKRIS: Do you think of songs as short stories?

RICHARDS: Some of them. I mean, things like 'Hand of

Fate' particularly, we got into a story. Others are just connections, almost stream of consciousness. One line doesn't really connect to what's gone before. People say they write songs, but in a way you're more the medium. I feel like all the songs in the world are just floating around: it's just a matter of an antenna, of whatever you pick up.

So many uncanny things have happened. A whole song just appears from nowhere in five minutes, the whole structure, and you haven't worked at all. You're playing and you're bored stiff and nothing's happening, oh dear, and you go out and 'ave a joint or something and *euhuh!* There it is. It's just like somebody tuned in the radio and you've picked it up.

Some people equate good work with being difficult to do, but a lot of the time it's the easiest thing. It just sort of flashes by you so quick that people virtually tell you. You didn't even see it yourself. 'Satisfaction' was the biggest hit we've ever had, and it just came *boing bang crash*, and it was on tape before I felt it.

BOCKRIS: It's obvious that everyone's life is very much involved at this point with drugs and increasingly so, and it's not going to get less . . .

RICHARDS: Oh, no way, no.

BOCKRIS: It's something that people have to talk about, it's something we need to know more about. Do you have any advice you could give people who read *High Times* about the drug situation, generally speaking, in America?

RICHARDS: I don't think I'm in any position to give any *advice*, as such, but maybe just by talking about it we can make things a bit clearer. It's interesting that they're lightening up on the marijuana laws slowly, and it's accelerating. I mean, since I've come to the States, New York is decriminalized, and once that sort of thing happens it snowballs. Already you hear talk of a commission looking into cocaine to give that a different status.

In a way I feel it's all a bit of a game because there's all this flimflam about decriminalization, which isn't legalization, and eventually what it comes down to is money anyway. If they can figure out a way of taking it over and making bread out of it, it'll be legal. The only reason methadone's such a big deal in America is because a lot of people are making millions on it.

BOCKRIS: But why can't they find a way at this point to make money out of grass and cocaine?

RICHARDS: Because I think they realize that even if they sell 20 filtered Acapulco golds, real grass heads will still be buying their stash from the man who comes over the border with it under the floorboards of his truck. If you want good tobacco, you don't buy Newports or Marlboros. You go to some little tobacco stall and choose your tobacco.

BOCKRIS: Then you think because of the quality differences, marijuana is a very hard thing to merchandise?

RICHARDS: 'Oo knows? Let's just say that I can't see myself, or anybody that I know, preferring to buy a packet of prerolled marijuana cigarettes when I know that it's going to be grade C.

BOCKRIS: But doesn't it seem more and more necessary to recognize that the human being is a chemical machine?

RICHARDS: Yes. I think that what we can really say is that anybody interested in drugs and wanting to take anything ought first to find out as much as they can about what it is that they're taking, what it is that it does to them, in order that they can compensate as much as necessary for what it is they're introducing into their systems. Even with grass, so many people don't take the simplest precautions.

I think that, personally, it's purely a matter of the person concerned. I mean, it's like a good blowjob. You know, in some states that's still illegal. It's just a matter of how far people are prepared to put up with so-called authorities prying into their lives. If they really don't want to accept it, then they'll do something about it because there'll be no way they can enforce it.

The other way, I think, is from the government. They ought

to do a lot more about educating people about drugs, rather than just trying to scare people by keeping them in the dark about everything, including possible ways of getting off really heavy drugs, because it can be done perfectly painlessly. That isn't the main problem. As they'll all say, disintoxication is 5 percent of the battle; 95 percent is keeping them off anything when you send them back. But 'ow do you know when all you're doing is keeping them on methadone all the time? You don't give them a chance that way.

BOCKRIS: Do you think alcohol addiction is as hard to kick as drug addiction?

RICHARDS: Yes, I think so. All these things are very individual. One drug'll have a different effect on one person than on someone else. I can booze for weeks and months and get lushed every night, and then, because I have a change of environment or whatever, I can stop and just not miss it. I just *can't* stop smoking cigarettes for the life of me. I'm as addicted to that as the biggest junkie is addicted to heroin. But then, millions of us are. That's something else.

Booze is something that I can take or leave, but it's a poison. I do feel there's that double standard that we all talk about. I consider booze to be far more harmful than any other available drug, far more damaging to the body, to the mind, to the person's attitude. The way some people change on it is amazing, and then, goddamit, every morning when you wake up you've got a cold turkey whether you like it or not. You know, just because it's called the 'hangover' . . . It seems to me to be the most uneconomical and inconvenient high you could possibly have, 'cos every morning you've got to pay for it. I mean, even a junkie doesn't have to do that unless he decides to stop or runs out of stuff, but even if you've got bottles of booze in the morning, you've still got a hangover. And it just seems so vague putting yourself through those constant incredible changes. That's what I think really does you with booze.

BOCKRIS: Do you pay a lot of attention to taking care of yourself physically, considering the amount of work you do?

RICHARDS: I don't pay that much attention to it, just because I've never had to. I'm very lucky in that everything's always functioned perfectly, even under the most incredible strains and amounts of chemicals. But I think a lot of it is to do with a solid consciousness of it in a regulatory system that serves me. I never take too much of anything. I don't go out for a big rush or complete obliteration. I sometimes find that I've been up five days, and I'll collapse and just fall asleep. But that's about the only thing that I do to myself, and I only do that because I find that I'm capable of doing it.

BOCKRIS: Have you read William Burroughs' statement in *Junky*: "I think I am in better health now as a result of using junk at intervals than I would have been if I had never been an addict."?

RICHARDS: Yeah, I agree with that. Actually, I once took that apomorphine cure that Burroughs swears by. Dr. Dent was dead, but his assistant, whom he trained, this lovely old dear called Smitty, who's like mother hen, still runs the clinic. I had her down to my place for five days, and she just sort of comes in and says, "Here's your shot, dear, there's a good boy." Or, "You've been a naughty boy, you've taken something, yes you have, I can tell." But it's a pretty medieval cure. You just vomit all the time.

BOCKRIS: What's the new cure they're working on in London at the moment?

RICHARDS: There's a Dr. Paterson who's been working on an electro-acupuncture cure that she's developed from a colleague in Hong Kong. Her husband was a Fleet Street journalist, a real hustler, so he figured they could market it. It's a little box about six inches by two inches with two wires coming out, one on each side. You plug one of these wires into each ear and they put out a beat that you can regulate yourself. As long as the beat is going on, you don't feel any pain. I

111

had Dr Paterson and her husband flown over from England, and they stayed with me during the cure. I kept this thing plugged in for 20 days. Anita and I did it together. You wake up in the morning and you feel all right. You can read a book, have a cup of tea. Things you could normally never do on first days getting off.

BOCKRIS: We live in a time where so much could be done medically to the system. With the correct medical information or supervision, we could take drugs all the time.

RICHARDS: Look at the astronauts. I mean, they're completely chemically regulated from the minute they start that thing until they come down. I think the sooner they realize that, they're gonna have to take notice of it and they start learning and they start teaching people more about certain things . . . I don't think any drug is harmful in itself. All of them have their uses and their good sides, so it's the abuse of them and the fact that, because of their so-called illegality, one has to get them from dubious sources, so you never know what you're actually getting. Maybe you're getting what you're after, but it's mixed with strychnine, which has happened to several people I know.

BOCKRIS: Have you ever been in a dangerous situation with drugs?

RICHARDS: No. I don't know if I've been extremely lucky or if it's the subconscious regulatory thing I've gotten, because I'm not extremely careful, but I've never turned blue in somebody else's bathroom. I consider that the height of bad manners. I've 'ad so many people do it to me and it's really not on, as far as drug etiquette goes, to turn blue in somebody else's john. You suddenly realize that somebody's been in there for like an hour and you 'aven't 'eard a sound, and I think it's such a drag, because I think it's a drag when people do it to me, thumping on the door: "Are you all right?" "Yeah! I'm having a fucking crap!"

But people do do it. I mean, if somebody's been in the

john for hours and hours I'll do it, and I know 'ow annoying
it is when I hear the voice comin' out: "Yeah, I'm all right!"
But sometimes I'm glad I've done it, because we've knocked
the door down and there's somebody going into the last
stages of the colors of the rainbow and that's really a drag.
The ambulance comes and ... clear everything up. Because
you can't pretend 'e's just fallen ill or something.

BOCKRIS: Rock is like drugs in a way, because people listen
to it to cure their pain. Rock music makes you feel good,
brings you out of yourself under any circumstances at all.

RICHARDS: It will do that for you in a way. Maybe why drugs
are so associated with rock music is that the people who
actually create the music no longer get that feeling from rock
unless they're actually playing it. I mean, they can't put a
record on and just feel good anymore because it's just so
much to do with part of their business. So you turn to other
things to make yourself feel good. It's a theory [laughing] ...
I don't know. That's my excuse, anyway.

BOCKRIS: But in a way, you're addicted to the guitar, right?

RICHARDS: Yeah. There's another thing. Now maybe it's
because rock and roll's such a tight formula. The most important thing is, because the formula is so strict, it's the variations
that come about within this format that are the things people
turn onto. Because it's the same old thing again, but there's
one or two slightly different ways of doing things that make
one record stand out different from another. And it's when
you're into it to that degree of trying to find ...

BOCKRIS: How much do you think you keep being successful
because you work so hard?

RICHARDS: I think it's probably got more to do with it than
even we realize, because it's very easy to be lazy when you
don't have to work. I've found it's very dangerous for me to
be lazy. I develop lots of nasty habits, which are not good for
me, whereas if I keep working – and in a way it's just like a
compulsion – I'll keep myself together. The minute I relax

and let it go, I just sort of drift. I can drift into anything. I'm fair game!

BOCKRIS: Well, I know Mick is, but are the rest of the members of the band into working like that?

RICHARDS: Yeah. Charlie loves to be at home, but that's his own little battle, 'cos he also likes to work. If Charlie could find a way of being on the road every night, but also being at home, he'd do it. Ronnie lives for nothing but playing, and that's the way Mick and I have always been. What we've got to push for now is a way to work regularly and to work a lot more varied venues in a lot more varied places, to get off the old warpath.

For instance, if they lay an American tour on us tomorrow, I can name 90 percent of the cities we're gonna go to. Rock and roll tours don't go to Wyoming, Idaho, Montana, North or South Dakota. They don't exist as far as rock and roll's concerned. But it can't be that people in there are not interested. They've got radio stations, and the same records are number one. It comes down to the agents and promoters who are totally into country music in those areas. So the only people who go there are country musicians.

It's amazing to me that in America, in this day and age, they can still keep these very rigid separate circuits. They are slowly breaking down, but I remember 10 or 12 years ago in America the black circuit was just totally separate. But the amazing one is the country music one, which is *still* rigidly separated from anything else. And for music which is in lots of ways so similar . . . when you come down to the basis of it and trace where it all comes from, one of the major influences on rock is white country music. That's 50 percent of it. The other 50 percent is black music. And the fact that those two just . . . it's apartheid, you know, so they're not white, they're rednecks.

BOCKRIS: Have you thought at all about doing a concert tour like Dylan's Rolling Thunder? Is it totally impossible for you to do that still?

114

RICHARDS: No. I think that's the way things have really gotta go. I can't see going around forever playing bigger and bigger baseball parks and superdomes. I think audiences have gone about as far as you can go with it. In fact, I think a lot of people probably don't go because they just can't stand to go to those places.

BOCKRIS: When you get off these exhausting tours, what do you do?

RICHARDS: Aaaahhh, that is the weirdest time. Yeah.

BOCKRIS: It must be a real difficult transition.

RICHARDS: That's my problem period. If I don't find something to do right away, that's when I've found that I've been getting incredibly lazy, but also incredibly restless because you're so used to being hyper every day, and suddenly you've got nothing to do and you think "Aaah . . . nothing to do, great!" And you sit back for five minutes and then you say "Phew!" You've got nowhere to go, and you walk around the room ten times and it's . . . it's . . . WEIRD!

BOCKRIS: Do you hang around with each other or does the group completely separate?

RICHARDS: These days everybody just fragments too, so suddenly you're alone from all these people who you've been incredibly close to for two or three months. Sometimes Ronnie and I are with each other for five or six days on the trot. Other people have been to sleep six times and we've seen six dawns. You can't even remember the last time you slept because you've got this memory . . .

It's funny, you know, when you sleep everything is so neatly put into compartments of that day and that day, and I did that on that day, but if you stay up for five or six days the memory goes back into one long period with no breaks at all, and days don't mean anything anymore. You just remember people or specific events.

BOCKRIS: If you all keep in good shape, do you think you have another 15 years?

RICHARDS: Oh yeah. I hope so. There's no way to tell. We know a lot of the old black boys have kept going forever. A lot of the old roots boys, the old blues players, and as far as we're concerned they're virtually playing the same thing. They kept going till the day they dropped. They still are. B. B. King's close to 60. Jimmy Reed died last year, and he was going to the end. Chuck Berry's still going. Muddy Waters just had one of his biggest albums ever. Howling Wolf kept going to the very end. Sleepy John just died last month: he was preparing to go on a European tour . . . I mean, Elvis was the one that I would have said, but he happened to have went early.

It's a physical thing. There's no denying that there's a high fatality rate in rock and roll. Up until the middle Sixties the most obvious method of rock and roll death was chartered planes. Since then drugs have taken their toll, but all of the people that I 'ave known that 'ave died from so-called drug overdoses 'ave all been people that've 'ad some fairly serious physical weakness somewhere.

Brian was the only one amongst us who would ever get ill. He was the only one of us who missed some gigs because of health, and this was before he was involved with any drug at all, and a couple of other guys I've known that have died from overdoses weren't particularly strong physically, and they probably went a lot quicker because of the fact that they were on drugs. But they're not people who you would have said would have lasted forever anyway. Meaning, I guess, that a lot of the time drugs just accelerated what's going to happen anyway.

BOCKRIS: At this point do you believe anything's going to get better, or do you think the Stones might not be able to continue doing what they've been doing?

RICHARDS: I can't see any real obstacles in the way as long as the Stones don't just sit on their asses, as long as we try and do things that we think are beneficial for all concerned.

BOCKRIS: So you don't worry about members of the group getting fucked up?

RICHARDS: No, not now . . .

BOCKRIS: I mean, you've survived so much.

RICHARDS: Exactly. The thing is that whatever's happened, nobody's ever felt alone. If anything's happened, somebody's always rallied around, and not just the Stones. Friends, other bands, other musicians and just other people generally, people not connected with the music business, just friends and people we don't even know, but you find they've been taking an interest in you. We all feel that as long as you don't feel isolated and completely cut off from everything, you're okay.

I feel very hopeful about the future. I find it all very enjoyable with a few peak surprises thrown in. Even being busted . . . it's no pleasure, but it certainly isn't boring. And I think boring is the worst thing of all, you know, anything but boring. At least it keeps you active.

BOCKRIS: Do you ever get worried that they'll finally get you?

RICHARDS: Well, if they haven't done it by now, no. It must be fairly obvious to everybody now that they've 'ad a go with trying. If they try again, I don't see any real way they can get away with it just because they have been trying to get me and it never works that way.

Terry Southern is one of the great figures to come out of the Sixties. He has drifted into oblivion largely because, rather than being associated with a single group, like the Beats, he was equally at home in the milieus of Hollywood, The Rolling Stones, The Beatles and the Beats. As he explains herein he was a man who did not believe in celebrity or collectives. His individuality is among his strongest characteristics, but cost him dearly in terms of his recognisability. Readers are encouraged to seek out his classic books, *Red-Dirt Marijuana, Candy, Blue Movie, The Magic Christian, Flash and Filigree* (least known and best), and see his films, from *Dr Strangelove* in '62 to *Easy Rider* in '69. He straddled that decade and was the greatest satirist of his times. A top draw, first-class act from beginning to end. We need more like him. Look for a forthcoming bio.

10

An Interview With Our Greatest Satirist: Terry Southern

In 1989, the day after returning from a book tour in Amsterdam, I drove up to Terry Southern's beautiful country house, Blackberry Manor in Northern Connecticut.

There he has resided these many years, and from there he has launched comic broadsides on the state of America, ranging from the madcap film Dr. Strangelove *to his novels* Candy, Blue Movie, *and* The Magic Christian. *His collection,* Red-Dirt Marijuana and Other Tastes *(being reissued this spring by Citadel Press), once prompted Norman Mailer to describe Southern's prose as "clean . . . and murderous", and hail him as the rightful heir to Nathanael West. My mind was full of questions about Southern's secret writing process as my car came to a halt outside his elegant 1756 house perched between green fields and babbling brooks. A grand scene lay before my eyes when I went inside.*

Terry Southern sat in a large armchair before a roaring fire. Books, magazines, papers, bottles, and ashtrays were strewn across the coffee table, atop which a large electric typewriter stood at the ready. Looking like a cross between Voltaire and a roué Mark Twain, the squire rose to greet me, emanating the charm and courtesy of a time gone by. We sat down to a groaning board of exquisitely prepared food, and he remarked, "You'll find that we know how to entertain our guests here at Blackberry Manor." Then, turning to his companion, Gail, he said, "Vic thinks it's an elaborate set-up for some weird intellectual sting." This serious/comic paradox, this magus of the sexual revolution, is also, of course, a man of letters deeply committed to writing in a fashion that has not been, and apparently cannot be, corrupted.

VICTOR BOCKRIS: As writers, you and I come from different worlds. You – as I understand it, correct me if I'm wrong – are the pure writer who eschews any relationship between successful writing and commercial success.

TERRY SOUTHERN: I think you're trying to draw a distinction between an artist and a professional. This is the difference between a party girl and a hooker. A party girl is somebody who does it for fun, but a hooker is somebody who does it for money. I'm just talking about the distinction this way so we can limit it to this dichotomy. I'm a party girl. No, I would prefer it, and that's on record now, if you would say 'party person'.

BOCKRIS: When you put a message on your answering machine, do you have a very strong sense of yourself?

SOUTHERN: I try to get away from myself. I don't know if you're familiar with this T. S. Eliot quote which I used as the prefatory quote in *Blue Movie*: "Poetry is not an expression of personality, it is an escape from personality. It is not an outpouring of emotion, it is a suppression of emotion – but, of course, only those who have personality and emotions can ever know what it means to want to get away from those things."

BOCKRIS: Therein hangs the focus of the interview – the conflict between your own being and celebrity.

SOUTHERN: I can tell you quite frankly, that is what put a damper on my keenness about writing: I saw that in the writing lies the trail of celebrity and damnable invasion. The only reason I'm granting this interview is because of my feeling of nonsexual endearment toward you.

BOCKRIS: Despite what you think of the life of celebrity, you've worked with many of the outstanding celebrities of our times, from Peter Sellers to William Burroughs. You worked with the Beats, with The Rolling Stones, and with film crews on so many classics, from *Barbarella* to *Easy Rider*, but you never became associated with any single group. You always remained true to your own person.

SOUTHERN: Well, I don't think a person should be given credit for something like that. It was probably just because I never came in contact with a group that appealed to me enough. I tried. At one point I actually wanted to be in a kibbutz with Mason Hoffenberg [Southern's collaborator on *Candy*]. Mason said, "Oh, we should go to Israel and be in this kibbutz." So we went on this ship. We had to clean out the furnace of the smokestack. It was the worst kind of work you could imagine, but it was very satisfying because you thought it was going to be an ideal community, one of these Shangri-La-type concepts. The first night this guy came in and he had been robbed. There were forty dollars missing from his foot-locker. So everybody was freaking out. People said, "My God, we gotta get locks on the footlockers." Then other people said, "No, no locks on our footlockers! That would defeat the whole notion of our unity. If that person took the money, he needed it." There was an immediate schism, and so we left the ship. The point of the story is that it's possible for me to admire and to try and join a group like that, but it's also impossible for me to join a group. You can probably never find a group that was more motivated than that group, but they split apart over a forty-dollar theft and a simple disagreement about whether the person stole the money or needed it. But I'm certainly interested in causes, as I know you are.

BOCKRIS: I am interested in understanding the process of your career. By the early Sixties, when *The Magic Christian* was published, your novel *Candy* was a runaway best-seller, but you didn't get any money from it because of an international-copyright mix-up that allowed millions of unauthorized copies to be published. Did this sour you so much on the publishing scene that you were cynical or detached when *The Magic Christian* was also successful?

SOUTHERN: What you are failing to realize is that I never had any notion at all that there was any money to be made in writing. Never – except for much later on, when I was approached to write film scripts. Any disappointments I would have had would not have been from the publishing aspect of it. Critical reviews might have upset me, but not the commercial aspect. You're thinking of it as though my view is like that of some career-minded writer.

BOCKRIS: But to go from writing *Candy* in 1958 to *Dr Strangelove* in 1964, and to get the enormous response that you got in such a short amount of time, must have had a big effect on the development of your career.

SOUTHERN: Are you saying that you can't comprehend creative work that isn't done to try to please somebody outside yourself? You seem to be – correct me if I'm wrong – ruling out any comprehensible stimuli other than peer-group approval, power, or just money. Don't you think that some of these things just happen, almost on the level of, say, doodling when you're on the phone? I have read enough of your work to know that you often write with a sense of delight about something and that you enjoy what you're writing. I can tell that you would write even if you weren't being paid. You're probably the sort of person who might keep a journal. Do you know those people who keep a journal, Graham Greene types, who don't assume, Oh well, this is going to be published? They're not going to show it to you and they in fact resent the intrusion if somebody snatches their journal, but great writing goes in there. I think Kafka's best writing is in his diaries, and he didn't want them to be seen by anyone. I'm prepared to invent a whole psyche, if you want, in which I'm a man possessed, a workaholic who couldn't stop writing.

BOCKRIS: What I'm interested in is understanding how you work.

124

SOUTHERN: I could tell you, as I have told many of my students over the years, that the way to do it is with some sense of method: if you write a page a day, you'll have a novel a year. How can you miss? A novel a year, wow! A body of work. We're talking Dashiell Hammett and Nat West. We're talking George Orwell.

Students want advice about everything. They say, "How do we do that?" And then you have to encourage them to establish a routine, such as the first thing you do is wake up. You wake up and you have the whole thing worked out where you have your coffee – maybe you have a coffee-timer thing so that the coffee is right there ready – and then *pow!* you sit down at your typewriter and you work for, it doesn't matter, two hours, three hours, four hours, or just until you turn out one good page. So you've got a page a day, and then you've got a novel a year.

BOCKRIS: Is that how *you* write?

SOUTHERN: No, that's how I *advise* people to write. I advise them to work like that and they can't go wrong. The work can even be bad and then the editor can rewrite it, but if you can turn out 365 pages of stuff, as long as it's clean copy, you've got a novel a year! After two years you've got two novels behind you, and then advances start rolling in, so you've got to keep up that pace. You've got to keep up that damnable pace of one page a day, which is not too unreasonable when you think of what football players have to go through, especially if you have your own typist. You can do it longhand and your typist can type it up, with you saying, "Make sure it's just one page."

BOCKRIS: The only person who could come close to you as a satirist is Lenny Bruce. What do you think he would say if he lived today?

SOUTHERN: Well, he often did say, "It is only corruption and injustice that allows somebody like me to make a living." My God, there's enough going on that he could satirize now:

the whole abortion thing, the damnable Shamir – that Grand Yahoo . . .

BOCKRIS: People miss you, Terry, and they want to know why they aren't reading new books by you anymore. Looking into the next decade, can we expect to see a lot more of Terry Southern in the 1990s?

SOUTHERN: [*Realizing that the interviewer is too thick to respond to the serious side of Southern's nature, Southern seizes upon his prior offer to represent himself as the Workaholic Writer, and launches into a routine.*] Yes! Norman Mailer once accused me of being a workaholic. He said, "Hey, can you slow down? Boy, are you cooking, you're smoking. Will you please slow down?" And Norman Mailer's no Mr. Sloth.

BOCKRIS: As a matter of fact, when I came into your quarters, I noticed a large typewriter next to your armchair. Apparently, even when you're relaxing you might want to type . . .

SOUTHERN: Well, if I should suddenly get seized . . .

BOCKRIS: After your great expedition into the film world, we're now happily looking forward to the return of Terry Southern into literature.

SOUTHERN: Yes, apart from the reprint of *Red-Dirt Marijuana*, with a new introduction by George Plimpton, I'm currently completing *A Texas Summer*, a hard-hitting novel.

BOCKRIS: Do you have plans for a series of novels?

SOUTHERN: Yes, now that I have a real facility for writing quickly, having written against deadlines, my new regime will be a novel a year.

BOCKRIS: So your intention is to go straight ahead.

SOUTHERN: Straight ahead, yes – no looking back and no darn breaking with this work ethic. What if I get into the Book-of-the-Month Club? What would Genet say about that?

BOCKRIS: He'd be happy to hear that you're going to commit to a novel every year starting in 1990.

SOUTHERN: I'm promising that; I personally pledge that to

you. I've never had good writing habits. You can say that I've been remiss and will shortly get back to the grindstone. God knows there's a demand, and it would be unreasonable of me not to respond to this demand. Let's assume that the price will be right, Vic.

BOCKRIS: You are a man who will respond to a letter.

SOUTHERN: I will indeed.

BOCKRIS: If someone sends in the right offer, you'll be there?

SOUTHERN: I'll be there with bells on, and wearing several hats.

The immortal William Burroughs limbering up on a massive medieval sword from the weapons collection of Chris Stein, chez Blondie, 1981. *(VB)*

Above: Liz Derringer, back of Warhol's wig, Jerry Hall watch Mick clowning during the disastrous Captain's Cocktail Party, NYC 1980.   *(Marcia Resnick)*

Above: Victor Bockris collapses during writing with Legs McNeil laughing hysterically, NYC 1979. *(Jeff Goldberg)*

Above: Chris Stein, Debbie Harry, Andy Warhol and Jed Johnson, July 4 1980 dinner in Harlem. *(VB)*

Above: Victor Bockris and Patti Smith, NYC 1971.

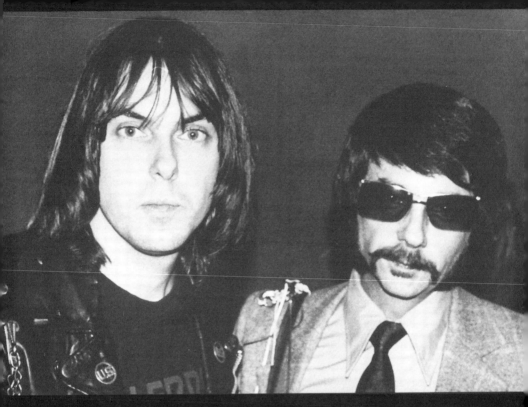

Above: Johnny Ramone and Phil Spector, LA recording session, 1978.

Above: James Grauerholz, Burroughs' amanuensis, late seventies NYC. *(Marcia Resnick)*

Above: Joey Ramone and Victor Bockris on the Bowery, NYC 1979. *(Marcia Resnick)*

Above: Party to end Nova Convention at Mickey Ruskin's Chinese Chance, NYC 1978. *(Marcia Resnick)*

Above: William Burroughs admires Chris Stein's weapon collection. NY, 1982. *(Victor Bockris)*

Above: Chris Stein and Debbie Harry make a triumphant entry into Mudd Club, NYC, as 'The Tide is High' is No. 1 in US. *(Marcia Resnick)*

Above: Victor Bockris and William Burroughs two days into the Nova Convention. Bockris shows strain. *(Marcia Resnick)*

Above: Chris and Debbie and the Mudd Club. *(Marcia Resnick)*

Joey Ramone chats up
Debbie Harry. Outtake from
Punk magazine's Mutant
Monster Beach Party, 1978.
(Chris Stein)

Nicolas Roeg is another maverick, like Southern, who was associated with Jagger, Bowie, etc via the films he made (*Performance, The Man Who Fell to Earth*). Among the greatest living film makers, he has been forced to support himself by making commercials, because he refused to kowtow to the Hollywood system, and because of his outspoken criticism of its creative book-keeping. If you ever get a chance to see a film by this man do not fail to take it. You will be well rewarded.

11

I Would Have Been A Soldier:
An Interview With Nicolas Roeg

I found Nicolas Roeg leaning on The Blue Bar of New York's poetic Algonquin Hotel at 6.35 one Friday evening in 1977. He was wearing a black and white check cowboy shirt, corduroy jacket and jeans over highly polished pointed high heel cowboy boots. In front of him on the bar hovered a precarious mound of documents ranging from a xeroxed catalogue of the Russian Film Archive to a 100 page love-letter-in-progress stuffed into a dog-eared manilla envelope. Next to him sat a beautiful young girl with a Botticelli face.

Born (1928) and raised in England, Roeg entered films as soon as he'd done his military service, starting as a clapper and quickly becoming a widely respected and successful cameraman. His first film (Performance with Mick Jagger) shocked the film-world, was heavily censored, confiscated by the US customs and blocked by its own producers for two years, but immediately became a classic on its release in 1968. Walkabout, Don't Look Now and The Man Who Fell To Earth followed, earning Roeg a reputation for innovation, the unexpected, and controversy, but a confirmed place among the most important film makers of his time because he manages to reach a large audience while remaining true to his own visions.

At 49, Nicolas Roeg maintains the spirit of a lyric, vagabond poet (his speaking voice is reminiscent of Dylan Thomas although he claims to be famous for a dull monotone rumble). He next plans to make Illusions starring Sissy Spacek and Art Garfunkel. But when I met him, he was in New York to direct a commercial for Revlon, and, typically, had no idea whether or when he was flying to London or

131

LA, but in a series of rapid phonecalls from his hotel, and a studio where he was viewing rushes of the previous day's shooting, he agreed to give High Times *his last evening in New York.*

After getting to know each other in the bar, and making a date to meet the girl with the Botticelli face for a late dinner, we took the elevator to the 11th floor and his elegantly appointed suite. While Roeg made a series of phonecalls to friends around the world, I plugged in my tape recorder and attempted to create an appropriate atmosphere by re-arranging the furniture and scattering a few books (Short Letter, Long Farewell *by Peter Handke and* From A to B and Back Again *by Andy Warhol) on the coffee table. At a nod from Roeg, I switched on the tape recorder, and this is what we said.*

VICTOR BOCKRIS: Are there only a handful of really good film makers in the world today?
NICOLAS ROEG: There are a lot, but only a handful are being looked at because film is a very young art. Have you read Mankiewicz's book *All About Eve?* In the preface he writes about the actor and where did action begin? One day in a deep dark cave everybody was sitting in their bearskin, leopard or tigerskin clothes and someone shrieked out, got up, stuck two feathers up his ass and danced around and behaved like a chicken. And then he went back and sat down and put on his tigerskin trunks. The next night someone said: "Why don't you do that again?" He said – "What!" And that's where acting is. It's not learning about projecting. Performing is a very serious thing. It begins in the cave when someone says "I've had it! I'd just as well run around and look like a chicken." I like the performer, and the nearest thing to a great performer is the balladier. It's not really so far away from its roots. The balladier's job was to tell stories and sing ballads. Richard Couer De Lion was saved by the balladier . . . I was asked about David Bowie: I'd spent twelve hours with him when we first met and when I went back to Los Angeles

someone in the studio said: "Well, it's very interesting, but can he act?" I said "But this man has had 40,000 people spellbound on his own, sticking a finger in the top of his trousers. What actor could command 40,000 people to look at them because even David says he's not Joan Sutherland. They're coming for his performance and what he has to say. They wouldn't come for Warren Beatty. So what do we mean by actor?"

BOCKRIS: Is there any way you can describe the difference between working with Jagger and Bowie?

ROEG: I think that's an amazingly static question. It's a question that I'm sure every woman – and damn it why not say this – is asked about their different men. Every woman is continually asked: "How can you go out with a little thin guy and also a big strapping guy?" I don't know. They're both interesting. There's no answer to that.

BOCKRIS: But don't you find that some actors tend to turn you on more than other actors?

ROEG: Of course. But at the time, it's like a love affair. You know, is it true? Were you really in love with him? Were you really in love with her? You can never say yes of course I was. You just say – "Not like you" – because the new one is the new one. Actually your question, to an individual like myself, is very much like life and can be applied to life. Which actor did you prefer? Which love did you prefer? Well I don't know. You fall in love two, three, four times, maybe twenty times, fifty times, one hundred and fifty times, three thousand times . . . it doesn't matter. I now love *you*. Let that suffice. I now am making *this* film. Let that suffice. All my energy is going into *that*. I mean, what past films meant are rather like love affairs. I wouldn't make a comparison between Mick and David. At the time they meant everything to me.

BOCKRIS: Does it give you a strange feeling to see actors or actresses you've worked with in other people's movies?

ROEG: Yes it does. Well, with Julie Christie it's a little different because I've known her a long time and I've worked in a lot of films with her, but since *Don't Look Now*, I think I would get jealous if I saw her in somebody else's film. I've been very lucky with the artists, because somehow the ones I thought would be absolutely right for the part after writing it, all agreed. With Sissy Spacek, for example, who's agreed to be in my next film *Illusions* (playing opposite Art Garfunkel), I first saw pictures of her. I'd seen *Badlands* and I was thinking about the girl. I went to see *Carrie* and then I met her. I'd already talked to her when I saw *Three Women* in Cannes. I thought she was wonderful and it confirmed my thoughts. She's extraordinary. We talked and talked. She knows the person who is in *Illusions* very well indeed. And to have an actress of that calibre, who is still at the point of developing her range, not playing the part that she's so right for is sad not only for me but for the movie business (Roeg has wanted to make *Illusions* for a year but is caught in a financial, legal bind). But I think if you really concentrate hard enough on something it will come true. But most people don't want a lot of things to come true, they want them to stay static. Don't rock the boat.

BOCKRIS: Did you see Mick Jagger in his other films?

ROEG: I saw *Ned Kelly* again recently on television. It's an excellent film, very underestimated. He's very good.

BOCKRIS: Did he indicate to you whether he was going to continue acting?

ROEG: He's reached an extraordinary position, Mick, hasn't he. Actually in his life, I suppose, he has everything materially that he needs. It's not publicised much, but he leads quite an extensive social life and I think he sort of gets satisfaction from that. He's got other things that give him satisfaction, to quote one of his songs. I'm only satisfied by one thing.

BOCKRIS: You're only interested in film?

ROEG: I'm interested in other things, but film's the only thing that gives me satisfaction.

134

BOCKRIS: That's what keeps you going?

ROEG: That and love.

BOCKRIS: I was wondering whether you saw various themes running through all your work?

ROEG: Yeah, you can't do a lot of things in life, you only really repeat yourself. You'd always like another shot at something. But you don't think about it, you don't change what you get, you can't find the finite. I always think in terms of some kind of love story and I just continue to make love stories really, I suppose, because it's an exciting human condition. What amazes me is that a lot of 'clever' people, especially critics, say "Oh, not another love scene." You never hear them say "Not another walking scene, not another eating scene, not another fighting scene." It's always a lovemaking scene that is 'another one'. And that's a much more interesting thing to be shooting than eating I think and a lot more can be said between two people. In fact it's very close to the edge of all contact. It's the greatest contact, so you get into very difficult acting. It's much easier to do other things than act love scenes.

BOCKRIS: You have that famous scene in *Don't Look Now* between Julie Christie and Donald Sutherland. I was told that you actually had them making love in that scene.

ROEG: That's not true. They could have if they'd wanted to. I would have let them ... It's rather flattering that people think they did.

BOCKRIS: *How often are you in love?*

ROEG: All the time. Yeah, I'm a sucker. I'm a sucker for it. Passion.

BOCKRIS: Which is your most successful film? Which made the most money?

ROEG: I really don't know the answer to that. I've got percentages in all my films and I've never seen one single check. And not one of them has lost money. Without arrogance, I know that a lot of people have seen *Don't Look Now*, a lot of people. I don't know anyone of the age of 28 who hasn't seen *Performance,* but the studio tells me that it's still losing. It doesn't really make sense, unless you realise that there is something between the shifting of the economic situation. Everybody in life has two aspects of their personality: desire and need. Desire is one thing, need is another. Corporations have a desire that a film makes good, and their need that it should. And if you have a whole mass of product you shift your need to desire and your desire to need and you balance your books. Well, that's a kind of legitimate thing, but I'm totally disinterested in it. *Performance* is supposed to be a minimarket: "Nobody has seen that film, nobody went you see . . ." And then I keep bumping into people who've seen it. I guarantee the guy in the lift has seen it. And yet it didn't make money. How do you work that out? You know, *The Big Balloon* made $12,000,000 . . . Well, beautifully, one must ignore that, because they know too it's a game. And that's why I'm staying in The Algonquin in a suite, because my movies lost all that money.

BOCKRIS: Was one of your films outstandingly difficult to make compared to the others?

ROEG: *The Man Who Fell To Earth* was the most demanding. I left a lot behind me when the film was finished. I was trying to do something with the syntax of film that at the time was very difficult to explain to the crew. The artists were wonderful. They realised what I wanted, but there wasn't time to help the crew to understand, and it made it a very isolated experience because gradually one found oneself cut away from any kind of observation from people who were close to you.

BOCKRIS: Is it true that there was a scene in the uncut version (the American distributors cut 22½ minutes from Roeg's original) where Candy Clark peed down her leg when David Bowie revealed himself as an alien?

ROEG: That's right. I've no idea why they cut that out. I don't think they liked it, but it's something that happens. "I peed myself with fright" is a phrase that has its roots in truth. It was a charming thing, she just "phizz!" did it wonderfully. And it was really a moment of absolute truth, it was such a big shock that a physical thing happened. BAAH! (Roeg throws himself back against the wall.) She almost flew against the wall.

BOCKRIS: Do you think fear is a major activating factor in people's lives in the United States?

ROEG: Yeah. I think it's a very interesting word, fear. I've never really heard someone say that before. I hate to say yes, because then one could rush off with a whole series of thoughts about why did I say yes, but . . . yeah, and then I don't think it's a bad thing. I suppose fear is a part of a lot of other emotions, isn't it? It's part of what makes people keep in a continual state of discontent. That's one aspect of its ability. What's that marvelous quote: "The only enemy I fear is time."

BOCKRIS: Do you ever get worried that you won't make another film?

ROEG: No. Because I think if it has to be it has to be. I really don't care to just go on shooting movies.

BOCKRIS: How old were you when you directed your first movie?

ROEG: I'll tell you something that my last movie was about: time. And the curious thing is this question is rather nice because of the obsession with time in the present day world, because actually it is a present day issue. Time is going. We're fading as fast, or as slowly, as we decide. Chatterton was dead at 21. Chatterton committed suicide and all his poems were scattered, half were burned. Shaw never wrote a play before he was 44. How old was I? How long had I been here? I'd been around for 36 years. For 36 years I'd been doing things. How old was I?

BOCKRIS: Why do you take so long between each movie? (Roeg has waited two years between each of his films, filling in his time and pocket directing commercials for Revlon.)

ROEG: After I finish a film, I get into a foolish state and I do foolish things. I recognise the stupidity of it, but I suppose I'm thrashing around trying to find some other aspect of the human condition I find I want to broaden myself with, to move about and around and to try and find a metaphor for. Because I like to try and hang onto things that particularly interest me. I'm not really what is pigeonholed as a director. I could just take a job directing, but I don't want to. I love making films, I feel most alive and I don't lead a foolish and stupid life. In between projects I can be very foolish. I'm stupid. But to encourage people into making films is a very difficult affair. They really want a man who takes a job and says he will direct their film. But having been a cameraman I could have stayed a cameraman to do that job because I love films and I would have photographed the things. John Huston said that film making is really a rather melancholy affair because you lose so much of yourself if you really put it into the film. You're continually being drained. So I suppose I get nourished in between films by behaving stupidly, waiting for something, waiting for Godot. I'm damned if I know.

BOCKRIS: Why are your films controversial?

ROEG: Something makes people uncomfortable about the underlying subject matter. However much it's covered up in terms of plot, the underlying truth is almost pagan. The premise of the thing makes people a bit uncomfortable. It makes me a bit uncomfortable.

BOCKRIS: What makes your films relate so specifically to the anxiety of our times. It seems like they portray the anxious edge.

ROEG: If you keep on and on about something – which I tend to do in my own life – you tend to reach the point of being close to crazy. I mean really intensely crazy, on the verge of madness in the tradition of Strindberg. I feel very sympathetic to people who get into that state. In *Performance*, for example, we had a scene where we wanted to use a real Magritte painting. We knew two or three people who'd got Magrittes and we wanted to borrow them, but they wouldn't lend their paintings. I was determined to get it. So we talked to the studio and the studio said, "Oh, that's quite ridiculous." And I said "We can rent one from a gallery, I know what gallery we can rent it from." And the guy said, "Are you crazy? You can get a print. Rent a Magritte! That's really . . . you don't know what you're doing." I said, fuck it, I am going to get it on that set. We are going to have a real thing. We don't want to photograph a print. So all right, if they won't get it we'll rent it ourselves. We rented it. When that painting came on the set it changed the atmosphere of the set. And Mick had a look . . . because the print wouldn't have done it. It was behind him. He takes down a fake painting and puts up the Magritte. Even the prop man was . . . "Cor, 40,000 pounds." It created a tension. I mean, Mick was performing in front of it and it gave a different tone . . . I believe that's true. We rented real diamonds for Anita Pallenberg to put on. It gives a different tone when someone feels the weight of them as opposed to the painted paste. They give a person a different authority than fake things do. Everybody says "Look at this, 180,000 pounds!" It's very different than saying – "Here's your diamonds dear. They're supposed to be real." It changes the performance.

BOCKRIS: What's been the strongest personal influence on your life that's affected you as a film maker?

ROEG: I'm not being facetious when I say this: I had a lot of Italian and French meals in Soho in London that changed my attitudes towards life and loving and affections. I guess it's only people that change your mind. It's all to do with human exchange. That's the biggest influence on me. When I thought about film, I thought about how I would want to see people behave on film.

BOCKRIS: Do you have any particular cinematic influences that you're aware of?

ROEG: I'm being influenced by this conversation! Actually, no. To be influenced by something is to copy and no one wants to intentionally be a copyist. I've got a lot of children, I've got dozens of children all over the world, and if I said to one of them "Did you trace it?" that's the most insulting thing I could say. Are you influenced by things is like saying are you copying someone else. Of course not. I'm only a child.

BOCKRIS: What was the first job you had when you left school?

ROEG: I was a pilot. I loved flying. Actually, you're the first person I've ever told that I flew. I liked the idea of parachuting.

BOCKRIS: What's it like?

ROEG: Very pleasant. Adrenalin is a nice thing to have. And I remember coming to the conclusion that it only runs in the veins once in a while when I was about 16: I climbed to the top of an Olympic Board in a place called The King Alfred Swimming Baths in Brighton to have a look. And there was this little girl that I was particularly fond of and she was swimming away. As I was standing on the edge just having a look with no thought of doing anything she shouted "Hey Nick, Nick!" And I knew that I had to do it, or else climb all the way down . . . and she was lying on her back waiting. I said fuck it and dived off. The thrill of it was desperately exciting.

BOCKRIS: You once said, you didn't mind your children watching television a long time because they'd learn to read stories through pictures. Do you think film will ultimately replace literature?

ROEG: How can I say this without appearing as outmoded as – oh damn it, why shouldn't I say it: McLuhan is only now beginning to be understood. The end of the Gutenberg Galaxy is the end of the press. Film makers aren't related to literature. I had a conversation once when I was working on this film script with Harold Pinter. We were having a drink during work and he said "Now look here," in an earnest voice, "what would you have been, Nick, if you hadn't been in films?" And I said "Well, it's a question I've often pondered to myself. It's easy for you, you know, because you're a writer. And so in the eighteenth century you would have been a writer, and what would I have been? I would have been a soldier, or an adventurer, a fellow who runs the church." The thing is, I'm not that static within these particular set of angles, but I guess I'd have been a soldier.

After the interview I made a fool of myself attempting to continue the interview in the back of a Checker cab and at Elaine's, where Roeg was trying to carry on with the girl with the Botticelli face (whom he had apparently met when she was six), who had come into his suite in the midst of the interview making it hard for both of us to concentrate. They finally got rid of me, but I felt bad about having cut into her time with him so invited Roeg to tea with William Burroughs at my flat two weeks later. The characters in the following transcript are identified by their initials: LM = Legs McNeil (cartoonist and writer for Punk *magazine); NG = Nick Roeg (don't know why he is identified as G rather than R); Bockris = Victor Bockris; PB = Peter Beard (like Clark Kent, an anthropologist, writer and genius); JG = James Grauerholz (William Burroughs' secretary); WB = William Burroughs; BG = Bobby Grossman (the photographer).*

LM: Did you like working with Bowie?
NG: Yes I did.
LM: Do you like him?
NG: Very much, yeah. He's a very good fellow.
LM: Really? Well like I really want . . .
NG: He has a wonderful . . . he's a great guy.
LM: Really? Seems like a real charmer.
NG: He's a very very extraordinary . . . very strange and different kind of human being. He's a great charmer, also very cold and not . . . what is really attractive about him is he has

no (Peter flushed the toilet and all conversation is drowned out by flushing toilet like Concorde landing) sentiment at all so that you're not . . . He is at the moment now . . . that's it. You can't charge it.

BOCKRIS: Candy Clark isn't in New York now is she?

NG: No.

BOCKRIS: Peter said he met her the other night at Elaine's.

NG: I know he didn't.

PB: (Screaming from bathroom where toilet is still roaring) WELL NICOLAS WHO WAS IT MAN? IT WAS THE OTHER ONE YOU'RE CONSTANTLY TALKING ABOUT!

NG: Oh God.

BOCKRIS: It was this girl he met at Elaine's and I was trying to tell him who it was.

NG: It wasn't Candy. I spoke to Candy today.

BOCKRIS: It wasn't Julie Christie, it wasn't Jenny Agutter. Who was it?

NG: I don't know. It's Peter that met her. I didn't meet her.

BOCKRIS: WHAT DID SHE LOOK LIKE? PETER! I have Candy Clark's new publicity shots I got in the mail today.

NG: Really?

BOCKRIS: Oh yes. Come here. They're on my wall.

NG: Well David Bowie is an excellent guy. (We walk into my room to look at photographs of Candy.)

JG: Well is one of you guys going to get it together to get out *Punk* Number Nine?

LM: Um . . .

WB: Well?

LM: *Soon.*

WB: What'd'ya mean by soon?

LM: Well . . . we're in between money.

JG & WB: YEEEEAAAAHHH . . .!!!!????

LM: Some guy offered us $50,000. The guy that bought CHERI and some other magazines. So we might go with him. I don't know though. You know.

JG: Somebody's trying to buy you?

LM: Well not buy us, but . . . but . . . in . . . you know. Who knows? But these people are always talking you know. TALK TALK TALK.

(Doorbell rings.)

JG: American Express is taking you over?

NG: (Strangled voice in distance from next room) But I was in that picture! I mean, they cut me out Peter . . . they cut me out!

(Enter Bobby Grossman.)

BOCKRIS: Oh Hi Bobby! Come on in (introductions).

PB: (Coming back into living room from bedroom.) He'll know who it was because as soon as I was introduced to her it was one of these girls that you're constantly rapping about so I said "Urh . . . I know all about *you*. Don't worry." And she said "OOOAAAAAWWWHHH, NICKLAS ROEG EYH?" In whatever accent.

NG: (Drily) She has a Texan accent. Candy's got a Texan accent.

PB: It wasn't Candy then.

NG: Someone else. It almost makes my heart want to stop when I realise that.

WB: (Talking about Graham Greene) It's a good book. It's got a strange shape. He's suddenly saying you're a bad Catholic. That's a very good book.

NG: I'm interested you liked *Brighton Rock* because that's very rare because that's an overlooked book in literature. Hands up who's read *Brighton Rock*? Good! Excellent! Go to the top of the form. And *stay* there till I come for you.

JG: What is that one about?

WB: It's about boys – seventeen-year-old boooooiiiyys. With razor blades strapped on their fingertips or something. I never got into that razor blade thing exactly . . .

NG: That razor blade . . .

LM: He's like a punk.

143

WB: Very very punky. He was in London . . .

LM: They're all English punks.

JG: Yeah. English punks.

NG: They have punks in California. But it's rather like Tamla Motown. Do you really believe that it's punk? I don't believe it.

(I have been in the bathroom during the last segment of conversation and now the explosion of the toilet commences again drowning out all conversation.)

WB: Do you know a writer named Jack Munro?

NG: Who was that?

WB: Well he was sort of the original punk and his father called him Punky. He died in 1948, he had a very serious motorcycle accident hitting somebody who was on a bicycle and . . .

NG: Well punk is a very good word. It's an old English word . . .

LM: I mean Shakespeare used it.

JG: What is the origin of this?

NG: It originally meant prostitute.

LM: That's right.

BOCKRIS: That was Shakespeare's use.

NG: No, punk is a very old English word.

WB: For a prostitute?

NG: Yes. It's in the dictionary. Very good.

LM: But no one used it, you know, it was nothing before we did the magazine.

NG: Actually in fact it used to be used in the Forties in the movies.

LM: Oh right . . . right. Oh well they use it every night on TV after these big chase scenes on TV they say . . . you know they can't say you silly motherfucker I'm gonna knock the shit out of you . . .

NG: So they say punk . . .

LM: Yeah right, then they bring him down to the . . .

(END SIDE TWO OF TAPE/SWITCH TO SIDE THREE.)

NG: I guess it must have different connotations in America. I love the subtle differences in the language. Americans are able to cut it down and make it much slicker where we say lift you say elevator.
BOCKRIS: I agree. That's good. Elevator's much more ... I don't know.
NG: It's quicker.
BOCKRIS: Yeah?
NG: Than lift?
BOCKRIS: Yeah much quicker. Somehow.
NG: Where you say automobile we say car.
WB: You say underground.
NG: Tube we say.
WB: Yeah, Tube. How did that get ... *tube*? I don't know. It doesn't look like a tube at all the underground. It isn't shaped like a tube. It's sort of like that (making shape with hands).
NG: I came over on the Concorde.
LM: Was it good?
NG: Incredible.
LM: Is it real skinny?
NG: It's very small, but it's quite amazing. It's quite thrilling. Three and a quarter hours ... and it's travelling at the speed of a bullet.
LM: Wow!
BOCKRIS: It's not. It's not travelling at the speed of a bullet.
WB: No, it's ...
NG: It is travelling at the speed of a bullet.
WB: It's travelling at the speed of a rather slow bullet, a bullet with not much muscle and a lot of ...
NG: It's travelling at fifteen hundred miles an hour.
BOCKRIS: That's the speed of a regular bullet?
WB: No, it's a ...

NG: That's a . . .

BOCKRIS: It's not a machine gun.

WB: No, it's the speed of the old black powder bullets.

NG: It's a bullet.

WB: Yes.

NG: So I mean it's marvelous to think that a bullet is just travelling along with you. Mind you it's not a bullet coming the other way.

WB: If you were hit by this thing you wouldn't even be able to see it because it was coming towards you so fast.

NG: When you think that this airplane . . . if a fighter from the Second World War went after it the bullet couldn't catch it.

LM: REALLY?

NG: It would just tap it da da da da da da da.

WB: Hmmmmhmmmmmhmmmmmmhmmmmmhmmmm

NG: And then it just goes tee tee tee tee tee teeeee that's amazing, it's beautiful. All those people in those black helmets with straps and goggles.

LM: Do they have stewards and like everything? Are they good looking on the Concorde?

NG: They're extra good looking.

This is an extract from *Making Tracks* with Debbie Harry and Chris Stein, soon to be republished in the US and UK.

12

Blondie On The Bowery, By Debbie Harry, Chris Stein and Victor Bockris

This crazy artist-magician we'd met called Eduardo invited us to rent a floor of his three-story loft building on the Bowery three short blocks from CBGB's; it was time to move from Thompson Street, and Chris abandoned his war zone crash pad on First.

We had the first floor, Eduardo lived on the second, and, for the first few months the third floor was empty. The Bowery was unheated funk, but the space was heaven. There was enough room for Chris and me to live, rehearse, and run the complex business of booking Blondie. The building had fittingly been a sweatshop, a doll factory employing child labor, which accounted, we figured, for a lot of the inexplicable things that happened there other than those caused by the actual physical inhabitants. The place was packed with poltergeists. After the doll factory it had housed Louis DeSalvo's private club. There were bullet holes in the windows of the back room, which had massive iron shutters that could have stopped a tank, even though the front of the building was completely unprotected. A famous philosopher's girlfriend, who was a very nice lady in great shape, with the Lauren Bacall look, had originally let Eduardo have this great space, and he asked us to move in when she moved out. But about a month or so after we moved in he started a downhill slide. He would go into a fake biker number, which involved not washing for days and sleeping in a piss-soaked bag with his boyfriend Alex. He worshipped piss and would piss into beer bottles, leaving half full ones all over his floor.

The cats, who moved from Thompson Street to the Bowery with us, were the first to suss out Eduardo's number. They just ran up to his floor and pissed and shit all over his drawings and paintings. He was a talented artist too and we liked his stuff a lot, but he was, like so many people who inherit money, incapable of doing anything with his own art. He was gone, but he was definitely an inspiration. He evidently inspired the cats too, but in their case only to greater heights of secret shitting and pissing. His floor of the house was basically a toilet. Despite this, our place on the Bowery became a center of action as the punk scene quickly began to develop.

First of all *New York Rocker* came out, edited by Alan Betrock, who produced our first demos and with whom we'd done various projects. He played an important part in shining some publicity onto the groups and keeping the whole scene exciting. Then near the end of '75 *Punk* magazine appeared and topped everything off. Editor John Holmstrom, and his living cartoon creature Legs McNeil, were two more maniacs running around town putting up signs that said *"Punk is Coming! Punk is Coming!"* We thought, here comes another shitty group with an even shittier name, but when we went out to the news stand one day there was this new comic rock mag that everyone loved immediately; it was always funny, very hip, and had lots of good pictures. I remember walking from the 82 Club past Phebe's to CBGB's one night with Legs, who was decidedly drunk on screwdrivers and started leapfrogging the parking meters. He did them all but when he jumped over the last one he just went, Nnnnnnnnnwwwwwwww bang! Landed on his head making such a loud cracking noise that everybody in the restaurant stood up and looked. But Legs got up, said

"Aaaaaaahhhhhhaa! Aaaaah!" and we helped him down the street. I don't know how he kept walking he was so fucking drunk. *Punk* became an organic part of the whole scene, as it was the most interesting magazine in the world when it came out. It was very cool to be in it, too. Chris contributed photographs frequently after the first issue. John once put a leather jacket and sunglasses on Jonathan, one of the dogs at CBGB's, and interviewed him asking, "How do you like it down here?" "It's horrible," Jonathan said. "It stinks of dog shit." *Punk* was a lot sharper than the other fanzines before it eventually collapsed under financial and personal strains.

We used to get some of our clothes on the street. New York has gorgeous garbage sometimes. Leather jackets, suits, and boots could be found in excellent condition. As a matter of fact, the famous zebra print dress that I posed in for an early poster was originally a pillow case rescued from the garbage by Eduardo.

I was feeling great for the most part during this period. We hung out and got along well with most of the other people/ groups on the scene like Richard Hell, The Heartbreakers, Ramones, Miamis, and Dictators. Most of them thought of us as an opening band and they thought I was cute, but never thought we'd get anywhere. I was still using props, like for 'Kung Fu Girls' I had some nine-foot-high cartoon monsters Eduardo painted, which I kicked through, jumping à la Bruce Lee.

By the end of 1975 we had got the band together to the point where we could go out to perform. Then Clem went to England for Christmas to visit his girlfriend Diane Harvey at Oxford. While he was there he called us collect from a phone booth in London to the phone booth in CBGB's and we talked about everything for an hour. Hilly didn't know any-thing about the call. Anyway, you can't do that anymore.

During the six weeks Clem was away we rehearsed and wrote new songs, hoping he would be back in time for us to

Beat Punks

do a New Year's Eve show. Clem didn't come back in time, so New Year's Eve 1975–1976 we didn't do a show. New Year's Eve was always a total bust for me as a kid. I never had a date, I always stayed home, bored out of my mind, watching the stupid ball on the Time and Life Building drop at midnight. Sometimes I would get drunk alone, or else at someone else's place babysitting. Traditionally the worst night of the year for me, New Year's Eve has now put Blondie to work in the oddest places. I felt it was very important to work on New Year's Eve.

One of the events that marked the real start of the New York punk social scene was Clem's arrival back from England with the first Dr. Feelgood album. We threw a welcome-home party for him on the Bowery. If there's one group that could take credit for giving direction to the New York scene, it must be Dr. Feelgood. Clem had seen them in London, and the fact that a band like the Feelgoods could pack the Hammersmith Odeon and make it onto the British charts gave many New York bands conviction to keep on. Unfortunately Feelgood stayed together barely long enough to catalyze New York's bands before they broke up.

What a great party. Several hundred people came, stood around, and got fucked up. That was the first time Nancy Spungeon (who would later die in the aftermath of the Sex Pistols) showed up looking hot. There used to be a lot of great parties in those days where everyone would be in the same place at the same time.

We lived on the Bowery for a year surrounded by the symbols of our struggle. One time Clem and Chris went out to the store and rushed back in yelling, "Hey! There's a dead bum outside!" He was frozen in the snow. Somebody had seen him walking around in the snow with no shoes on earlier in the day. His eyes were open, he had a little white beard, and he had turned blue. Everybody ran into the street to look at the frozen bum until an ambulance came to scrape him up.

One bum we called Lon Chaney was always smiling. He would wear a top hat and pink overalls. Once he had on a pair of white men's longjohns, except they were all dabbed with paint à la Jackson Pollock or Larry Poons. Or he'd have on a military outfit. There was an abandoned storefront across the street from us, where all the bums would crawl in and sleep. One day another bum came along with a big stick and commenced banging on the front of the place, and screaming for hours. The view out our front window often had the surreal look of a Fellini set, though the rotting decay of the Bowery was eerily peaceful after the local restaurant supply store closed in the evening.

Meanwhile things were continuing to develop. Danny Fields began a regular column in the *Soho Weekly News* and started giving some publicity to the downtown rock scene. Famous people started coming to CBGB's. Jackie Onassis was said to have dropped in one night, and it became very cliquish. The first time Danny wrote about us in his column was when we were in *Vain Victory*, a play by Jackie Curtis, which was made up of lines from old horror movies. Tony Ingrassia directed it. Blondie did the music and I played Juicy Lucy. This was an important move for us, introducing Blondie to yet another audience.

On July 4, 1976, we drove back from Boston and arrived in New York at seven-thirty in the morning. We returned our rented station wagon uptown, then travelled downtown on a bus. We were bleary-eyed, stoned out of our brains, and fucked up from doing this big gig the night before, and the bus was full of these bright-eyed chipper old ladies wearing red, white, and blue American pinafores, who'd struggled in from Missouri to see the ships. When we got back to the Bowery we found a three-hundred-pound bum taking a two-hundred-pound shit on the front step. We took it for a genuine Bowery Bicentennial Welcome. Masses of patriotic tourists strolled through town all the day as we watched the boats and walked around. The Bicentennial was reminiscent of Godard's movie *Weekend*. There were throngs of people thronging all day long, like a big ant colony.

Eduardo's boyfriend Alex was a really sweet guy who was also fucked up on biker imagery. He had long hair, a blond beard, big muscles, and looked like a biker but used to go off five days a week to a normal computer job. He'd come back in the evening, put on biker drag, and sit in the piss-soaked loft smoking huge joints of angel dust after work. Then Eduardo would come home and he'd smoke two big joints of angel dust too. I don't think they had to do anything else, because we did a little of the angel dust occasionally and it was different than the shit that went around later. It was more psychedelic. Once Chris had ESP and saw Chairman Mao in the cats. One night he took a joint of angel dust to CBGB's and dosed everybody, pretending it was a regular joint. It only took one or two hits to get you fucked up so you were hallucinating and didn't know what was going on. Although I must say, we don't think angel dust is too good. It's akin to smoking a plastic bag, or Elmer's glue.

Eduardo and Alex finally sucked another victim, Steven Sprouse, into their environment. Poor Steven moved all his shit in before he realized there was too much shit already and something was definitely wrong, when Eduardo just kept him up all night. Quite coincidentally, if you believe in coincidence, Steven Sprouse was a young, unemployed designer/painter and he did live on the third floor for a while until he was half frozen.

Mod clothes were cheap in thrift stores, and Steve loved the 'op' clothes of the Sixties, too. Oh for pegged pants, narrow lapels and small collars! None of these items were for sale new in New York when Blondie started, so finding a supply of pointed shoes in mint condition was a major event that could eclipse finding King Tut's tomb, causing en masse pilgrimages to Hoboken. Everybody in the band got a short haircut around the same time. Gary was first. This was all part of the process of jettisoning the Stilettoes style and dressing Blondie in the mod mood. I had worn a pair of black shorts once and Steven said that this was the right look for me. He gave me a pair of thigh-high black leather boots and black tights to go with the shorts. So as soon as we got back into the black I was right at home, everything clicked.

This was the first of some fifty interviews I did with Debbie Harry.

13

An Interview With Debbie Harry

New York City 1979

Debbie Harry and her boyfriend Chris Stein came over to my apartment in West Greenwich Village at 4 pm to show me some photographs he'd taken of her. Chris has been doing photo sessions with Debbie ever since they met in 1974. They had just heard that Call Me, *the theme song from American Gigolo, was a top five AM Radio Hit.*

VICTOR BOCKRIS: What's the story with that song? Giorgio Moroder wrote the music?

CHRIS STEIN: He wrote the music and Debbie wrote the lyrics, yeah.

DEBBIE HARRY: They asked me if I wanted to and I said sure I'd love to. We went over to the hotel and he played us the movie on video and I just got my impressions of it and I tried to think of what it would be. Giorgio's original idea was to call it *man machine* because the man was just like the sex machine, and he had these lyrics he had written but he definitely wanted me to write something better.

STEIN: Debbie's lyrics are much more subtle than what he wrote. His thing was very direct like saying *I am a man and I go out and I fuck all the girls.* Debbie's lyrics are a lot more subtle and the movie in a way is not that blatant, it is sort of subtle.

BOCKRIS: So how do the lyrics come to you?

HARRY: I was just listening to Giorgio's music and I had my visual impressions from the film which really helped a lot, it's really cool . . .

STEIN: Yeah in that kind of situation it helped a lot. I was just talking to somebody about doing movie music. It's so easy to do music for a movie. Like it was so easy to do 'Union City' because the mood of the picture was all there and everything and I just had to fit the music to it.

HARRY: *American Gigolo* has some things that are really nice about it, it has a very great look. The thing that I was really fascinated by when I saw it was the muted tones and high tech look of it, so that was the first verse about colors. *Color me your color baby/color me your car.* It was like teasing too because the thing about the movie was that he was always – "Call me! Call me if you want me to come to you." You know, "Cover me." And it was like these little commands had this macho quality through being a male hooker, you know that kind of demanding business. So it really fell in easy for me. I got real enthusiastic. The first verse came real fast and then the others were just there.

STEIN: She made up the song in the studio.

HARRY: I loved doing it. It was like being hired to do a jingle or something. You know, you get your assignment. And now everyone's predicting a top five hit. It's a stroke, it's a definite stroke.

BOCKRIS: How did you write 'Heart of Glass'?

HARRY: I don't know how it happened. Chris wrote this song you know and he was playing it to me de de de de de de and he was sitting there with the guitar. I mean sometimes with the guitar I used to have to fight about me getting space on the bed or the guitar. Because sometimes he was just there with his guitar and nothing else. Like sometimes when he starts playing something over and over again and that just came out and we didn't really think about it the music was just there.

BOCKRIS: But how did the words get written?
HARRY: That's what I'm talking about.
BOCKRIS: You mean you came out with the words just sitting there listening to him play?
HARRY: Yeah. Sometimes notes seem to suggest certain words.

One evening around nine I went up to Debbie and Chris's Penthouse apartment just off Central Park and taped a further conversation with Debbie.

VICTOR BOCKRIS: Do you have any experiences that stand out as your most extreme psychically?
DEBBIE HARRY: When I was a really little girl I thought that I killed Eleanor Roosevelt. Somebody in my family was just raking apart Eleanor Roosevelt and I was sitting there saying I wish she was dead. And I wished and I wished and I wished and I wished and I wished for days that Eleanor Roosevelt would die and then she died. And I just felt really bad afterwards. But I knew I didn't kill her.
BOCKRIS: Also there was that story you told me about when you were in Bangkok.
HARRY: Oh yeah, Chris was tossing and turning and he was like awake and I was sound asleep and he was just asking himself a question mentally and I sat up while I was sound asleep and I answered his question and then I lay back down. But Thailand is very sensual a lot. The climate is very sensual, the people are real sensual. Everything's really sensual there.
BOCKRIS: Is it very different to play Bangkok?
HARRY: Yeah. It's very general communication. Communication is just basic human attitudes or human experiences: happy, sad, rational, irrational. That kind of stuff versus intellect.
BOCKRIS: But does it effect the way you feel performing?

HARRY: I guess I have to go out of myself more in Bangkok, try to reach out. It's like the difference between having an audience that's fifteen to thirty-five and an audience that's three years old to eighteen years old. Because they're less involved with intellect. Their existence is more sensory and that's it.

BOCKRIS: You do have a large following among little kids.

HARRY: It's because I'm old enough to be their mother.

BOCKRIS: I think it's because little girls always choose bigger girls to admire and be like. [. . .]

BOCKRIS: Have you ever wanted to have a child?

HARRY: Yeah. Sure.

BOCKRIS: Have you decided not to?

HARRY: No. I haven't decided not to. I just haven't decided to.

BOCKRIS: It's one of those things that has always been taken for granted, but it seems like a lot of people are deciding not to.

HARRY: Well everyone's being poisoned to death with all these fucking chemicals and nuclear shits going around it's just a natural instinct not to perpetuate life in a fucked up environment. It's not natural to pollute one's environment. I mean nobody pisses in the water you're going to drink but everybody drinks piss, you know? It's really true. I was trying to think about what are the basic differences between men and women and I think that that's probably one of them that women are more involved with just basic physical survival techniques whereas men can play around with all these deviations and have all these little . . . their existence is much more abstracted.

BOCKRIS: Do you have any girlfriends? Everytime I come up here the place is full of guys.

HARRY: They're all Chris' friends. I guess I don't have any girlfriends. I have friends, but I don't have any constant girlfriends. I mostly just hang out with Chris. I guess you just come here when there aren't any girls you know. Maybe I don't have any girlfriends. Uh oh.

BOCKRIS: Is that a problem.

HARRY: OH NO! I DON'T HAVE ANY GIRLFRIENDS!

BOCKRIS: What makes you really mad?

HARRY: Sometimes I really fly off the handle. I just scream and yell. Stamp my feet.

BOCKRIS: Do you throw things?

HARRY: Yeah. Sometimes. We used to have really great fist fights. We used to punch each other me and Chris, we used to punch it out. But we don't do that anymore. I guess we just got over it.

BOCKRIS: But I know you like sex in the supermarket best. Could you tell us just one story about sex in the supermarket?

HARRY: One time I came in and there was this woman – you know how they always have these men or women doing demonstrations. You know like sometimes they have a man with the mop and glow or the bissel rug cleaner or they have the lady with the hors d'oeuvres, the kind of paté you can make out of cornflakes. So well one time I went into this 24-hour supermarket on route 17 in Ramsay New Jersey and there was a lady there with a huge van of cherry jello. I guess that was probably the ultimate sex experience I had.

BOCKRIS: What happened?

HARRY: Nothing.

BOCKRIS: Just seeing the cherry jello?

HARRY: This *huge vat* of cherry jello. I mean it's not really sex in the supermarket, there's no body contact, it's very . . .

BOCKRIS: Actually the 24-hour supermarkets are the ones that are exciting. There's something about anonymity which is very sexual, when people walk around anonymously by the cucumbers.

HARRY: Yeah I guess the heaviest sex if you really want to talk about physical sex in the supermarket usually it only happens in the parking lots. It never happens in the store.

BOCKRIS: What, when the guy comes over and says can I talk to you?

HARRY: Well, you know, it's like you're trying to get into your car and somebody comes up and tries to steal your purse or something, pushes you down into the car and just tries to rape you. Or one of the checkers carries your bags out to the trunk and brushes up against you, but that's just about it. At least it is for *me*. Maybe some ladies hang out with the butchers and stuff.

BOCKRIS: Are you surprised by the number of girls you know who've been raped?

HARRY: No.

BOCKRIS: You don't find it particularly high?

HARRY: I guess it's high, but I mean that's just the story of being a cunt. It's either you get it or you give it, right. Girls always get it. Do you know any guys that have complained of being raped?

BOCKRIS: No.

HARRY: Well, there you have it.

BOCKRIS: I know guys that have been raped by guys, but they don't complain about it.

HARRY: No? Well the thing is, I don't know, when guys get raped by guys I think it's different than when a girl gets raped by a guy. Because a guy who rapes a guy there's going to be a certain . . . well no, I guess not. Guys that get raped are really in trouble. What are *they* going to say when they go to the police. "I've been raped"? The police are just going to laugh the guy right out of the station house. Kick him in the ass a few times.

BOCKRIS: But the way rape is handled in this country is such a big joke.

HARRY: It is awful.

BOCKRIS: It's pretty bad. It's nothing like this in England, for example.

HARRY: I know. Girls don't have so much problem going out

and stuff like that. I mean it really isn't like this anywhere else in the world.

BOCKRIS: In the last year I've discovered that almost every girl I know has been raped at least once.

HARRY: I don't know what to say. I don't know. That's why they should legalize prostitution, they should legalize that. I mean let's just get sophisticated here, really! I mean every other country in the world probably except Australia and Canada has legalized prostitution. Every other country, right? I don't know about Japan, but they've always been very sexually liberated. They've always been open for lesbianism and homosexuals really they always have the Japanese. The Chinese are real rigid. I heard there is no pre-marital sex. It's not encouraged. All kinds of sexual contact is really discouraged.

BOCKRIS: If you could invent sex all over again, what would you change?

HARRY: What would I change? I would make it have more flamboyant ritual. Torches, silk robes, so that it would really dig into your libido.

BOCKRIS: Do girls ever attack you because they're jealous?

HARRY: Yeah. But only if they take downs.

BOCKRIS: You're the sort of person that draws attention.

HARRY: Oh yeah. I guess I know what you mean. I used to get followed home a lot.

BOCKRIS: Is that nothing to do with you?

HARRY: Yeah. That's that other girl.

BOCKRIS: Which one is that?

HARRY: That's A.

BOCKRIS: Do you have any memory of a particularly crazy thing that happened to you?

HARRY: I guess the craziest one was in the middle of July when my girlfriend was about seven months pregnant and she was like huge and we were walking down 1st Avenue and we were crossing 14th Street going south and he was walking north and he passed us by and I looked at him and he was dressed for winter and it was about 95 and he was sweating and I just like looked at him and said Oh My God and then he came around behind us and stuck a knife on my girl-friend's stomach. He held this marine knife to her stomach and hailed a taxi and forced us into the taxi. By the time we got to 23rd Street the taxi driver got hip and he drove down a one way street weaving and driving like really crazy and then a cop car came past us, pulled us over, and by that time the guy had the knife on my stomach and then all of a sudden this gun came through the window of the taxi. You know "Police! Police!" It was really fast and really scarey. The Naked City. I hopped out the other side really fast. We talked to the cops, but we just got out of the car as fast as possible.

BOCKRIS: Do you find the situation you're in now means that you can meet a lot of people and are they more interesting than the people you used to know before you made it?

HARRY: I don't know. I think it's the same. I can't help it. Maybe I'm fooling myself. I think that I'm just meeting all the same people. They're all the same. Everybody's idiots. I'm just meeting the same idiots all over the place. Uptown, downtown, Japan, England. They're all the same, but it's like everybody even looks the same that's the freakiest part of it. There's people I mean that are living in New York and LA that have their replicas performing the same functions in other places in the world or the country at the same time. You know, there's more than one Fast Freddie. I don't know if he likes that . . . I don't know if anything you know happens particularly fast. Except natural disasters or explosions.

BOCKRIS: You think speed is possibly an illusion.

HARRY: Yeah. Speed. Size also.

BOCKRIS: Well size is almost definitely an illusion. I mean it's a totally subjective thing. Do you think America is the most modern country because it's the richest country?

HARRY: Definitely. And it's also extremely what everything is based on. The culture doesn't have much base other than

166

expansion and production. I don't think our agricultural period was really very strong. It was kind of more stable.

BOCKRIS: We push money more than anything else so by our standards its important, but then is it as important to people in Russia?

HARRY: We went to the airport in Moscow. Did you ever go to Moscow? What was it like?

BOCKRIS: Moscow? It was great. I really liked it a lot.

HARRY: I just think everything is the same everywhere. I mean the only place that was anything different for me of any place I ever went was Thailand because I saw things and it was like you know it wasn't as clean and it wasn't as modern, but it's like funky. I never saw that before.

BOCKRIS: So what are you doing for like the next month or so?

HARRY: I'm waiting to hear about a script. I'm trying to . . . get organised. Our home life is never very organised I don't know if it ever will be. There's always piles of papers around and it's just maddening.

BOCKRIS: Your place always looks like you just moved in.

HARRY: You should see what happened today. I mean the amount of mail that we got today which is like a sixtieth of what we get because they just sent some of it over from the fan club, they thought we'd like to see some special things, but I mean I just can't keep up with it. I need a secretary now! I can't keep up with it. I want to answer these letters, I want to communicate to these people, but I just don't have the time.

This interview was done for my book on William Burroughs in which only a few of its lines were included. It was one of the most enjoyable, relaxed taping sessions I've ever done largely because of Debbie and Chris Stein's roots in the Beats. They were and are essentially Beatniks!

14

Blondie Meets Burroughs

In 1980 I invited Chris and Debbie back to my apartment for dinner with William Burroughs. The conversation took some interesting twists and turns.

If you are too young or too dumb to know who Burroughs is, a brief perusal of your local bookshop's shelves will tell you that he's one of America's greatest modern authors.

He invented the infamous 'cut-ups' writing technique by reshuffling the words of his novel, The Naked Lunch *to make three more books,* Dead Fingers Talk, Soft Machine *and* The Ticket That Exploded *and has had several other bestsellers, including* Nova Express *and* The Wild Boys. *Along with Jack Kerouac and Allen Ginsberg, Burroughs was in the vanguard of the Beat Movement, and at the time of the interview Burroughs had just returned from a conference in Italy and completed a new novel,* Cities Of The Red Night. *For his part, Chris Stein is in the studio producing the Lounge Lizards and Walter Stedding & The Dragon People whilst Debbie reads scripts for a possible movie role and vacuums their apartment.*

VICTOR BOCKRIS: So are you getting lots and lots and lots of invitations these days to go out and stuff?
CHRIS STEIN: Yeah, we're pretty busy. It's nice having a phone machine.
DEBBIE HARRY: Yeah the phone machine is very nice. We just got it last week and it's much nicer than an answering service. It's sort of perfect.

BOCKRIS: Someone calls and if you want to talk to them you can turn it off and talk to them?

HARRY: Yeah. Plus the fact that when you play it back it's so entertaining.

STEIN: Yeah to hear five of your friends . . .

HARRY: Shrieking into the phone and stuff: "WE KNOW YOU'RE IN THERE! WHY DON'T YOU ANSWER THE PHONE!"

WILLIAM BURROUGHS: I used to have several of them that worked in different ways. I have no feel for these sort of things. I dislike telephones anyway. In order to survive I have to talk to certain people on the telephone. I know I have to do it and I do it, but I don't like it. And something I've always deplored is the practice of visiting over the telephone. It just drives me crazy to have someone visiting over the telephone. Say I'm in a room and somebody I want to see about something is busy on the phone for three quarters of an hour. It drives me crazy!

HARRY: Oh I can't talk for that long. Just brief hellos and stuff like that.

BURROUGHS: Well I feel the briefer the better. My feeling about phones is deliver your message and get off as quickly as possible. See, your message may be complicated, you may have to dictate something over the phone. I've done that. It's excruciating, like having to dictate a telegram.

HARRY: It's hard, yeah, spelling and everything.

BOCKRIS: Debbie and Chris just came back from London and they always fly on the Concorde.

HARRY: Sometimes we do. If the record company pays for it we do. It's great! It's the greatest.

BOCKRIS: What are the other people like on the flight is what I want to know!

STEIN: We chased Lord Somebody out of his seat. He was smoking a cigar in the No Smoking section so we told the Steward to chase him, and the Steward came back to us and said, "That guy told me 'Don't you know who I am!' " and it was Lord So-and-So.

HARRY: Yeah. Lord and Lady So-and-So.

BOCKRIS: Nicolas Roeg said all the people look like old businessmen.

STEIN: Yeah, mostly completely businessmen.

HARRY: No! We saw Willie Nelson! Wasn't Willie Nelson on the flight?

BURROUGHS: Well I don't know. Who is Willie Nelson?

HARRY: Country and Western guy. And I saw this blind guy. One big huge blond guy sat there and we didn't know what was wrong with him, but he was like so fucked up he just sat there in the seat and he was like, you know, "GUUUUUYUIIIMUUURRRGGGHHH!" And they led him off the plane at the end. We didn't even know he was blind; we just thought he was completely stoned, so stoned that he couldn't even get around. They drink a lot on that flight too. Free booze. You can drink forever.

BURROUGHS: I don't know anything about Concorde. What's it like?

HARRY: It shoots up in the air like a rocket ship. It takes three hours from London to New York.

BURROUGHS: Unless you're looking for a tax write off, I can't see why anybody would . . .

HARRY: Well, it is an experience because there's like a club of people that are like fans of the Concorde, and because there are such a small number of planes in the fleet of Concorde planes and they only carry 100 people at a time, it's a real thrill. And remember when they show those things of the moon launches, how the rockets jettison different parts? The plane sort of does that when it shoots into a higher surge of power. The plane sort of goes thwoom! and approaches space, and everything is sort of nice. It makes you want to be an astronaut.

BURROUGHS: Well, I would leave the piloting of the plane

to someone else, but I sure would like to go on it. I don't believe any of that stuff about "I won't go on unless I know how to pilot the plane," although I used to be a private pilot, a very private pilot. It's easy as driving a car to fly a simple plane. I'm not talking about a big airplane or anything like that, but one of these jobs that land at 24 miles per hour and cruises at 65 miles per hour.

HARRY: They have these little two-seater helicopters now for just about the same price as a car. You know those executive helicopters for about $12,000.

BURROUGHS: Helicopters are difficult and dangerous to fly. They're much more dangerous than regular planes.

STEIN: You know what hang-gliding is?

BURROUGHS: Of course. I know what it is. They used to take off across this plateau. You can be 10,000 feet in about half an hour outside Boulder, so these guys are up there taking off the cliffs. It's very dangerous. All my pilot friends say no, no, no, it's like trying to drive a car without a steering wheel. A lot of people have been killed, worse yet injured, terribly injured. You know people say "Oh well, suppose you do get killed." Well there are a hell of a lot of worse things that could happen to you than get killed. But it must be an absolutely great feeling if you can come down alive, because I have seen them up there and at first I thought they were buzzards.

STEIN: My friend told us he saw a guy dangling from a hang-glider hanging from the electric wires in California.

BOCKRIS: Have you ever had a bad electric shock? You've had them obviously.

BURROUGHS: No, I haven't had any electric shocks.

BOCKRIS: Not even just touching a toaster with a knife or something?

BURROUGHS: No, not even that. The most I've had is walking around on the rugs. That's what we used to do as kids, shuffling around on the rugs. But I don't know about these shock treatments. I know a lot of people who've had them and I didn't see anyone who was permanently improved.

BOCKRIS: Bill just returned from Italy. He said it's very calm over there, and there's no tension at all.

HARRY: Yeah, they like this new Pope.

BURROUGHS: Did you read *Day of The Jackal?* Remember that great scene in *The Day of The Jackal* where De Gaulle got through because of this time fuck up and the grenade had just shattered the glass and he gets up just brushing glass off himself and says, "Encore une fois." Really magnificent. "Once again." He was a completely fearless man.

BOCKRIS: Everybody hated him in England because he was so . . .

HARRY: So French?

BOCKRIS: Don't you think the French are the most awful people in the world?

STEIN: I wouldn't agree with that.

HARRY: Yeah, but I like that.

BURROUGHS: I think in many ways the English top them.

HARRY: AAAHHHAAA defend yourself!

BURROUGHS: America will also have . . . you know we can produce . . .

BOCKRIS: A close second.

BURROUGHS: American monsters, the industrialist and so on.

BOCKRIS: But the French are so long-winded.

BURROUGHS: I wouldn't say long-winded at all. The French are utterly ruthless.

HARRY: No, but they're so secure . . .

BOCKRIS: In their Frenchness?

BURROUGHS: I understand people being miserly, but a lot of people, particularly wealthy people, have an absolute complex about anyone asking them for even the smallest loan.

HARRY: I used to live with somebody like that. Remember Chris! Somebody who really had a lot of money, but was really uptight about lending money. You know what I mean?

BURROUGHS: Yeah, they get a whole production going as soon as anyone asks them for money. Like suppose somebody I know very well says, "I need $5 for a day Bill to go and do this, that and the other," I wouldn't think twice about it, but if you ask a rich person and then he says, "Oooohh, well I don't happen to have it on me." I've also had them say, "I DON'T LEND MONEY."

HARRY: Well, what do you lend?

BURROUGHS: By the time they're in the house . . .

HARRY: How about your watch? Would you lend me that?

BURROUGHS: . . . and closing the door. They don't want to know about this. "Have you no pride!"

STEIN: We used to live in this cheap building on the Bowery. We all almost got killed one night. The whole place cost $350 a month 'cos there was no heat at night and there was only one bathroom. I used to have to go down about eight in the morning to get the boiler going, then it would start up and go the whole day until they would close the liquor store at six, then there would be no heat until the next morning. Well, one night the flame in the boiler went out and all the gas just got pumped up through the radiators, and when Debbie and I woke up we had black soot around our nostrils.

HARRY: The cats woke us up though. That was the most amazing thing. The cats woke us up.

STEIN: We would have been dead in another half an hour.

BURROUGHS: I'm lucky, I'm a light sleeper see, the slightest thing wakes me up.

HARRY: I think I'm a light sleeper.

STEIN: It's really not true though, she goes out to sleep, she sleeps good.

HARRY: Sometimes I do and sometimes I don't. But our cycles are completely the opposite, so that when he's sleeping really well, I'm usually awake.

BOCKRIS: Bill told me that if you have these strange dreams or sexual visitations at night and you want to break the train of events, the thing to do is get up and have a cup of tea.

BURROUGHS: If you want to. Yeah. Well, nightmares, for example, I feel you fall right back into. You know the kind of dreams where you're struggling to move and you do move and you're awake. Then if you just close your eyes and don't get up you're going to have it again, but if you get up . . .

BOCKRIS: Most people apparently want to go on with it because most people don't get up. They stay there.

BURROUGHS: Well, they're probably too lazy.

HARRY: It's because it's a physical change, right?

BURROUGHS: Yeah, you just get up, maybe have a glass of milk, or if you still have that terrible habit, smoke a cigarette, walk around a couple of times, then you may or may not break it, but nightmares will come like that, one after another, the same one of being paralyzed, held down . . .

BOCKRIS: It almost suggests that if you feel any kind of physical tension, and you can move into another dimension, it would cure it.

STEIN: Have you ever witnessed any flying saucers? Do you know any UFO people?

BURROUGHS: No. I never saw one. I guess I have talked to people who told me directly that they had seen one, but I can't exactly remember. But there was this bit about the strange animal who tore up the table at a friend's house in Boulder. It was a strange thing. He had this table out there in this courtyard, and it was made out of a chicken coop with a piece of plywood on top. They heard this weird howling and then they found that the table had been moved and the top was neatly placed down on the floor with everything on it, which means that no animal could have done it because they couldn't pull it out without spilling everything on it. And this happened a couple of more nights and then the table was completely destroyed. They rushed out there as quickly as they could and heard this unearthly screeching, but they could never get out there fast enough to see whatever it was. Logically it had to be something that could have taken the top of the table and put it down. There were no eccentrics in this very small town, and this got written up in the Boulder newspaper on cattle mutilation and flying saucers.

On a 1978 visit to Los Angeles to write about the filming of a Jack Kerouac biopic (based on *Heartbeat* by Carolyn Cassidy, the wife of his best friend), Burroughs flew up to San Francisco where he was interviewed by Search and Destroy's Ray Rumor, aka Raymonde Foye.

15

Burroughs On Punk Rock

"Los Angeles is a charming place to visit, but charm is a power that is hard to pinpoint," I was thinking as I stood on the veranda outside my room one evening when a spectral form glided up, a vodka and tonic (no ice) in its right hand. My eyes travelled to the spectacles of William Burroughs as he looked out over the city and said "I will tell you about it. The sky is thin as paper. The whole place could go up in smoke in ten minutes. That's the charm of Los Angeles."

When I flew back to New York to work with Tom Forcade on some 'Hollywood deals', Burroughs flew up to San Francisco where he was interviewed by Ray Rumor in a punk rock newspaper called Search and Destroy. *The introduction to that interview begins: "William Seward Burroughs has been mentioned by more bands interviewed in* Search and Destroy *than any other thinking writer – to punk rock he is something of a major provocateur."*

RAY RUMOR: What are your feelings about 'punk rock', politically, or musically, or visually?
WILLIAM BURROUGHS: Well, I think it's an interesting important phenomenon. I am very much a fan of Patti Smith. But it's always been my feeling that you get much more if you're *there*, than you ever can with a record, because I can't get the real impact of Patti Smith and the vitality that she produces in the audience, and the whole electrical energy that's in a performance doesn't always come through on record.

RUMOR: Do you think it's making a dent in the establishment?

BURROUGHS: Well, the establishment is full of dents! I don't think there IS an establishment anymore. I mean, who is the 'Establishment' in America? There IS an establishment still in England. Which is sort of an anachronism, but it still exists, as people still do want the Queen and the royal family. And there are still these five or six hundred very rich and powerful people who really control England. That's why they can't pay anyone a living wage. By the time the people at the top get through splitting it up there isn't enough to go around. But in this country, I don't know what you'd say was the establishment.

I am not a punk and I don't know why anybody would consider me the Godfather of punk. How do you define punk? The only definition of the word is that it might refer to a young person who is simply called a punk because he is young, or some kind of petty criminal. In that sense some of my characters may be considered punks, but the word simply did not exist in the Fifties. I suppose you could say James Dean epitomized it in *Rebel Without A Cause*, but still, what is it?

I think the so-called punk movement is indeed a media creation. I have, however, sent a letter of support to the Sex Pistols in England because I've always said that the country doesn't stand a chance until you have 20,000 people saying bugger to the Queen. And I support the Sex Pistols because this is constructive, necessary criticism of a country which is bankrupt.

Richard Hell, perhaps the most perceptive writer to emerge from the punk milieu, was the greatest Burroughs fan of all. This seminal piece shows why.

16

My Burroughs
By Richard Hell

I consider Burroughs the real Rimbaud. Rimbaud's program to banish the ego and destroy the controlling, classifying, structuring function of the brain ("derangement of the senses" in order to "become a seer." – AR), was self-evidently desirable, came naturally to Burroughs. "The ego is excess baggage," he wrote. (AR: "I is another.") Burroughs' life was one long cultivated coma.

As a writer he was also utterly unpretentious, workmanlike, scientific ("What is Art," Ginsberg asked him in the Forties. " 'Art' is a three-letter word."). To Burroughs writing was another way of subverting that which would control him. He postulated the Word – language – itself as the ultimate form of control: a virus (a virus being a mechanism that commandeers the cells of its host, transforming them into factories for producing copies of itself), and intended to mess with all the ways he could find that writing would influence people and their realities. Writing was a way out of his own control as well: he always described himself as recording rather than writing: much of his material came from his own dreams ("An artist is in fact transcribing from the unconscious.") (AR: "I am a spectator in the flowering of my thought.") (which, as a junkie, often doubtless meant 'nods'); he further subverted any egoistic function of writing with his cut-ups; as well as exploiting and exploring the technical magical/inoculative/therapeutic possibilities of writing –

neutralizing horrors by revealing and describing them, looking for prophesies and new realities in the cut-ups ... He spent his workdays in the mines – his dreams (nods), others' writings (which supplied many of his lines), cut-ups.

The first thing I'm always hit by in reading his writings is his fearless unattachment. He has no vested interest in how things are or the nature of his own responses to them. (I remember when I was a teenager being stunned to learn from Burroughs' writing the concept of the hidden "vested interest" – the doctor's vested interest in disease, the cop's in crime, the general's in war ...) He treated himself as a specimen. (His highest value seemed to be minding your own business. "The mark of the basic shit is that he has to be *right*.") It's like he was a detective sent back from death. He had nothing to prove, only to discover. His detachment from his own humanness, his unsentimentality, was outrageous. He did not want to be human (earthlings "insect servants"). But neither did he want to die. He resented even mortality as another form of control. He wanted to write his way out of it all.

What is the meaning of his narcotics addiction? Many people don't realize that he was an addict till the end. The Lawrence years were spent on methadone – synthetic heroin. Well, it's who he was, you can't get around it – it's not the sort of thing you'd call incidental about a person. I think it's got to be called the central fact. And, just as one would expect the writings of a slave, or a quadriplegic, or for that matter a billionaire, or a champion athlete, to reflect a world view that followed from such a special status, it's only natural that this is so. It gave him his metaphor. To the actor all the world's a stage, to Burroughs it was a torture chamber of alien manipulations to his organism (and he wanted to escape it).

He was a kind of classic addict type – a person who despised himself, found the world greatly paining, and who wanted out. He said that he'd always felt that within himself

186

"there was a basic wrongness somewhere," that "other people are different than me and I don't really like them," and he felt great guilt and self-hatred for "mistakes too monstrous for remorse" – killing his wife, never visiting his mother in the nursing home, his neglect of his son. "I have crippling depressions. I wonder how I can feel this bad and live. Very few people are ever in contact with that area of human despair. I've survived by confronting it. I let it wash through me." He described numerous occasions in his life of being overcome, broken down, by final relentless sadness, in freezing convulsive sobs, usually from loneliness and guilt at having failed others. I think he himself feared that deep down he really was the "sheep-killing dog" that he was said to resemble – by the father of a schoolmate – before he was even twelve years old. Addicts tend both to hate themselves for their self-absorption and emotional distance (tending to be 'sensitive', but to their own feelings, not others'), and to exacerbate these failings in the flight from them into narcotics. Hair of the dog. It's complicated.

And of course addiction makes for a complicated attitude to addiction too. Burroughs was confused about how to conceive of narcotics-use himself. He would affirm the citizen's right to use drugs and he would mock and curse governments' efforts to control, while at the same time he would acknowledge addiction itself as a horrible control – the very model of control – and describe addiction as resulting from mere exposure to a narcotic substance. There was also a lot of death and misery around him wherever he went, and no doubt much of it was due to vulnerable souls taking Burroughs as a model and trying to live up to the metaphysical glamour of his "nothing is true, everything is permitted" program. I think of Burroughs as a soulful and decent guy – even an old-school gentleman – a 'Johnson', and don't think he should be held accountable for the weaknesses and cluelessness of some of his followers, but I do think that it's useful to remember that a lot of what you hear when you listen to Burroughs comes from bottomless despair and narcotics. Thing is, it makes a lot of sense, little as he wanted to.

Then again, maybe this is obvious and I'm just muttering to myself. His writing is beautiful and of course hilarious: meticulously seen, sawn, and nailed, deadpan, fearless, matchless ear. He's among the most select (Joyce, Beckett) in having a style so refined that you can generally recognize him in a sentence. But just as great is that freedom from ties, from debts to, from vested interests in virtually anything. When you're coming from no assumptions, not even of the virtue of human existence, what you see here on earth could well make pain-killing dream-inducing drugs a preferred option, no matter what the sacrifices. Think about it, or as Bill'd say, "Wouldn't you?" (1997)

© 1998. Richard Hell

It turned out that Susan Sontag was another of Richard's favorite writers. When I asked her if she would like to have dinner with him, Susan, who was intrigued by the punk phenomenon, immediately and happily accepted. This is one of my favorite and most enduring pieces.

17

Susan Sontag Meets Richard Hell

New York City, 1978

It was the evening of the fifteen-foot snow blizzard in 1978 and SUSAN SONTAG was due at my Greenwich Village apartment from her 107th Street penthouse at seven pm. Feeling certain she wouldn't make it – or shouldn't be expected to struggle through it on her own – I had gamely offered to pick her up in a cab. Everyone laughed, but when I stepped out of my apartment, allowing ample time to scour the streets for any vehicle, a large empty Checker was idling at the curb. Consequently I arrived fifteen minutes early at Sontag's residence.

Fifteen minutes of cab driver talk later, Susan appeared looking ravishing, having completely recovered, after recent visits to Venice and Paris, from two investigatory operations. As we rode downtown she brought me up to date on her apartment-hunting travails. "Basically," she reported, "there are no apartments available in New York."

Meanwhile, RICHARD HELL was struggling through the snow-drifts outside his Lower East Side apartment, trying to find a cab. I had insisted on keeping the interview dinner date since Hell is in the middle of making a movie with German director Ulli Lommel, and Susan is working on three books all to appear this year. It had been difficult enough to find an evening which they both had free.

However, in the cheery ambiance of my apartment, with a fire roaring in the grate and a chicken roasting in the oven, we thawed out pretty quickly while Susan and Richard, who were meeting for the first time, found numerous common interests to chat about.

191

SUSAN SONTAG: Are you from New York?

RICHARD HELL: No, I'm from Kentucky. Where are you from?

SONTAG: I grew up in Arizona and Southern California, came to New York when I was twenty-five.

HELL: You look really great. I was expecting to see you sort of wasted looking, you know . . .

SONTAG: No I feel okay. I don't know, I feel terrific.

BOCKRIS: Did you see the story in the *Voice* about asexuality? Unless you have a full time live-in person, most people don't have the time to get sex.

HELL: I think it has to do with nature; it's the overpopulation. I think people want to have less and less children because it's an evolutionary step.

BOCKRIS: But John Waters (film director – *Pink Flamingoes* – ed.) said that it's a classical thing when societies break down that there's a separation of the sexes. I never heard that in history, have you?

SONTAG: No. I don't think it's true. I think on the contrary that the sexes have always been separate and that's one of the things that's wrong with the past. I think there's probably less separation now.

BOCKRIS: Isn't it possible for a man and a woman to have a relationship . . .

SONTAG: I should hope so.

BOCKRIS: . . . where they don't have to live together or get married, but where they can see each other naturally or something?

SONTAG: I like the way you say "naturally". Yes, sure it is.

HELL: That's the only way to live.

SONTAG: But there's something that happens to people when they get older, which is that they start accumulating things.

BOCKRIS: Accumulating what, people?

SONTAG: Accumulating things: accumulating their lives;

Above, below and overleaf: William Burroughs demonstrating how to draw and fire a handgun: three stills from Howard Brookner's documentary, *Burroughs.*   (VB)

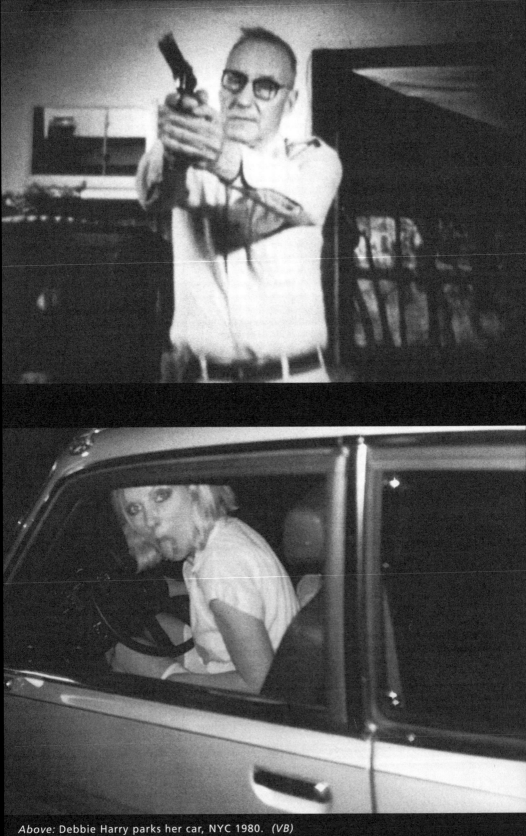

Above: Debbie Harry parks her car, NYC 1980. *(VB)*

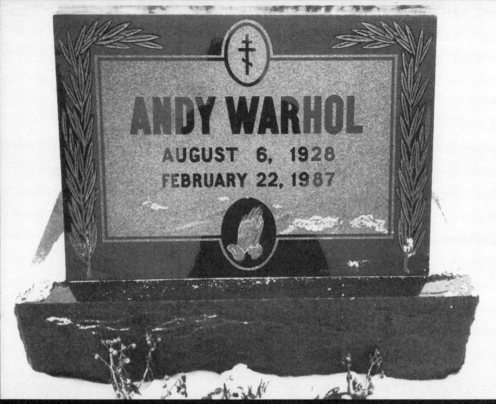

Above: Andy Warhol's grave, Pittsburgh. *(VB)*

Above: Jagger, Burroughs, Warhol, Bockris at the scintillating Captain's Cocktail Party.
(Marcia Resnick)

Above: Ondine, star of Warhol's movie Chelsea Girls, star of Warhol's *a, a novel,* and Billy Name, Warhol's Factory manager, 1960s editor of *Chelsea Girls,* editor of *a.* NYC 1989, during filming BBC documentary on Warhol. *(VB)*

Above: Ramones' lighting man/choreographer and painter Arturo Vega with *Punk* magazine's cartoon character and writer Legs McNeil, NYC 1978. *(VB)*

Above: Mary Woronov, star of *Chelsea Girls*, seen here in the great *Rock 'n' Roll High School* directed by Alan Arkush, starring the Ramones.

Above: Stein, Harry and Walter Stedding, the electronic violinist who Andy Warhol managed and Blondie took under their wing in the late seventies. *(Marcia Resnick)*

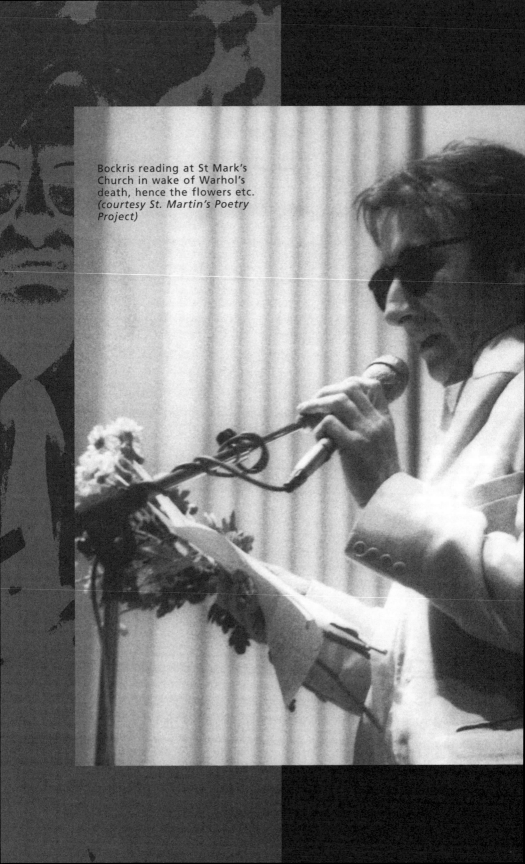

Bockris reading at St Mark's Church in wake of Warhol's death, hence the flowers etc. *(courtesy St. Martin's Poetry Project)*

Manuel Gottsching, Mr Ashra of Ashra Tempel, Berlin 1978.

Richard Hell, aka Richard Meyers. This man, like his counterpart Patti Smith, was and is primarily a writer. A poet, novelist, essayist he also wrote and performed the song, 'The Blank Generation', which in 1976 telegraphed the Punk movement to the media just as Allen Ginsberg's 'Howl' telegraphed the Beat movement twenty years earlier in 1956. 1980. (Marcia Resnick)

accumulating their responsibilities; it's less and less easy to change.

BOCKRIS: You're twenty-eight, aren't you Richard?

HELL: Uuuuhhhaah . . . I'm twenty-six.

BOCKRIS: Oh, yeah, I told Susan you were twenty-six. Do you remember what it was like Susan?

SONTAG: *I was* having a terrific time. I did something inadvertently very clever, which is that I got married at seventeen and divorced at twenty-five, so I had all that behind me. I had never had an adolescence, and at twenty-five my adolescence began and lasted until I was thirty-five. When did you come to New York, Richard?

HELL: When I was seventeen.

SONTAG: Do you still have folks back home in Kentucky?

HELL: They've since moved to Virginia. I have a sister who's moved to Mexico. She's a year and a half younger than me, pretty and she's a lesbian, which just last year got her completely cut off from my mother who regards herself a feminist and is leading all kinds of strikes and stuff on campus at the school where she teaches. My mother couldn't deal with it.

BOCKRIS: I think it's really still harder to be a lesbian in America.

SONTAG: Well it's just harder to be a woman.

BOCKRIS: I was talking to Chris Burden (conceptual artist – ed.) the other day and he was saying how he really hated his girlfriend, and I realized that I really hated my girlfriend.

SONTAG: Does she know?

BOCKRIS: Yeah, I told her.

SONTAG: You mean you broke up!

BOCKRIS: No, no, we still see each other all the time.

SONTAG: Why do you see somebody you hate?

BOCKRIS: It's more exciting.

HELL: Do you have a napkin or something?

BOCKRIS: Toilet paper.

SONTAG: Bring me some.

BOCKRIS: Sorry, this is so embarrassing. This is a cross between a punk dinner and a chic dinner. We have a fire, we have a reasonable apartment, it's okay, we have flowers and everything, but then we do have the punk sensibility as well.

(Richard goes into the bathroom, comes out with a roll of toilet paper, and passes around wads of it.)

HELL: ... anyway, the difference between popular art and elitist art is elitist art is too judgmental. Elitist art is satisfied with itself aesthetically only. Popular art is the kind of art where you want to affect your culture and to have some influence on the way people think. That's pretty clear, that distinction.

SONTAG: I don't know. I mean Dostoyevsky had an influence on people. Yet I'm sure that when he was writing he must have thought he was doing the best thing he could do, just satisfying himself in a room.

HELL: The distinction has to do with your own personality whether you're interested in affecting the culture, or whether you're just interested in creating something beautiful. You see, the way I feel is that the generation I belong to has more in common among its members than any other generation that ever existed because of television and public school systems. What I'm relying on is that if I go as far as I can *being* myself that it will arouse something in all those people, but the problem is that you then become *merchandise* – another essential difference between popular art and elitist.

SONTAG: You know if you would talk to most writers or most painters or most serious musicians, they would probably complain about the same thing. There are privileged moments when it all comes together. I mean you've written a book of poems. But you know that the lyrics of your songs will have an audience far beyond the poems that you might publish because they are carried by music. People will either take those words in, or they won't, but the music is something that people will relate to. It has a kind of energy or sexual feeling so you'll be giving them two for the price of one . . .

HELL: But I wasn't complaining about it. I'm *not* complaining . . .

SONTAG: Alright you were implying . . .

HELL: Let me finish what I'm saying: you realize that as a commodity, who also has all the same intentions and attributes of somebody who's working in high art, the way to protect yourself is to regard celebrityhood as being your *real* art form. It's just your personality that's the commodity and not your work. That's the only way to escape being packaged by the merchandisers. They then become your tool rather than you becoming theirs.

SONTAG: I didn't mean to say you were complaining about it. Most people who are involved in so-called high arts, if they have any degree of success, would describe very similar things. One way of being a celebrity is to make yourself totally inaccessible and never manifest yourself and never do anything and be as pure as the driven snow. Your purity will become a product, and it can be sold and it can make your reputation. It has to be consistent, it has to be of a certain volume. Let's say, your absence could have a certain weight, somebody like Salinger or Pynchon here, or Beckett in France.

HELL: No, no, no. I don't think so. Salinger, Pynchon, Beckett . . . those names would mean nothing to the man in the street.

SONTAG: No that's not true, but they are within. There's an awful lot of writers who think they have to break their asses to go out on publicity tours and have interviews etc. In fact, it can be done in a smaller way.

HELL: But these are not popular artists, Pynchon and . . .

SONTAG: But listen . . .

HELL: Beckett does not affect in any way the way people feel.

BOCKRIS: No, Beckett has enormous influence. People don't walk around saying "Oh, this is because of Samuel

Beckett," but they're picking up on things that Beckett has put into the culture without knowing it was Beckett.

HELL: I don't know.

SONTAG: I think Victor's right. It's true that it isn't direct in terms of names and recognition. Look at surrealism . . .

HELL: I think Bob Dylan had an infinitely greater impact.

BOCKRIS: Bob Dylan stole most of his stuff from Jack Kerouac, there are many lines that come straight out of Kerouac.

HELL: Kerouac was pop.

BOCKRIS: But I mean the thing is that you get people like William Burroughs and Beckett whose language has infiltrated the culture to such an extent that people are quoting them without knowing they're quoting them. That's even more extreme than quoting a line from Bob Dylan.

HELL: We're talking about a scale, we're drawing a line between people who have impact and people who don't, and there's bound to be a no man's land in between. The difference between Beckett and The Beatles is so great there's no way they could possibly be . . .

SONTAG: It's certainly true the names aren't as well known, but I was thinking of an example of the surrealist artists of the Twenties and Thirties. Very few people could name the names of the famous surrealist artists, but you just have to look at the windows of any major department store and you will see their impact.

HELL: It took forty years to be assimilated and it's dead by then – completely superficial. The fact that it's in the store window is a symptom of how totally it's been absorbed. That is banal. Look how big an influence Kafka had. He was at a frontier in his period and thirty years later that frontier has arrived as the environment.

SONTAG: That's a very good example. Everybody else catches up. Somebody said that the artist is the early warning system. But do you think, Richard, that rock has really changed people?

I know it has changed me, but then my whole being is interested in being changed by what I experience. I'm open to change.

HELL: Oh yeah, incredibly. By marijuana legalization, by Jimmy Carter getting elected, by hair lengths. The fact that on the radio every day during the Sixties there was this information coming across that affected what happened to the world . . .

SONTAG: But I remember popular music when I was a kid. This is before rock and roll, when I really only got interested in popular music around the time of Johnny Ray . . .

BOCKRIS: He was the guy who cried all the time, right?

SONTAG: Yeah I . . .

HELL: His career was ruined when he was found in a motel room with a guy in some place.

BOCKRIS: With a guy?

SONTAG: Oh really, I didn't know that. Anyway, he was the first one that I paid any attention to. What I remember as a kid, is that I wasn't interested in popular music. Pop music was something you played when people came over and they wanted to make out – purely background for making out. It was not something that had any real autonomy.

HELL: There weren't teenagers then.

SONTAG: Well they weren't in the same sense, right. But then what happened in the Sixties was really interesting. People started buying records and listening to records the way they were buying and reading books. You'd play a record and listen to a record by yourself and talk about it. That did not exist before the Sixties.

HELL: There was an extraordinary number of teenagers in the Sixties. There became this thing where suddenly there was this specific period of life – teens. There was acknowledged a period between being a child and being a grown-up and this became power.

SONTAG: Then, it didn't occur to me that there was anything in between.

197

HELL: It is a very subtle consciousness, being a teenager . . .

SONTAG: Which can last to approximately thirty-five.

HELL: It's the most attractive consciousness to speak with. It's the most sensitive because it hasn't solidified yet.

SONTAG: It hasn't completely sold out. Essentially what's happening is that everybody's got ten more years, that's my idea. In other words, for a woman to be in her early forties now is just like to be in her early thirties a generation ago. It used to be when you were over thirty you were old, you were out of it, finished. Now people start to have that anxiety at forty, and even at forty they manage to stave it off and go on. Also it's terrific how people have a much longer time in their lives to be young and they look better.

BOCKRIS: How old are you?

SONTAG: I'm forty-five.

HELL: The way I feel, I want to encourage in my songs and stuff, that feeling of being an adolescent throughout your whole life, of rejecting the whole idea of having a self, a personality.

BOCKRIS: Are you writing a lot of songs during this period while you're making movies?

HELL: I just wrote one last night: 'The Kid With The Replacement Head'. No, I haven't actually written any since the album came out until last night because I have been working on this movie. What I usually do really as a policy is to do it at the absolute last minute. I figure you know more at the last minute than you did at the next to last minute.

SONTAG: I always put everything off until the last minute too, but it's just that I'm so disorganized I can't get myself to do it. I'm supposed to turn in a book tomorrow, literally tomorrow morning. It's this essay on illness, it's going to be a little book, and I was supposed to make some changes in it. I'll do it when I get home . . .

BOCKRIS: Oh yeah, you'll do a lot of work tonight when you get home, sure.

HELL: I was just thinking about that essay on illness today when I was thinking that I was going to come over here. And the fact that you had cancer means now . . .

SONTAG: That I'm interested in illness . . . exactly.

HELL: And that cancer is going to become . . .

SONTAG: Well, it is a big subject, but people don't know how to talk about it.

HELL: It would not have happened if you had not gotten cancer.

SONTAG: Sure, if I were in a plane crash, I'd probably be writing about planes now . . . I mean that is the way I do it.

HELL: It's just ideas, like the way you . . .

SONTAG: No, no, I'm not writing about my experiences. I said if I were in a plane crash I'd be writing about airplanes, not about plane crashes.

BOCKRIS: I bet you'd write an article in relation to the possibility of their crashing.

SONTAG: No, I don't think so because the fun of the essay is not to write about my experience, which is very banal, the fun is getting interested in the subject.

BOCKRIS: I think the most interesting thing about you as a writer is the extent to which you prefer writing fiction to writing essays.

SONTAG: Oh I much prefer it, but I can't help getting interested in all these subjects.

HELL: Did you write anything outside *Death Kit*?

SONTAG: Yeah, I wrote a novel before that called *The Benefactor*, and then I've written some stories, which are going to come out this year as a book, and I'm working on another novel and a couple of stories.

HELL: How about movies, are you still . . .

SONTAG: Yeah, I'd love to make movies but I had a very discouraging experience with distribution. I had a very good experience making them. I'm not enough of a business-woman to know how to do this distribution thing. You know there aren't any theatres anymore; that's something you're going to discover with this movie you're in, Richard, and I hope it goes well. That's the most heartbreaking part of it. You have this thing, and then maybe it goes to some festivals, okay, and gets some reviews and where is it? It ends up in some colleges.

HELL: That's my base fear.

BOCKRIS: College kids?

SONTAG: A lot of theatres have been taken over by sex films. There just aren't the theatres where they can be shown. I mean even Fassbinder, how many people have actually seen a Fassbinder movie?

HELL: But you could say that about somebody like Godard. How many people have seen Godard movies?

SONTAG: More, a lot more, a lot. Godard was really a major event, he changed movies, single-handedly. You can say before Godard and after Godard. Fassbinder, all these people, would have been inconceivable without Godard. He changed the whole media. I mean you can't say Beckett or Burroughs changed writing.

HELL: That remains to be seen.

BOCKRIS: Do you think anyone ever had an idea which was the happiest country?

SONTAG: Well you know hundreds of millions of people have thought that America was the happiest country. And then I read one writer who said, "Happiness stops at Vienna." I thought that was a wonderful line, everything east of Vienna is just a continental tragedy for a thousand years.

HELL: I bet America is the happiest country.

BOCKRIS: I bet it is, I would never live in England because everyone in England is so miserable.

SONTAG: Yeah, but England is a particularly miserable country.

BOCKRIS: Particularly miserable, and probably always has been.

SONTAG: That's why they like it so much when there's a war. Everyone in England says how great it was during The Blitz.

HELL: That's the only subject that arouses any interest in the whole country. Even the First World War still stirs their interest.

BOCKRIS: It's because then they felt the pulse of English life. It was wonderful because the English love to be told what to do by a thundering person like Churchill; his speeches were just like Hitler's.

SONTAG: Only if you don't have a politics. I think it makes a difference what the context of the speech is. I mean, Churchill was a bastard and a terrible racist and an imperialist and everything but I mean those speeches were heard in a certain context and they inspired people to feel good and to behave well to each other and to carry on in a correct way. Hitler's speeches made people hate each other and aroused all kinds of ugly feelings. You can't be such an aesthete, Victor, that you really hear two people shouting and say they're shouting the same thing. I mean, God, I never thought if I lived for a hundred years I would defend Winston Churchill, but I must, you know, if you compare him to Hitler.

BOCKRIS: A lot of people do.

SONTAG: Well I think that's a really shallow attitude. You said this even before Richard came, because we were talking about England. You said that England wants a leader. I mean if you think the English were so hypnotized by Churchill and they had such a gas in the Second World War, how come they threw him out in 1945?

BOCKRIS: They were bored and Churchill told them that the economic situation was very bad and that things would be horrible for a while and his opponent said it was alright, don't worry. It was very English, totally economic. The English are very economical people, they don't buy drugs ...

SONTAG: And that's why they're in the ...

BOCKRIS: They just buy cheap pills and things.

SONTAG: If they're such an economical people, as you put it, and that word's very ambiguous, why are they in such a pickle now?

BOCKRIS: Because they're too economical, you know, if you don't take any risks . . .

SONTAG: America may be the happiest country, but I don't think Americans are happy. I guess there aren't any happy countries.

BOCKRIS: Do you think that a person should have an opinion or an attitude towards something? I really don't.

SONTAG: No, I'm not interested in opinions.

BOCKRIS: Yes you are. You're saying if I don't have an opinion or an attitude . . .

SONTAG: I think you *do* have an attitude. Listen, I *hate* opinions. I've begun to think that one of the reasons I write essays – and I really don't like to write essays – is to unload my opinions. If I can just write it down then I don't have to hold that opinion anymore.

HELL: Opinions as opposed to what?

SONTAG: As opposed to energy, as opposed to feeling, as opposed to sensations, as opposed to perceptions. Opinions are like some kind of crust that grows on things and you want to kind of peel them off.

HELL: I don't think you can just separate opinions from feeling for instance. I think you're saying you shouldn't have prejudices.

SONTAG: No, they could even be true opinions. Like we both agreed a while ago how terrific Godard was, that's an opinion. My impulse is if I like Godard that much and I think he's that interesting then I want to write an essay on him which is what I did. I want to keep on making space for other things. I think that's important.

BOCKRIS: Do you think people are still fascinated by space, or do you think that fascination has been killed?

SONTAG: I'm always amazed how unfascinated they are. I

mean about the reality. In 1969 when people went to the moon it was amazing how unimpressed people were.

HELL: You'd think there would be the fascination of traveling. The only kind of travel which is available now in space is not available to anyone but these astronauts, so it's really boring. Who cares about it if you can't go and the only thing is to watch it. My biggest ambition is to get out into space as soon as possible.

BOCKRIS: I know that Burroughs wants to leave as quickly as he can get off the planet.

HELL: I've got this fantasy which says when I get to be forty they won't just be choosing guys who are astronauts to go. That's why I want to establish my reputation as a poet, so I can convince people in Congress that you gotta have a guy who can explain what it's like to be there . . .

This is an extract from a 5,000 word piece called *Negative Girls*, which pins the punk experience through the point of view of the seminal punk chick.

18

Notes Of A Punk Rock Groupie

That's when I started going down to Los Angeles and hanging out with musicians at Rodney Bingenheimer's. Then we went over to the Ramada Inn because we wanted to meet Kiss. That was when Kiss first came to Hollywood. When we were hard up for money we would go to the hotels and see what bands were in. Then we went to the coffee shop and ordered whatever we wanted and just signed somebody's name and room number. So we lived off the bands without the bands really knowing it. They probably were so drunk and stoned all the time they thought they had eaten . . .

When I was hanging around the Hyatt House one time I met The Kinks. I was hanging around with Dave Davies. Leo Sayer was there. B. B. King was there. Led Zeppelin came in. Foghat was there. I just walked around and I would hear party noises coming from all these bands. I would just knock on people's doors and people would always invite you in. I stayed with Davie Davies for two weeks. He had quarts of vodka and gin. I used to walk around the hotel with a quart of some alcohol or bottles of champagne and of course if you had that much alcohol and knocked on somebody's door, they always invited you in for sure. At this one Kinks party they took this girl and they got her totally undressed and these two roadies held her upside down and spread her legs and somebody poured the champagne on her cunt while somebody else took pictures. We would sit around with BB guns and shoot out the lights. We tore chairs attached to the walls outside the elevators out of the walls and plomped them in front of Robert Plant's door. When I was with The Kinks we threw a bed out of the window. These people from Leo Sayer's room took my girlfriend Lisa and they pulled her pants down and they took shaving cream and made a face on her butt and stuck a cigarette in her ass and took a picture, and you really couldn't tell it was an ass. But then Lisa's mother, who was fucking this guy in Silverhead, was at the Hyatt and she ran into somebody from one of these bands and they said, "Look at these pictures ⁀ have of this girl Lisa." And it's like she goes, "That's my daughter!" And then she blamed it all on me because I was older.

On the plane to New York I was sitting next to a Hell's Angel and he asked me where I was going. I said, "East 3rd Street," and he goes, "Oh, I live on East 3rd. What's your address?" It turned out he lived next door. I said, "Well listen, I will be frank with you, I am terrified of the Hell's Angels." He said, "Hey, listen, I will tell everybody you are the new kid on the block and nobody will mess with you."

The apartment on East 3rd was really disgusting and I got a horrible job at Burger King. One day I could not get into the apartment to get my check and I was really pissed off. So I told my Hell's Angel friend and he went into the apartment above mine and said, "We have to use your fire escape." He got my check and my clothes and said, "Come on. I will take care of you." He introduced me to Terrible Ted and his wife and they took me in as their housekeeper.

They kept their guns under my bed. In the middle of the night a guy would come in and say, "Oh, I am sorry to disturb you," and he would reach in and pull out a gun. The first time it happened I am like, "Oh my God I am sleeping on top of artillery!" But I got used to it.

On the eve of my 21st birthday we went to CBGB and Anya introduced me to Sylvain Sylvain and then he said, "Well, I am going home. You coming?" So I went out with him and I had a really good time and the next morning I woke up and it was my birthday. I said, "Oh, it is my birthday." He went, "Oh, great," and he ran out and got me a scrambled egg sandwich and coffee and made me take a bunch of vitamin B. He said, "You know when you drink a lot you have to take your vitamins." Then he told me all these stories about Japan and the early New York Dolls when they had a lot of money and went through heavy duty drinking. Then he walked me back to Anya's at 101 St Marks Place.

That night we were going to see Talking Heads at the Ocean Club. Anya talked me into taking acid. I said, "No, no, no." She said, "Yes, come on. It's your 21st birthday you got to take acid." So I did. She dressed me up in skin-tight purple satin peddle pushers, black stiletto high heels boots with caribou feathers around the top and a really tight angora sweater and we went out. I made her buy me a bottle of Jack Daniels because I told her if I started freaking out I wanted something to come down on.

They were videotaping at the Ocean Club that night and we were at a very fun table trying to share a shrimp salad. It looked really horrible. The lights were so bright I could not stand to look at anybody. Then Joey Ramone came in. So I told him, "Look, I don't have any money and I am just coming down off acid. Can you help me out? Buy me a couple of beers or something." There was this girl following him around and she kept saying, "You're talking to him too much. I want to be with him. Please go away and let me have a chance." I said, "I am just drinking with him." I didn't like plan on going home with him or anything but it ended up Joey was trying to, like, ditch the girl. So he says to me, "Come on let's go to CBGB and drink there." It was well after five in the morning. I go, "But it is closed now." He goes, "It's not closed to me."

On the way to CBGB I held my coat so nobody could see

him take a piss, and this girl is still following us. She is, like, practically crying. So Joey said, "Come on with us," and the rest of The Ramones were there and Hilly and a bunch of people like Roberta Bayley and we were playing pinball. I was sitting on the pool table and Joey asked me to watch his beer because he had to go to the bathroom. He comes running out of the bathroom and jumps on top of me and spills beer all over my pants. And he starts kissing me. And I am, like, going, "Oh my God this is really exciting. I got Syl last night who I always wanted to fuck and now I am getting Joey." And the girl is, like, crying, "Oh, that's right! Why don't you just drag me all over town and then just ignore me!" And he is like, "Oh, we are going home now." This girl was following us right to the door and he goes, "Well, we are going to bed." She goes, "Oh, that's it. I take the train all the way to the Bronx." And it's like, "Okay, come on up." So we are sitting on his bed giggling and kissing and she is sitting on the corner of the bed crying. So Joey said, "Hey, do you want to watch TV? Just keep it low so Arturo don't wake up." She goes off and we hear her fumbling around in the dark and she knocked a bunch of stuff over and Arturo jumped up screaming and threw her out and me and Joey were just laughing our heads off but trying to be quiet so Arturo doesn't scream at us.

I ended up fucking Joey but it was, like, really awkward the next morning. He was looking for his glasses. I couldn't find my bra. It was like really, "Oh God!" We were both really embarrassed and I couldn't wait to get out of there.

I once accompanied Norman Mailer and his wife Norris to a Ramones concert at CBGB. After the third song, Mailer, who was standing on a chair to get a better view, turned to me and yelled, "Heroic!" This single word perfectly summed up the aura of the Ramones. I met Joey Ramone in 1977, and we became fast friends. At the time I was juggling three careers, working with Andy Warhol, William Burroughs and working with Blondie. The Ramones were one of the hardest working bands of the Seventies, and Joey spent most of his time on the road. As a testament to the value of our friendship, we communicated largely through letters. The two short pieces that follow were originally published in my apartment's house journal, Traveller's Digest. The third one comes from a piece I wrote with Joey for High Times. He is still the coolest, most intelligent, funny guy I ever met in downtown New York.

19

Joey Ramone: A Literary Relationship

After the people I've written books about, the coolest punk celebrity I met in New York is undoubtedly Joey Ramone. John Holmstrom, then editor of *Punk* magazine (this was in '77) now publisher of *High Times*, introduced me to him in ace punk fashion. Joey was staying with the band's lighting designer and a talented painter Arturo Vega, around the corner from the renowned punk club CGBG. One night after a gig John and I came careening out of the club and took turns creaming Legs McNeil, who had had the affrontery to recently attempt to sleep with my girlfriend when I was in Australia! I guess he thought I was far enough away that he was out of danger, but no such luck! Immediately we had left Legs lying in the gutter, where he had been attempting to pick up a chick, I found myself following Holmstrom literally straight up the face of Vega's building via those metal screens that close across windows at night keeping hoodlums out. Entering the loft through a second storey window we charged the unsuspecting Ramone, Vega and a couple of their friends but soon found ourselves getting the worst of the altercation. Joey had me pinned to the floor, one bony knee plunked on each shoulder demanding I surrender. No sooner had we introduced ourselves than we became fast friends. Everybody loved Arturo, but Joey was clearly something of a loner. A wildly creative, intelligent guy surrounded by a lot of less intelligent guys (not Dee Dee who he got along with best), he liked nothing more than to settle down in a comfortable bar or apartment around three am and spend the balance of the night solving the problems of the world. The problem was, I tried to explain to him, I was desperately trying to make a living as a nine-to-five writer. Consequently we met much less often than I would have liked, but even when he was on the road Joey made a real effort to keep in touch, as one can see from these two letters:

"Hey ol boy whats the doop?" he wrote from LA where The Ramones, in perhaps their single most productive period were making an album with Phil 'The Great' Spector, and filming *Rock n Roll High School* with the great ex-Warhol Superstar Mary Woronov (*Chelsea Girls*). "What's doin. Hanging out swatting flies recordin the album it sounds incredible really explosive!! cant wait for ya to hear it though its only ½ done. Just saw a picture of Wayne County" (which Joey thoughtfully included) "with his new operation he looks more like Debbie Harry everytime I see him. Saw Robert Gordon & Spedding he's great – say hi to Jeff and everyone. See ya soon. Hi from everyone here. P.S. Los Tacos is the best Mexican dump in LA better than Lucy's. No bands. No gas. Aggressive flys. They repainted The Trop pool black and filled it with turquois green shitty water it looks like a lagoon Joey Ramone."

In another missive from the road he wrote: "Last nite I saw somethin on TV that really flipped me out. This was the first report ever let out in the whole US bout cloneing. This guys puttin out a book called Who Will Be The Next God. Anyway Upjohn the Quaalude Corp. & 20 other major drug corp have gotten the rights from the Federal Gov to syntheticaly create & clone & own!!! people & that until recently only frogs could be successfully cloned. But some scientist from New York has just successfully created a 14 month old kid thats an exact replica clone of himself. That's fuckinamazin that's really weird. I mean when ya think about it. Anyway I thought you should. They said that this would come out

nationally in June. Hanging out in N. Carolina. Don't understand what people do here since I haven't seen one person
outside of the hotel. Last night went to see High Anxiety. It
sucked but was really great, I'm really into Cheap Trick.
They're fucking incredible. Listen to their 1 & 2 album. Legs
story in new Hit Parader was fucking riot. Best thing he's
done fantastic. See ya. Joey Ramone."

In fact, perhaps appropriately considering he wrote songs
and I wrote celebrations, our friendship turned into something of a literary one: the next thing I found myself doing
was collaborating with him on an editorial he had been commissioned to write for *High Times* in 1978. This is the first of
its eight pages:

> "Living on the Bowery's very exciting, people are getting
> stabbed and murdered all the time. It's very exciting, lots
> of atmosphere. Tomorrow we're playing The First World
> Festival in Toronto with Ted Nugent and Aerosmith, a
> whole day affair for 100,000 people. Gotta get up and fly
> at 5.30 am.
> Excerpt from: *The Diary of Joey Ramone.*

I just saw The Who movie *The Kids Are Alright*. It's fucking
fantastic. It doesn't come off as just another documentary, it's
loaded with charm and character, excitement and the genius
of The Who (if you love The Who as much as me). But for me
it was more of a movie that reflects the current sad state of
rock and roll. After seeing *The Kids Are Alright*, I felt really
enraged.

The Who are the perfect example of what Rock & Roll
stands for and was always meant to be. Whether it be 60's,
70's, 80's or 90's the definition of rock and roll is: Daring.
Exciting. Going out on a limb. Very visual catchy and melodic
tunes. *Not* ½ hour boring guitar solos or mindless songs
about sex: She Left Me. Who the fuck cares!!! The kids of

now are being deprived, cheated and brain washed bad. It's not their fault, most of them just don't know better. Rock and Roll is dying 'cos the media is trying to kill it as it's always been trying since the days of Elvis and Gene Vincent (50s). They're spreading propaganda about how youth listening to this music have their minds poisoned and turn into habitual sex crazed hard core tri-sexual, mindless pill popping pot smoking drop out mass murderers, which we all know is bullshit, but it's always worked successfully to promote the clean-up-the-image campaign. Remember Pat Boone and Doris Day – the soft decor public image that parents will approve of. Rock and roll is for rebels and outcasts. *Rock music was not meant for your parents pleasure.*"

As well as being a great painter, film maker, publisher, journalist, photographer, trendsetter and icon, Warhol was a great writer. His novel, *a*, which will be re-published in 1998, will give us all a chance to read what I mean. Grab a copy. It tells you more about Warhol's Factory in the Sixties than any other book. It is a bonechilling read.

20

Andy Warhol The Writer

I was first introduced to Andy Warhol through his voice in 1973. I was working with a writer named Andrew Wylie in New York City. Wylie had interviewed Warhol and was trying to convince me that Andy was not only the most important artist of the twentieth century but also the greatest person in the United States. I was *not* convinced of this and argued with him about it. Wylie then played for me, on a cheap tape recorder, a cassette of the interview he had done with Warhol a couple of weeks prior. I listened to that voice for approximately one minute and was *immediately* convinced of both of these assertions.

In his writing, Warhol was most interested in depicting what I call 'voice portraits'. I discovered this when I went to work for Warhol at *Interview* magazine in 1976. He told me that the best way to do an interview was to visit the subject, ideally in their own home, with no questions and no preconceptions – with as empty a mind as possible. This way, the interviewer will get the most accurate and revealing image of the subject via the topics he or she chooses to discuss, as well as the grammar, syntax and vocabulary used. If a tape is transcribed very accurately, with each 'uhm', 'err' and 'but' included, what is redacted is a voice portrait. Warhol demonstrated this in the distinct interviews he did for *Interview* magazine between 1974 and 1982.

The first book Andy wrote, and probably the most obscure in his catalogue of fourteen books, is called *a (a novel)*. One day, in August of 1965, through the kind of serendipity that decorated Warhol's career, Andy received a package in the mail from Philips Recording Company containing the first cassette tape recorder. Warhol was told that he could keep the machine on the condition he do something to publicise it. Andy instantly decided that he would write a book with it. Everyone at the Factory laughed and thought how stupid he was, because that's not writing, that's tape recording – or as Truman Capote said about Jack Kerouac, "That's not writing, that's typing". Apparently, 'language' is not writing, words have to be written in some kind of preconditioned manner to be considered true writing. Andy didn't agree and approached his favourite superstar, Ondine. Ondine was not only Warhol's court jester but he was also the most articulate, funniest, fastest-talking person at the Factory. Warhol proposed that he would record '24 Hours in the Life of Ondine' (the reference to *Ulysses* is inescapable, and Andy knew the implications of writing a novel which would cover twenty-four hours in the life of a man), and he told Ondine that the book would make him famous. Ondine, who was a great person and wanted to be as famous as he was fabulous and loved Andy, was happy to do it so they agreed to meet a few days later on a Saturday morning. When they met, both ingested some Disoxyin pills – Ondine took ten (a superstar-strong dose), Andy took two – and off they went, living in what in those days was a normal day in the life of Andy and Ondine. They went to the Factory, they went to visit people in their apartments, to restaurants, they rode in the back of cabs to clubs . . . and Andy recorded it all on his brand new toy. After twelve hours, however, Andy tired and went home. The book was not completed until two years later during a second marathon session in August of 1967. *a* is, by the way, undoubtedly the most accurate written portrait of the silver factory. It is typical of the blindness of the publishing industry that while facile books on Warhol tumble into print yearly this echt document remains almost entirely neglected although available (through Grove/Atlantic who own the rights). What makes it so puzzling that the book is out of print in the celebrity-soaked USA is that it contains an all-star cast. Ondine dominates the text but Edie Sedgwick makes some fascinating appearances twittering a series of the trippiest titters in the book like "gone down from divinity to star to somehow the mockery walks get in."[1] And Lou Reed makes a guest appearance. Since a book about Edie was a bestseller and there are several books in print about Reed, it is inexplicable that a book *by* Warhol about these people remains out of print (and don't give me that 'it's hard to read' routine; it's easier to read than *The Naked Lunch*). It looks like another part of the denial of Warhol's genius. Although he was, in my humble opinion, as creative with words in 1965–7 as William Burroughs, Richard Brautigan, Thomas Pynchon or Susan Sontag, to name but a few of the stars of the day, nobody takes him seriously as a writer. And he was an industrious one.

Once the recording had been finished, Andy had to get the 24-hour tape transcribed. And it was in this step that the book was transformed from a good idea into literature. Rather than asking one person to transcribe, Warhol chose a bevy of (mostly) women to do the vital work. He gave the tapes to various people including Maureen Tucker, the drummer for The Velvet Underground who happened to be a super typist, and Gerard Malanga's secretary, Susan Pile. Warhol also hired a couple of high school girls to come to the Factory each afternoon after school to type.

A number of inconsistencies occurred in the process of transcribing the tapes. Maureen Tucker refused to type up any swear words, so every time there was a swear word Maureen left that blank (there were a lot of blanks). One of the little high school girls had a tape confiscated and thrown into the trash when her mother overheard the language used – so one entire section of the book was lost. Susan Pile and Paul Katz, who were privy to the inner workings of the Factory and knew everyone there, felt strongly about some of the nasty things that were said about certain people on the tape, so they changed them to nice things. They also felt strongly about some of the nice things said and changed those to nasty things. Throughout the transcription words are misspelt, including 'and' and 'but', and grammar is confused; sometimes there are sixteen colons in a row or paragraphs with six brackets that open but never close. In this sense it is the 'worst' book ever written, just as Warhol's films are the 'worst' films ever made. However, the films have, albeit grudgingly, at least been recognised for changing the form and content of American cinema, and The Velvet Underground's first record produced by Warhol has been recognised as among the greatest rock records ever recorded. *a* is just as important a book as *The Chelsea Girls* is a film or *The Velvet Underground and Nico* is a record and should be recognised as among the most accurate, creative, influential novels of the Sixties. It is a useful, revealing, funny, educative book. To ignore it is a cultural crime, is to rewrite history incorrectly. It should be included on college reading lists in anthropology courses and history courses as well as English 101.

In August of 1967, Andy was handed the six hundred page manuscript to read in preparation for publishing the book. He was astounded by what he received, but contrary to what was expected, rather than take the pages to someone and have them properly re-typed, Warhol embraced the transcription exactly as it was. This is fantastic, he said, this is great. He read it six times from beginning to end.

In preserving the manuscript's shattered state Warhol was actually presenting the precise aura of the conversations. Because as we know, people don't actually speak in sentences, and there aren't always periods of complete silence when one person speaks and others are supposed to be listening. Instead, there is always some sort of babble going on during a conversation. Language is broken, people literally don't 'spell' words right when they speak them, words are spoken incorrectly. In *a* Andy created an accurate picture of a day in the life of the Factory in the Sixties.

Although the book was completed in 1967, it was not published until after Warhol was shot, in the fall of 1968 by Grove Press, which also published Warhol's *Blue Movie* (the script illustrated by stills of its stars Viva and Louis Waldron making love in the shower and in bed). Thus, although *a* was the first book Warhol wrote which was published, another book written in 1966, *Andy Warhol's Index (Book)*, was published first by Random House in December 1967.

Andy Warhol's Index (Book), which is an expensive rarity today, was another portrait of the mysterious silver factory as a schizoid funhouse. It consists primarily of photographs, blank pages, joke pages and a pop-up cut-out of a medieval castle inhabited by Warhol's superstars above the logo 'We are constantly under attack'. The text is a rambling, seemingly random, classically monosyllabic interview with Warhol. Although it stands today as an essential report on the Warhol factory, the *Index* book operates on a different level entirely than *a* inasmuch as it does not rely primarily on language.

In fact, 1967–8 saw the first stream of Warhol books: apart from *Andy Warhol's Index (Book)* and *a*, there was *Screen Tests: A Diary* (in collaboration with Gerard Malanga); *Intransit: The Andy Warhol-Gerard Malanga Monster Issue*, as well as the famous catalogue of the Svenska Moderna Museet in Stockholm with the flower paintings on the cover, popularly known as the telephone book because of its thickness, that contained some three hundred photographs by Billy Name and Stephen Shore as well as ten pages of Warhol's most famous aphorisms: 'I don't believe in love.' 'I want to be a machine.' 'I don't like to think.' All these books had a single purpose – to popularise Warhol just as the Bible popularises God. Only *a*, however, succeeded as a work of art on a par with his films, music and painting. As I see it, *a* is part of a trilogy that is married to, and is very similiar to, the film *The Chelsea Girls* and the record *The Velvet Underground and Nico*. It was made at the same time and based on the same people. The stars of *The Chelsea Girls* and the stars of The Velvet Underground are in *a*; and *a* follows the same themes and subjects as do *The Chelsea Girls* and *The Velvet Underground and Nico*.

a stands, I suggest, among the ten greatest books of the Sixties, along with *The Naked Lunch* and *A Clockwork Orange*. As is all great literature, *a* is a record of contemporary human speech. (Go back and read *The Goncourt Journals*[2] or *The Diaries of Samuel Pepys*[3] – the authors are reporting patterns and kinds of human speech.) *a* is a complete insight into the workings of the Factory and of the Warhol world and, as such, is tremendously successful. When published in the aftermath of Warhol's shooting, it was well reviewed in (the highly intellectual) *The New York Review of Books* – at length and seriously for exactly what it was. But inevitably, *a* was treated as were *The Chelsea Girls* and *The Velvet Underground and Nico* – recognised as an underground masterpiece it was largely ignored, and was probably read by as few people as have seen *Sleep*.

Andy believed the tape recorder could change writing as much as the camera had changed painting. In the mid-Seventies, Warhol turned the machine on himself in another attempt to create literature. Hence, we get his second string of books: *The Philosophy of Andy Warhol: From A to B and Back Again*,[4] *POPism: The Warhol '60s*[5] and *Andy Warhol's Exposures*[6] (of which I wrote the first draft).

In the Eighties Warhol wrote three more books – I like to think he saw his books in the Sixties, Seventies and Eighties as trilogies mirroring each decade, but that is perhaps overwarholising Warhol – *America*, *The Party Book* and the posthumously published *Andy Warhol Diaries*,[7] which was his only bestseller (what he had hoped *a* would be). The diaries were edited by one of the most talented, least known 'lifers' at the Factory, Pat Hackett, who had revealed a flash of brilliance in writing the scripts for Andy Warhol's *Dracula* (1974) and *Bad* (1977), with George Abagnolo, which is one of the reasons they captured Warhol's voice so well artistically and commercially. *America* and *The Party Book* were primarily photo books with a text dictated by Warhol on tape mixed with interviews with a number of the photo subjects. Compared to their peers in the Sixties and Seventies they indicated a dire falling off of Andy's interest in publishing books. Books were too much work for too little money. In fact, in 1985 when Andrew Wylie, by now a powerful literary agent who owed a good deal of his success to what he had learned from Warhol, approached Andy with a proposal to get him a one million dollar advance for five books that were for the most part already written – *The Diaries*, his play *Pork* (1971), the text of *The Chelsea Girls* and other factory documents – Warhol refused, somewhat bitterly, on those grounds. One could not help getting the impression, however, that the real reason behind Warhol's rejection of Wylie's super offer was the treatment Andy had received over thirty years from the publishing industry – from the editors to the reviewers – which had been, in a word, 'stupid'.

a, *The Philosophy of Andy Warhol* and *The Andy Warhol Diaries* are in my opinion the three great books that Andy Warhol wrote. (*The Diaries* successfully take you back to the Eighties, as *The Philosophy* takes you to the Seventies, and *a* takes you to the Sixties.) They are 'the essential Warhol'. And we hope that in time some enterprising publisher like Penguin or Vintage will put out a portable Andy Warhol, doing what they have done for so many dead writers: by presenting a well-edited selection of his work with an instructive, informative, entertaining introduction, to make available to the reading public around the world a book that could place Warhol in an appropriate, well-earned context as among the most influential reporters of his times. Such a book would of course include extracts from a number of his 'voice portraits' in *Interview* magazine as well as from interviews he gave throughout his life. For more than any other writer of the period, Warhol made out of human prose a poetry as vital as Allen Ginsberg's, as tough as William Burroughs' and as delicate and passionate as the writings of Malcolm X. When I read the histories of the Sixties and note with astonishment that the attempted assassination of 1968 (coming right between Martin Luther King and Robert Kennedy's assassinations) is ignored and his influence on film is ignored and his influence on journalism and literature is never mentioned (despite the fact that back in 1974 *Newsweek* noted that *Interview* magazine had given birth to *People*, among others, and Warhol has inspired at least one hundred books in the last thirty years), I begin to grasp what it means to say that Andy Warhol died of neglect.

Notes

1 Andy Warhol, *a (a novel)* (New York: Grove Press, 1968).
2 Edmond de Goncourt, *The Goncourt Journals, 1851–1870* (New York: Greenwood Press, 1968).
3 Samuel Pepys, *The Diary of Samuel Pepys* (New York: Crosup & Sterling, 1892). This citation describes the first publication fully transcribed from the shorthand manuscript in the Pepysian library. However, numerous other volumes of Pepys's diaries have been published at later dates.
4 Andy Warhol, *The Philosophy of Andy Warhol: From A to B and Back Again* (New York: Harcourt Brace Jovanovich, 1975).
5 Andy Warhol and Pat Hackett, *POPism: The Warhol '60s* (New York: Harper & Row, 1980).
6 *Andy Warhol's Exposures*, ed. Bob Colacello (New York: Andy Warhol Books/Grosset & Dunlap, 1979).
7 *The Andy Warhol Diaries*, ed. Pat Hackett (New York: Warner Books, 1989).

When Martin Amis first came to New York in 1977 I was assigned to interview him for Warhol's magazine, *Interview*. Andy thought he was "really great". He turned out to be right again.

21

An Interview With Martin Amis

"You write your first book, actually, to say to the world: 'Here I am, I'm nice and interesting and have me round, I'll go to bed with you'," says English novelist Martin Amis on his first visit to New York ("It seems to me an easy place to live") since he was ten, to celebrate the publication of his second book* Dead Babies*. *A first,* The Rachel Papers, *written when he was 21, had served as an effective introduction.* "I think that writers write about what it's like to be a certain age, maybe only tiny bits of being a certain age." Dead Babies *was written when he was 22–23. It is about an English country house weekend ("The most civilized thing you could possibly do, but telling a seventy year old woman my book's called* Dead Babies, *I do feel a bit of a pervert"). "People in America will think it's a shitty, vicious book,"* he says, *"but in England I'm known as a writer with civilized attitudes and not just a sick scribbler." His favorite American author is Joseph Heller whom he recently interviewed in London.* Interview *interviewed him in extremely civilised surroundings – the Upper East Side flat of Jon Bradshaw, the Michael York look-a-like English author of* Fast Company, *a book about gambling in the US. Martin has borrowed the flat for three days while Bradshaw is out of town.*

"Oh there you are," he says, opening the door before we knock. "Did you get my note?" *No. It has fallen off the mail box, which is why we had not known how to open the front door.* "The door is open" *read the note.*

Inside the flat is dark. Suitcases, books, and bottles of whisky are carefully spread out on the floor. Martin's girlfriend July (the British representative of Woman's Wear*) is kneeling on the floor with a* *telephone arranging cocktail dates. It's three thirty and just as cold inside the flat as on the street.*

"It's cold. You've managed to bring England to New York."

"Yes, it's just that temperature in here. And there's no TV, no stereo, no radio, no heating and no lights," Martin nods, satisfied.

"I was looking for a heater and I didn't see any."

"Isn't that some unit over there?"

"No, that's the air-conditioning unit."

"Would you like a blanket?"

Straw chairs perch around a glass coffee table in the middle of a starkly furnished lounge. Sitting in the fading light and fighting off the cold with the Haig, I asked the 26-year-old son of Kingsley Amis these questions.

BOCKRIS: When your book appears are you very keen to do as much as you can to [publicise it].

AMIS: I'm very unpushy with my publishers – I don't hustle the publicity department, I don't ring them up and ask how's it going every ten minutes – it's embarrassing to be too interested, especially financially.

BOCKRIS: That's a very English attitude. In America, it's "Are we making money right now?"

AMIS: They can't believe how casual I am about it. They say "We might have another review in this morning, why don't you ring up and check." And I say, "Just send it to me in due course. I don't want you to make any effort." But I'm sure if I said – "I think this is the greatest book written since *Hamlet,* I happen to believe it sums up the modern human condition," – I would get a couple of hundred sales out of it. Because in America you say you're great and you're great. In England it's the reverse.

BOCKRIS: You say you're great and everyone says . . .

AMIS: You're a loudmouth. And you say you're lousy and people say you're great because they're discovering you.

BOCKRIS: So you're not coming to America like Oscar Wilde who made a very carefully planned trip to release his personality on the country?

AMIS: Yeah, but he was Irish.

BOCKRIS: Speaking of Oscar, do you ever get scared that as a writer you'll get out of shape and fat?

AMIS: Well, actually, if you look around the writers in England, they all never do any exercise.

BOCKRIS: But they're all so poor . . .

AMIS: They're poor, they don't eat right . . .

BOCKRIS: But you probably won't be that poor . . .

AMIS: Well I've got a job.

BOCKRIS: . . . being successful.

AMIS: I think I'm a pretty athletic figure compared to most of the English writers. It is a worry, but they all seem quite fit. They live a life of such anxiety that it keeps them in some kind of shape.

BOCKRIS: Do you do any exercise at all?

AMIS: Yeah, I play tennis, swim a bit, walk up and down the stairs and everything.

BOCKRIS: Did *Dead Babies* actually come from an experience you had?

AMIS: It was based on a weekend I went through before I'd written my first book, where a lot of people were drunk, screwing, stoned, lying, and for about half an hour it seemed like hell. I thought there was a book there. Then it got stylised in my imagination and two years later I wrote the novel. Throughout writing my first novel I was thinking about it all the time. In fact, everyone agrees that part of writing is subconscious and that does a lot of the work for you. You can have terrible problems in a novel – you just don't know how you're going to get from A–B – then don't think about it for a few months and it's all ready without your being aware of having attacked it.

BOCKRIS: How long a period was there between your

finishing the first novel and getting started on the second?

AMIS: I began the next day. And after finishing *Dead Babies* I began the next day on my third. It's the only defense against a terrible post-natal depression and tristesse.

BOCKRIS: Do you feel much more confident and sure of your powers and abilities now that you've done two books?

AMIS: No, I don't think one grows in that way at all. I may worry about different things, but I do the same amount of worrying. I never feel I can relax. It's not that I want to get on or anything, but I feel uncertain about how good I am, how much talent I've got. I'm more aware now of just how likely I am to be second rate rather than first rate. A sort of sadness enters your work at this point. When you're writing your first book, it could be anything; it could be King Lear or it could be nonsense. And then you get an idea of how good it is and it's quite good, but it's not very good, and will you improve at all? You hope you're learning, but you also hope you're not getting more timid and that you won't try for bold risky effects. So you've got to fight against caution as well.

BOCKRIS: Do you think *Dead Babies* is going to be very successful?

AMIS: I shouldn't think so, no. I can see reviewers playing it cool about the decadence. "We don't want anymore bad news." I told my publisher that my next book would be about a puppy that won the love of the village. He was very keen and said, "That's the sort of book people in America want."

BOCKRIS: What is an average day in your London life?

AMIS: I live with my girlfriend in Pimlico in a flat. Three days a week I go to the office of the *New Statesman* about ten, do what needs to be done there and meet friends for lunch, work through the afternoon and come home, perhaps go out to a party, or dinner, or stay in and write. So, quietish but with a fair amount of incidents. I'm talking to writers a lot, which is sometimes exciting. I'm throwing ideas around all the time, and that's good, and actually having, as far as I can see, a fucking marvellous time compared with everybody else. I'm aware a hundred times a day what a horrible life everyone has compared with me, although, of course, no one's perfect. But it's buzzing a bit in London and actually I find it quite stimulating the way everyone is re-examining life from the point of view of not making enough money and the mild danger you live through every day. It's not a bad decade to be in London.

BOCKRIS: Do you still have a job for economic reasons or do you want to keep having a job?

AMIS: I like the idea of two bases; a home and an office.

BOCKRIS: Why not rent an office and go write in it?

AMIS: I need company. It's a very nice office, there are a lot of people there I like, and there's gossip.

BOCKRIS: Would you say perhaps the major reason you live in London is because it's a good place for you to work?

AMIS: It's more natural caution. The idea of movement seems like a wrench to me, a frightening prospect.

BOCKRIS: Do you think it would throw you off your rhythm to move to New York for a year and write here?

AMIS: Yes, it might do. I'm very conscious, in spite of the subject matter in my book, of working in a tradition, and the British is a more sedentary tradition than you have in New York where I keep getting electric shocks.

BOCKRIS: Do you make more money from your books in the States or in England?

AMIS: If your book gets to number fifty on the American bestseller list, it's selling twice as well as the number one book in England. So I sort of can't help but make more from here. I think it's about three or four times as much actually.

BOCKRIS: Can you make enough money from your novels to live on if you want to?

AMIS: Just about, but I would never like to try and do that because then writing becomes work and not a mixture of work and play which is the way I want to keep it. You could imagine yourself rushing through a book just to get the advance and I don't want to go in that direction. No doubt I'm going to end up that way.

BOCKRIS: Have you ever met anyone else whose father was a writer?

AMIS: Auberon Waugh. Evelyn Waugh's son.

BOCKRIS: Do you talk about that much between yourselves?

AMIS: We would both be embarrassed to talk about it. I always knew I was going to be a writer, that's what I always wanted to be. I think from the age of twelve I would start looking at life as possible novel fodder.

BOCKRIS: Do you feel a lot of pressure on yourself because people are obviously expecting a third book?

AMIS: Only pressure from inside. I have an image of myself as middle-aged and people say "He wrote two novels in his early twenties and look at him now." You don't want that to happen to you. But I think people are actually rather wary of talking about it. My father, for instance, never gave me a word of encouragement, *bless him,* you know, from that point of view. When I told him I was writing a novel he just said "Oh really?" And he didn't see it until it was published. People treat me with a bit of reserve in that way, which I'm grateful for. It's probably not the same in America where everyone is much more concerned with what's going on and it's not a private business, as it is in London, until publication.

BOCKRIS: What's your vision of yourself in the next 5–10 years?

AMIS: I think I'd only stop writing novels if I dried up or if I was very short of money or something like that. Then you get into the Norman Mailer circuit of having to write more crap than good books. I think you should tap your central energy first which for me is fiction. That's the stuff that falls upon you and there's no one else involved. If you get tired of that perhaps write some other sort of books. When I'm old and fucked up and can't write anymore and no one wants to see me and I've been rejected by all my friends, I'll write those other books.

BOCKRIS: What do you do if you desperately need to relax?

AMIS: Drink. Do you want some more Scotch?

High Times sent me to Berlin in 1978 to pick up on the vibe in that strange, alienated city. My visit coincided with a Patti Smith concert and the opening of a German film on punk rock. After London, it was the punkest city in Europe.

22

Berlin Rocks

It's easy to get there.

This is a daily diary I wrote up each night during four days investigating the structure of Berlin for *High Times*, 1978.

Friday

Friends in London had warned me not to take drugs into West Berlin under any circumstances: "The customs agents will undoubtedly search you because they are so uptight about terrorists and *you* look like one. Just give your stash", they said, "to us." So before I flew to Berlin from London on a Dan-Air Charter ($120 round trip) last night, I had cleaned out my pockets and cases.

Squeezing down the aisle of the aircraft, I wondered who would be in the next seat for the one-hour-fifty-minute flight into Germany, but she was more than I could have expected: a Berlin teenager returning from an English boarding school to join her parents for a skiing vacation in Innsbruck. Not only did she (16) speak excellent English, but – to my surprise and delight – her father was the eminent low-temperature German physicist Professor Klipping. Christine reported that Berlin "is full of drugs and I am very shocked even to find my schoolfriends now are all drugs taking, yes even LSD. Of course, they all are hash smoking, you see." She loves Berlin where "there is no poverty and everyone is very happy because it is a beautiful city full of parks and benches to sit on and admire the views." She gave me a list of places to visit and said she would like to invite me over for a drink with her famous Dad, but was unfortunately departing at 7 am the following morning for the skiing. I accepted the hospitality of this beautiful girl as a good omen.

Passing through German Customs: a large German with a flat face asked me if I had anything to declare, I said "No", he said "You can go." Cursing my London connections, I took a cab to the Savigny Hotel on the Brandenburrgerstrasse, checked in with the nightclerk, and went to bed (hadn't slept the previous night doing London drug scene).

This morning, after getting up too late for breakfast, I hurried down the Kurfurstendam (abbreviation: Kudam – the famous major thoroughfare) toward the Autoren Buch- handlung at 10 Carmerstrasse, a centre for poets and writers, whose address Allen Ginsberg had given with a recommenda- tion to make contact with a certain man who spoke English and would fit me into the picture.

As I crossed a vast street I noticed a huge yellow sign saying *Deutsches Commerzbank.* One thing about travelling is to always make a careful cockpit check before exiting your hotel room and entering the new atmosphere. You should always, for example, carry your passport, because it is the only proof that you exist since *nobody knows you,* and also if you want to cash any traveller's checks you will need it. I did not have my passport on me and it was midday on Friday (when, nobody had told me yet, the banks close at 1 pm) and I suddenly realised I better get some cash for the weekend. I walked in:

"Cashen sie die . . .?"

"Ja."

I rapidly signed four and laid them out on the table.

"Passport, bitte." I knew this was going to happen, but my American Immigration card is a fine-looking technical document full of serial numbers and a photo, so I laid it down and said "Take this, it is good." I was not at all upset when she replied negatively, because, in the process of digging the immigration card out of the depths of my wallet I had found one big fat joint of very good grass I'd rolled up and forgotten to discard in London. I managed to cash my cheques further down the Kudam at the seminal Kempinski Hotel and reached the Autoren Buchhandlung around 12:30. A helpful lady, who actually didn't speak much English, gave me the phone number of a man she said would be able to help me, and suggested I visit a bar this evening called the Zweigelfisch on Grollmanstrasse.

I walked from the Autoren Buchhandlung along the Kant-strasse and stopped in a small cafe for lunch. I told the patron to recommend something because he could speak English. I find it hard to understand the Germans when they talk. You look at them and go "WHAT!" And they look at you like you're being rude. So he brought me an oval-shaped glass of beer with a three-inch head on it, and a plate of cold potato salad plus an order of sliced potatoes and a piece of meat covered in potatoes ($5).

Further down the Kantstrasse I stopped outside a movie house that said THE GERMAN VERSION OF PUNK ROCK. This is obviously the hip cinema and here it is in a good central location. Further on down the Kantstrasse the lights on the stupendous Cafe Mohring are blinking on and off. I bought a copy of *The Paris Herald Tribune* and went in for coffee. Everybody looked at me. The clientelle was made up of content, rich young people dressed in expensive Italian or German (undefinable as yet) clothes, and old homosexual couples. At one table, an elegant fifty-year-old son was discussing a financial problem with his dowager seventy-year-old mother. Across the street Hot Tuna, Patti Smith and Ritchie Havens are advertised for upcoming performances. A headline in the informative weekly *ZITTY* magazine proclaims *BERLIN HAS A BABY AND ITS NAME IS ROCK AND ROLL.*

It's funny to come to a city where you know no one simply to look at it. The people seem at first to be living in another world. They can see you but they don't recognise you, so there isn't much feeling of connection to others on the street. One experiences the isolation of the man in the single room. But Berlin feels like the right place to do this study, because I believe the best way to look at it is suddenly by surprise. As I walked back to the hotel, having read a disappointing *Herald Tribune*, smoking the joint down a quiet street on the way helped. In Room 93, I looked at myself in the mirror and said "You're in Berlin." *On intuition,* and because many people had said "Berlin seems interesting." Also, while Samuel Beckett and David Bowie have both moved here in the Seventies, the big guns of current German Lit, Gunter Grass and Max Frisch, both keep apartments in Berlin. I.e. a lot of hip people live here.

My room is a high-ceilinged white box with light grey Victorian wallpaper. At 4.45 this afternoon, I decided to imagine what it would be like to have sex in Berlin and jerked off on the cold grey and white bathroom floor. Outside, I could hear the birds, and it *was* more exciting because it was in Berlin. I think if you actually had sex with someone here you'd lie there afterwards thinking "I did it in Berlin" and feel more fulfilled.

Next to my bed there is a sign that shouts:

HERE YOU GET BEST TELEPHONE SERVICE.
USE IT.

The telephones are very modern, so I picked one up and made a few calls. On the phone it's actually easier to speak a foreign language because the person can't see you. I made an appointment to meet Herr Herbach at the bookshop 11.30

tomorrow morning. (THE PHONES WORK PRETTY WELL! – stoned note scrawled on back of book.)

Around 5.30 I went to the Kant Kine for Wolfgang Busch's *Punk in London,* to see how it was being presented to the Germans. It's a fairly straightforward documentation of British punk but almost totally lacking in humor, except for an excellent film of The Clash playing Munich. They said they hated Germany because the police had thrown them out of a hotel. Rodent, when asked about Germany, said "Lots of money, isn't it? Lots of Deutschmarks" (which sums up the English attitude). But I find it very hard to criticise a country when I'm alone in it because someone might arrest you and you don't know anybody so you're fucked. So far I have not seen any policemen but Berlin is an extremely law-abiding city: everyone is rich. But when I looked in the shop windows this morning, there were big pictures of BERTOLT BRECHT and big books about CHAIRMAN MAO. Berlin is "the cradle of electricity" but I haven't felt any in the air. Evidently the people are not dedicated to the sound of punk rock, but they take a rather studious content view. There were ten in the audience, twelve waiting for the next show – no punks.

It quickly becomes evident that Berlin has a very good supply of everything, no over-crowding, comfortable accoutrements and virtually no street-crime. So if you lived here you might be content too. "But not bored," argue Berliners because Berlin does have an edge about it. After all, it's an international centre and has had an extreme recent history. According to Baedeker "On 3rd February 1945 1,000 acres in central Berlin were turned into a sea of flames in less than one hour." And: "80,000,000 cubic metres of rubble covered Berlin on May 2nd 1945 when the Russian guns ceased bombardment, after two weeks of fighting hand to hand, door to door, street to street." Yet today, while tweedy Londoners still offer "I had Jerry in my sights when . . ." stories, Berliners have clearly put the war behind them and their city is now one of the most luxurious and modern in Europe.

I had a very bad night at the recommended 'hip writers' and artists' bar' Zwiegelfisch, where I was surrounded, just as I had feared, by middle-aged men with beards. There were two interesting looking guys, both gay, with short hair wearing heavy make-up, but I didn't get a chance to talk to them. I did overhear an American soldier telling two German girls "America is a drug society, everybody's into drugs." I wonder if he knew that Berlin is a central point for drug traffic coming from the east on Aeroflot flights?

Quote for the day:
   "In Berlin a guy can live in the same apartment for forty years, there isn't the same pressure . . ."
   Iggy Pop in conversation, New York 1978

Saturday

I got up fairly early this morning and went along to breakfast, the only meal this hotel serves (for $3.00 extra). A waitress approached me with "Ja?"

"*Er, sprechen sie Englisch?*"

"Nein."

I presumed there was either a set breakfast of scrambled eggs or at least a menu, so said "Tea."

"Zo." She returned two minutes later with a big bowl of rolls, a big jar of jam, two small pieces of butter, a small plate with some cheese and coldcuts on it and a small bowl of fat black grapes, accompanied by a pot of tea. I got hold of a couple of Kraut dailies from the sideboard – at least I could look at the pictures and make out the captions: *"Today Princess Margaret is 47. Her boyfriend has internal bleeding. She returns from the hospital after visiting him."*

I laughed through the complete breakfast, collected my

equipment and hit the Kudam, smoking the second half of the joint – snapping pictures of passers-by, telephone boxes, street signs – heading for an 11 am glass of sherry at the Kempinski. Unfortunately I had borrowed the camera from a lady in England who had failed to inform me that it didn't work, so, while sitting in the lobby of the Kempinski waiting for my sherry, I found myself unwinding the totally exposed role of film and pulling it out of the sprockets. Next time, I decided, I will stay at the Kempinski, where the whole staff speaks English. It felt very comfortable, international and discreet. The lobby is decorated in black with dark browns and greens, but all three colors are picked up by heavy gold lights and fixtures. It's a presentation of stolid elegance. I mean, I think the Germans are a little heavy. Everytime I go out I run into stolidity. And the standard smart thirty-year-old German is a pretty brutal-looking character, with his curling lip and blond wolf-do (Deutsch version of the shag cut) . . .

All the pieces that make up a city are beginning to appear. This morning I actually saw a beggar sitting on the Kudam (very rare), and three excited kids jostling in a pinball shop next to the peep show (promising young models from all over the world) opposite a cinema showing *Achilles*, a very violent German film. The waiter brought the check: it cost $3.25 to have a glass of sherry in the foyer of the Kempinski Hotel.

I met Kepi Herbach (who turned out to be a jovial public relations man from The Academy of Art) at the Autoren Buchhandlung. He introduced me to the Turkish poet Aras Oren, and the two of them gave me the following pertinent information about West Berlin.

1 There are 2,000,000 people in Berlin and it was built for 4,000,000.
2 It's very important to understand that Berlin life functions around social clubs (called Kneipes) and that these,

though often informally based in bars are strictly divided among the working-class, older people, and artists (who think of themselves as 'the outsiders'). There is only minimal social exchange between these two groups.

3 The 'working class' are the people who run (as in 'work') the city. There is no industry except the nightlife.

4 The rest of the West Germans are a little pissed off with Berliners because they realise that they're paying for this city which has no means of supporting itself. West Berliners are aware of this disdain and return it.

5 On television they run their commercials in fifteen-minute blocks so as not to interrupt the programs/there are a lot of political discussions, and the news comes on three times a night.

6 Berlin is an extremely well organised metropolis. Everything is very fine and runs smoothly. Berliners were astonished by New York's inability to deal with last winter's blizzards.

7 Berlin and Berliners lost their identity when the city was pounded into "a sea of flames" and they are always looking for a new one, this makes the inhabitants of the city very open-minded.

8 100,000 Turkish people live in West Berlin. Beginning in the Twenties the Berliners imported Turks to work but "recently a very big number of Pakistanis came to Berlin and it caused a problem because they imported too many of them, so the government put them back in the airplane and paid them all some money to start again in Pakistan."

9 Samuel Beckett has been personally directing his plays in Berlin since the late Sixties, has a flat in the Akademie Der Kunst, and can be seen walking daily the four kilometres from the Akademie to the Schiller Theatre. If approached, he will speak.

10 Two good magazines to buy are *TIP* and *ZITTY*.

11 There is a special desire on the part of the government to

promote arts here. After New York, London and Paris, Berlin is the most important cultural centre.

12 David Bowie's favorite restaurant is *Exiles,* a place where Austrian writers, who find their own climate extremely puritanical, gather to eat Wiener Schnitzle. In the German edition of *Playboy,* Bowie said he considered Hitler to be the first rock star. "We were quite surprised by this, we couldn't understand it," Herr Herbach tells me.

13 In Berlin, there is no closing time.

14 The best Drag Queen Club is Chez Romy Haag's on the Fuggerstrasse. There are a lot of gay restaurants and a big number of gay people in Berlin. "One place you might think interesting for very simple people is the worker's drag queen clubs," Herr Herbach tells me.

Before saying goodbye, Kepi and Aras invited me to a party at the atelier of a writer who was leaving Berlin the following day. After the party, they suggested, we might go to the Zwiegelfisch and then onto Romy Haag's.

I went back to the hotel, made some notes, and hopped a bus down the Kudam towards the Tiergarten: the buses are slightly more spacious and modern than the London double-deckers with cream exteriors and red interiors. The receptionist at the hotel gave me the wrong directions so the bus didn't take me to the Tiergarten, but it was fun to ride. The driver had a very clear intercom system through which he told the passengers which stop was coming, and not to misbehave. I got off halfway to Kreuzberg – the 'hip' section of town – and walked across town to the Tiergarten, Berlin's version of Central or Golden Gate Parks. At one end you can stare across the 100-yard dividing-point into East Berlin.

I walked back along the historic STRASSE VON 17 JUNI in a blazing sunset which illuminated the black and gold Wagnerian statues of gods in the gardens on both sides of the avenue, and then suddenly came upon the spacious modern-office-buildings in the centre of Berlin in the twilight. There was just the thinnest slice of moon as I walked and walked looking at every sign, building, pedestrian, car, and getting, what Jamie Wyeth refers to as, "indigestion of the eyeballs".

I particularly enjoyed the large dinner I just ate at the Bratwurst Stand. I had two big sausages each accompanied by a crispy roll and a big spludge of mustard with a side order of French Fries covered in a white sauce that looks and tastes like a cross between fresh whipped cream and mayonnaise. I was standing around an outdoor counter in a light rain with a bunch of people all sniffing and going mmm mmm mmm as they munched on their brats, brots and brunts. It cost $2.50. The patron asked me if I was French and when I said "Amerikan, aus New York", he launched into a panegyric saying now that the airfare between New York and Berlin had just been lowered to $325 round trip he planned to go for his summer vacation. Another man eating a bratwurst chipped in his two cents: "I was there for a week and it only cost me $1,000, very reasonable."

This afternoon I felt that it was probably something of a privilege to be a Berliner – at least, within the confines of Europe, they seem to have a more realistic financial scene than most. I have to count every pfennig and plan my excursions like minor military operations to make sure I don't get stuck with a big bill I can't pay.

Quote for the day:
"No place that I have been to exhibits more democracy than West Germany, but the eyes of the world are watching to see if they can deal with this problem while at the same time increasing democratic liberty."
Max Frisch in conversation, Berlin 1978.

Sunday

Apparently I didn't plan *last night's* excursion very carefully because I woke up this morning very angrily and had no idea where I was because I was dreaming about renting a car in England and these two girls are giving me a hard time about getting a nice car because they think I'll smash it up so I go down to the local cafe for a coffee and they give me their last cup which some mad lady snatches and runs away with so I go back up to the office and the girls are laughing hysterically, but actually this was the hysterical laughter of three chambermaids who had turned on six vacuum cleaners outside my room in order to WAKEN ME UP! And were now hammering on my door yelling WHEN ARE YOU GETTING UP? (in Kraut). I winced and moaned, searching for memories of last night's bash, and mumbled "Soon, soon" but Germans are determined to get a precise answer. So I yelled out "IN EINE HALBE STUNDE!" and started to have a hate affair with the maids.

I took the fall and landed next to the lamp and my wallet, which was luckily still filled with money. Stumbled into the bathroom, took a look at myself, screamed, climbed into a pair of jeans, pulled on a shirt, slammed sunglasses around my face, yanked open the door and stared at THE MAID, dangling the key in my hand. She threw up her hands, shrugged her shoulders, and said "Ja, aber jetzt ist est ganz genug" ("Yes, but it's already too much"), and turned on her vacuum cleaner. So I went out to the receptionist and threw the key into her face and ran out the door and she chased me down the street yelling "WHEN ARE YOU LEAVING?"

I had to go to East Berlin. There was no orange juice, no eggs, no refreshments for this research. I miss everyone in America. Today I started to think "Berlin sucks". The party I went to last night 'for artists' was the same scene you see everywhere. Here was the same man hating the same woman and later dancing with her ecstatically, the same overweight men with mustaches, complaining about the success or failure of their latest book, asking to be interviewed. "Berlin attracts many people who never made it," Edgar Hilsenrath, a German-Jewish author (of *The Nazi and The Barber*) recently publically interrupted by the NPD., which he said is made up of very young or very old people and is not really a serious threat but something to pay attention to, told me. I felt as if I had seen enough.

I got a bump on my head last night, must have fallen over, came home and wrecked my room, it's a wonder I got here and I don't remember how. Rudolf Hess is still in Spandau. There was this guy last night telling me how successful he was so I said "Yeah, but how come you have hair on your nose?" I don't like the People who run my hotel. The thin blonde behind the counter is giving me these "I know your number looks" and I'm beginning to feel uncomfortable.

These are some notes I made this afternoon while taking the subway into East Berlin:

This subway is by far the best in western world, ranks second only to Moscow's/clean fast efficient neat. The trains are bright yellow and the seats are green. I haven't paid yet – don't understand that bit. They sell alcohol on the subway platforms in little bottles. Stops as I pass them: Blissesstrasse/ Berlinerstrasse . . . It's very easy to use because everything is very clearly signposted in big letters and numbers. A Turk just got on beating up on his kid who didn't want to get on. No smoking on the subways/no cigarette ads in Berlin. Automatic photo machines on every platform, we just stopped in a station but the doors didn't open. Berlin, cradle of electricity, city of machines. You open the subway door yourself. A guy just did it. Everytime the train pulls out of the station a cat shouts "ZURUCK BLEIBEN!" (Stand back.) The thing about the Germans is they understand machines, as do the Japanese, and that is why they are so far ahead of everyone and proud of it ("You might know of course Germany is the richest country in Europe and with the lowest unemployment", Kepi Herbach told me yesterday morning). A beautiful chick just got on with her DOG who is leaping about playfully, amusing the passengers. A really cool guy wearing high heel shoes, red socks and a short corduroy zip up jacket just got in and sat (the train is getting crowded) next to me. He's reading an occasional romance comic book, the dog is barking. Here's my stop.

I am cool because I just got off the train and I could have gotten on the wrong train but I felt deep down inside CAUTION, read the sign, and it said "Go upstairs and get on the other platform for Tegel asshole".

ON NEXT TRAIN: I just saw on the Friedrichstrasse platform there's a guy with a microphone directing the whole thing. We just passed the first stop in East Berlin without stopping, a totally wrecked derelict station covered in dirt and broken pieces of wood presided over by a fat guard slumped against a pile of rusty boxes. I have to stop writing now because I'm about to go into East Berlin on the subway and I don't want to make a fool of myself or get arrested for taking notes . . .

40 MINUTES LATER/ABOVE GROUND/EAST BERLIN:

I'm here. This is really weird. I've walked about two blocks and keep reflecting on the weirdness. First thing strikes you is silence of East Berlin because many fewer cars and less excited chatter. Next thing so many more older buildings that look like they were once grand and think "This is all because of Hitler".

Coming across is also eerie. They take your passport *away* from you and give you a piece of paper – oh by the way I never did pay the subway, it seems like you can choose not to (but if you get caught it's a $10 fine) – with a number on it and you stand in a room with fifty other people until they call out your number (takes 15 minutes) and give you all these other pieces of paper and you give them 5 marks ($2.50) and then you walk over to a stodge face guard who looks at you to make sure you're you. If it is he stamps all these pieces of paper and gives you some of them.

Then you go to another fat soldier and give him 6.50 West German marks and he gives you 6.50 East German marks (which you *have* to spend) in a little cellophane bag. Real cute. Then you come out past a bunch of thin teenage soldiers in hats that are TOO BIG. Then you're here blinking in the sunlight on the Friedrichstrasse. There are punks in East Berlin – kids wearing jeans rolled up to mid-calf, bare leg, some sock and big big black boots. They look dirty and good. Intellectuals here wear long black leather coats and are unshaven. Basically you can always tell an adult communist because of the grim look, shabby clothes and stodgy gait.

I had forgotten how sad life is in a communist country, how the people get run down by their personal series of disappointments and of course the poor men drink surreptitiously out of little bottles wherever they are standing. I was just in a line in this cafeteria where I got an enormous plate of poor food for $1.25, so bought it just to taste, even though not hungry. The girl behind the counter – blonde and really very pretty eyes in a plain face – got very angry with the timid British couple who couldn't understand the menu. She just threw up her hands in disgust and said "Das ist Alles!" (That's it.)

A man comes to my table about 56–60 and poor, tries to talk to two old ladies about the pleasure of sitting in the sunshine, but they just stare moodily at their dishwater tea and think probably he is drunk. He just tried again. And the lady said "Zoo". But now they have begun to chat about the patterns the sun makes in finished voices and suddenly it's so horrible here I'm getting chills. Another thing I'd forgotten about the east is that there are informers everywhere. You have to be careful about who you talk to and what about especially in public because the waiter might report you . . .

The kids are very good looking though, maybe better looking than in West Berlin, because they have that lean and hungry look which is always so popular. I wonder if there are any drugs here. Someone last night at that party told me, emphatically pounding a fist on the table "THE WALL IS OPEN NOT FOR PEOPLE BUT FOR DRUGS" (the 100 deaths from heroin in West Berlin last year is considered high). THE WALL is a wonderful symbol, but you can't actually *see* it. I mean, it's there, but you don't keep bumping into it.

I came back from East Berlin via the subway and went straight to the Neue Welt theatre on Hasenheide to see Patti Smith's concert. The group was doing the sound check. I bumped into J. D. Daugherty (the drummer) and he said "Welcome to Berlin, stay around I'll talk to you later." I sat down. Mario, the tour manager, asked me what I was doing and I said I was from *High Times* and could I have a backstage pass. He said sure (*High Times* has a very good reputation by word of mouth in Germany). Mario told me that every concert in Germany was sold out. Then this really beautiful girl called Rozi came over and told me all about her best friend Manuel Gottsching who was the originator of Ashra Tempel and gave me his address suggesting I call him tomorrow and go over for a chat before leaving town.

Howard the publicist from Arista records, took me up to the group's dressing room from which I got expelled ten seconds into a conversation with Ivan Kral by a tight-assed English roadie. Howard came out with his mouth full of food frantically apologising and saying that he didn't realise they wanted to keep the room very empty, but it's actually better to get thrown out than thrown in.

Anyway, it was more interesting down in the chairless auditorium, as people began to pour in. Very proper little old ladies in waitress outfits wandered around serving trays full of big cups of beer. The audience was very good looking, a lot of well-dressed punks. Also I notice a kind of Bertolt Brecht look, which is skinny hair, black leather, and horn-rimmed glasses on a thin nose.

There was certainly evidence of a lot of drugs. Five guys next to me were dancing on acid, everyone smoked hash throughout the concert (no police evident), there were even the occasional sympathetic huddles around 'a bummer'.

Patti's concert was perhaps best summed up by the Berlin paper the following day: they complained about the hype, and said the music wasn't much fun to listen to and the lyrics were indecipherable but she had a good voice. The group was made uptight by the silence and immobility of the majority of the audience. At one point Patti said "I ain't impressed with you, I sang in front of 14,000 people so 2,000 people doesn't mean shit to me," but nobody understood what the poor thing was saying. However, the proof of the audience's actually extremely positive reaction came with the hysterical 10-minute *political demonstration* demanding an encore (I kid you not). The manager of the theatre told Patti there would be a riot if she didn't come back.

I couldn't help but compare seeing The Ramones in London to seeing Patti in Berlin. You have to hand it to the Berliners for their organised serious consumption of the concert combined with a clear presentation of their approval, but Londoners like to ROCK OUT.

Quote for the day:
    "The weather is uncertain."
    Father Romeo Panciroli, commenting on the Pope's decision not to celebrate the traditional Palm Sunday mass in St Peters, due to the terrorist kidnapping of a major Italian political figure. In conversation, Rome 1978.

Monday

I tried to eat a big breakfast, in preparation for a long day, but got put off by the half-page close-up photograph of a corpse in Tel Aviv. Funny how reading the news in another language you wonder if it's true. My impulse was: "I must catch up and check on this." I think the Germans are rather attracted to terrorism, but I mean I don't know what that means.

You'll remember perhaps that I mentioned the Berliner's love of machines? I got an interesting look at it this morning. If you think the German walks his dog on a 'leash' you would be wrong. He has instead a small machine which looks like the circular plastic casing for an electronic kite handle. It is red and the dog connected to this thin metallic lead, can walk as much as thirty feet in front of the stroller. As he changes positions the machine adjusts the length of the lead so all the stroller need know is the dog is attached to him at all times. I saw this on the Carmerstrasse this morning coming out of a store where I had bought some notebooks and postcards.

I went back to my hotel, packed, paid the bill ($84 for four days, I think pretty reasonable for a very clean, efficient, if somewhat stolid hotel), and made an appointment to visit Manuel Gottsching at 3:30, which just gave me enough time to say goodbye to the lady at the Autoren Buchhandlung and have a nice lunch.

If anything hit me continually with a negative twinge in Germany, it was the heaviness of their objects, particularly the furniture, cutlery, clothes and buildings, but the character of a people is awfully elusive: as soon as one feels one has pinned it down, the impression is totally contradicted by a series of others. For example, in saying Germans make heavy things one ignores the delicate mobility of a Porsche. The beauty of German girls is largely based on their solidity, which does not sound like an attractive quality but can be, juxtaposed to . . . Naturally their problem lies in running to a little fat, but those who escape the rigid potato diet and maintain their lightness have a double-barrelled attraction, because of a supreme confidence in their superiority.

After lunch I went to Manuel's and waited in his lounge while he made a long-distance call to an electrician. He has a beautiful apartment with two enormous sparsely but tastefully furnished rooms, a music room (where he records his solo albums) and kitchen (where the remains of breakfast – boiled eggs and coffee – sit complacently on the table). The bathroom, done in light pink, is full of Rozi's OPIUM perfume. Manuel also has a cat who seemed to know more about the German rock scene than anyone. And this cat was actually staring at me so I felt a little unsettled, but thought "anyway, this is my last contact in Berlin".

Manuel finished his telephone call, offered me a glass of French Cinzano, and explained that the Berlin-born rock scene, as represented in its individuality by Kraftwerk, Tangerine Dream, Ashra Tempel and Klaus Schultze (going under the label "space rock", after rejecting the earlier "cosmic rock"), has very little support from the German press and businessmen. Their records have consequently sold very poorly. One label called OHR (translation: ear) had originally released all their records, but the owner of the label, a Herr Kaiser, quickly developed such a bad reputation for being crazy that all his artists found, even though they liked him and he was the only one who understood what they were doing, they couldn't afford to have anything to do with him.

256

According to Manuel (who is often called Mr Ashra because he was *the* man behind Ashra Tempel and has gone on to produce three excellent solo albums, the latest of which, *Blackouts*, is just out on Virgin), this music did grow out of the explosion of political feelings created by the students from 1968–69.

"In West Germany, the Bader-Meinhof gang is a very small group of militant revolutionaries that can call on a few hundred people for logistical help but otherwise is completely isolated politically."
New York Times, March 1978

But "Radio and TV are VERY CONSERVATIVE and change is *very slow* in Germany. Most of these German groups had their first success in France because the French public is open to new things whereas the German audience is very critical and mostly concerned about how 'correct' the musicians are. This", says Manuel wearily, "is part of the German mind you have to contend with."

Prior to 'space rock' the German music scene was *so dead* that musicians had to create something *so strange* that it might get some attention, and that is why the sound of German music is so specific, though Manuel agreed that it was also a fair representation of the mechanical nature of the German intellect. However, he is now surprised to find that no new groups are forming.

Manuel is an excellent guitarist often compared to the most innovative American and English players, he also seems to have a clear understanding of what he wants to do with the guitar, combining the monotonic Teutonic style with complex interior progressions, and hopes to go to New York in the Spring to do the music for Berlin fashion designer Claudia Skota's show there, but, although he feels very positive about the future, Manuel is clearly exasperated by the 'nothingness' of Germany. N.B. He loves Berlin, and seems to have a pleasantly cultured and tuned life there. He and Rozi were certainly the most interesting, hospitable and attractive (apart from Christine Klipping) people I met during my weekend in Berlin. After our conversation and exchange of addresses, they kindly drove me back to my hotel in a comfortable yellow Mercedes. From the Savigny, I took a bus for 60¢ to Tegel Airport, twenty minutes from the centre of Berlin.

The bar at Tegel was very pleasant and the whole airport is generally excellent. But, again, security precautions are rudimentary. A middle-aged Jewish businessman in front of me was made to unload his whole briefcase and demonstrate that his cameras, a regular Nikon and a Bolex Movie Camera, work, whereas I, dressed in black leather, was passed through without the slightest . . . and I am carrying a tape recorder which could easily conceal a Derringer or explosive. At best, travelling is as dangerous as it always has been.

I had a very interesting conversation for the last forty-five minutes of the flight with a lady sitting next to me who told me my German was very good and that got me going. We ended up discussing the beauty of German women as opposed to the beauty of Americans, who she said she found mostly too fat (!?).

She was in Berlin in 1943 during the bombing, and when the Russians came in, and she showed me a little book she bought then – a tiny English/German dictionary – she thought she would need it. She spoke a little English and she is a very good example of the resilience of the German people because she said "Well, when I got back to Berlin I found my man was dead. Well he was dead. First I thought I would go away, but then my friend and I we came back to Berlin . . . I had to get on with my life and I did. Now I have many friends . . ." and she smiled.

Quote for the day:

"The Germans have survived wars with the Romans, attacks by Huns, Magyars and Mogols, The Thirty Years War, Frederick the Great and Napoleon – and they will no doubt survive even my rule."

Adolf Hitler in conversation, Berlin 1945

Christopher Isherwood has been my favorite writer since I was fifteen years old. I read every one of his books at least twice. His Berlin stories are still the best account of what it was like to live in that city in the 1930s.

23

Christopher Isherwood
Meets William Burroughs

Christopher Isherwood has flown overnight from Los Angeles and is in town for four days to promote Christopher And His Kind *(Farrar Straus & Giroux $10). When I meet him at the Algonquin at 6 pm, he has not slept for 24 hours but shows no sign of strain. At 72, he appears fit and trim, looks younger than his years and seems buoyant about the attention* Christopher And His Kind *is receiving. He is here with his friend of the last twenty years, the artist Don Bachardy. Both wear casual ties, jackets, slacks, buckle shoes, and bracelets. Before walking out into the street to get a cab, Christopher puts on a double-breasted tan military-style raincoat and as the taxi pulls away in the direction of the Bowery, he begins the conversation by noticing my Qantas flight bag. I ask him if he's ever been to Australia.*

CHRISTOPHER ISHERWOOD: Several years ago. Tony Richardson was making that ill-fated *Ned Kelly* picture with Mick Jagger. We had an awful lot of fun. The journey down was wonderful. We flew to Tahiti, and then we went over to Bora Bora, and then we went to Western Samoa, then we had a sort of peep at Auckland, and finally got to Australia. And, of course, they were shooting out in the back country which – although it's not very far from Canberra – might just as well have been the proper outback. It's so empty there when you get outside. We were working on another project, so we made an excuse to make it into a business trip.

BACHARDY: Well, it actually was a business trip because he wanted the script right away.

BOCKRIS: Was that the *Frankenstein* film?

BACHARDY: No, it was a script of *I Claudius* that he was going to make. It was only prevented by his not being able to raise the money. He wanted Mick Jagger to play Caligula. And, actually, I think, after *Ned Kelly*, he and Jagger had a falling out, so it was then very difficult to raise money. He wanted Nichol Williams to play the part of Claudius. Apparently this new one that he's just finished *Joseph Andrews* is ah . . . I hear nothing but good things about it. Even he is pleased. And he's the first one to talk his own work down.

ISHERWOOD: Oh we're great admirers of several pictures of his, even ones that haven't done very well, like *Mademoiselle.* Did you ever see that? It was quite extraordinary.

BACHARDY: It's one of the films he made with Jeanne Moreau.

ISHERWOOD: I worked on *The Loved One* several years ago with him. As a whole it was a mess, but it had very amusing things in it. Some by Waugh and some just completely invented from elsewhere. It sort of rambled about all over the place.

BOCKRIS: It's rare that people make good movies out of really good books though, isn't it?

ISHERWOOD: Yes, I think it is. I happened not to like that particular Waugh nearly as much as some of the others. It doesn't hold up very well. There's a lot of plain old rather boring kind of anti-Americanism, anti-Californiaism. But we had the most awful amount of fun making it.

The cab pulls over on the deserted Bowery. It's very cold outside.

BOCKRIS: This is it right here. (*Cab stops in front of the locked iron gate of William Burroughs' headquarters, referred to by himself and his entourage as 'The Bunker'*). A foreboding entrance, but this is it. We can all hop out. *(Pays cab)* Give me twenty cents! Let's see . . . thanks a lot.

CAB DRIVER: *THANK YOU.*

BOCKRIS: *(On street)* Now. It's rather hard to get in here sometimes, it depends on whether the gate's open or not. Ah . . . the gate's not open. We have to go across to this bar here and telephone. Hope you don't mind . . .

BACHARDY: And he comes down and . . .

BOCKRIS: He comes down and unlocks the gate, yeah; it's not too frightening.

BACHARDY: Is that because it's a bad part of town?

BOCKRIS: Well, I mean, I don't think that's the reason actually that they have it locked. It's just that it's a big building and they lock the gate. He doesn't personally lock it.

We walk across the street to a bar half a block away. Icy wind. People wrapped in blankets leer out of doorways.

BOCKRIS: Now this bar's perfectly safe, perfectly safe. *(Open door, go into bar, loud noises of laughing, shouting, breaking glass, screams.)* I'm going to run to the back! *(Christopher and Don run very close behind. Voices from various conversations appear on tape: "That's my two dollars" etc.)* Is there a telephone in the bar?

BARTENDER: Nope.

BOCKRIS: *(Surprised)* There's not a telephone in the bar?

BARTENDER: No. There's one right there across the street.

BOCKRIS: Oh, okay, fine, thank you. Little mistake there. *(We thread back out of the bar stepping over a maze of broken glass, sawdust, blood and spittle and come out into street.)*

ISHERWOOD: *(Gleefully)* It's so Eugene O'Neill it's not true.

BOCKRIS: *(Running across street)* Can we make this? I think we can. Just! *(Christopher is dodging cabs beside me.)* Right, here we go again. *(Open door into second bar. Repeat of above atmosphere. Voices drift in and out of the tape: "You and me are gonna meet*

Allen Ginsberg at William Burroughs' Bunker, minutes before leaving on a three week
national tour of US campuses. What was he thinking? 1986. *(VB)*

Above: The girls gym class led by PJ Soles works out to the beat of *Rock 'n' Roll High School.*

Above: Brion Gysin, WSB, Albert Goldman, Keith Haring, Prudence Crowther. Kneeling

Above: Still from *Rock 'n' Roll High School* with the Ramones. Highschool blows up in background.

Above: Debbie Harry and Terry Southern at the Nova Convention, NYC 1978. *(Marcia Resnick)*

Above: John Girono escorts Allen Ginsberg out of the Bunker as Al hits road for three week US college tour, NYC 1986. *(VB)*

Above: Victor Bockris and his companion Lisa Krug at the Groucho Club in London, 1989. *(courtesy Hutchinson)*

Above: Bockris poses in front of Warhol's Electric Chair with *Making Tracks* in arms, illustrating a feeling authors often have on completion of a book. *(Stellan Holm)*

Above: Velvet Underground lawyer Christopher Whent has his copy of *Uptight* signed by Gerard Malanga, Sterling Morrison and Bockris. *(Bockris Archive)*

Above: WSB blows out birthday cake candles for his 70th at The Limelight, NYC 1984. VB cheers in background. *(Bockris Archive)*

Above: Burroughs and Bockris entertain The Police at Bill's 70th birthday. William thought they were real policemen. *(Bockris Archive)*

Above and below: Bockris and Burroughs sit on steps in front of Burroughs' house in Lawrence, Kansas. *(James Grauerholz)*

Damita Richter, America's No. 1 Punk Rock groupie and the author's companion during writing *With William Burroughs*, NYC 1979. *(Marcia Resnick)*

tomorrow, you better believe it! When your friend ain't around. I've had enough of your shit! All your goddam friends!") This is part of seeing William Burroughs though, isn't it? *(VOICE: "You're just a Puerto Rican Irish punk." VOICE: "Now wait a minute . . .")* *(On phone)* Hi! James. We're down on the corner here . . . righto . . . *(hang up)* Okay, they're coming down *(walk out into street)*. Is it worse to be a drug addict or an alcoholic do you think?

ISHERWOOD: God, I don't know, ah . . . I never tried either.

BOCKRIS: You do see more alcoholics in the world, generally, in these kind of areas, completely broken up, which means, I suppose, that either drug addicts just die or else they don't get in such bad shape.

ISHERWOOD: I've drunk rather a lot during my life, but I never came anywhere near to being an alcoholic. I don't know why, I guess it's just . . .

BOCKRIS: Here we are. James! *(Burroughs' secretary James Grauerholz appears behind the iron door with a key.)*

GRAUERHOLZ: How do you do?

VOICE IN STREET: Ah shut up!

BOCKRIS: *(Stepping aside)* Don Bachardy, James Grauerholz. Christopher Isherwood, James . . .

GRAUERHOLZ: It's a little bitter out there.

BOCKRIS: It's getting really cold and it's going to get colder. *(Walk up a flight of stone steps)* I'll lead the way *(walking into William Burroughs' spacious apartment)*. I love this white floor. Isn't it spacious? Hi Bill, nice to see you.

BURROUGHS: Nice to see you.

BOCKRIS: Christopher Isherwood, William Burroughs, Don Bachardy . . . *(shake hands, nod, smile)*

BURROUGHS: Why don't you take off your coats gentlemen. *(All put coats in Bill's room next to his pajamas which are lying neatly folded on his bed, come back into living room and sit around large conference table that Burroughs has in the kitchen section of his apartment, in a series of office style orange armchairs.)*

GRAUERHOLZ: Can I get you a drink?

EVERYBODY: YES!

ISHERWOOD: *(Looking around)* This is a marvelous place.

BURROUGHS: There are no windows. On the other hand there's no noise. This whole building was a YMCA. This used to be the locker room. The man upstairs has the gymnasium and downstairs is the swimming pool. It's a furniture shop now.

BOCKRIS: Where are sort of the mass bathrooms and things like that? Are there big rows of urinals?

BURROUGHS: Well there are two urinals right in there *(pointing toward bathroom)*. That's possibly all they had.

BOCKRIS: This is a real flying visit for you, you're just in for three days?

ISHERWOOD: Yes, we have to go back on Saturday. It's terrible.

BOCKRIS: Do you always come to New York when you have a book out?

ISHERWOOD: No, not really. I forget. Well, I did last time, that's right, but, no, they were just very good in that sort of way, they really get behind all that. *(Turning to Burroughs)* I'm going through a phase of being very pleased with Farrar Straus and Giroux, they seem to be interested in a really kind of behind you in your corner way.

BOCKRIS: Roger Straus has a great reputation for giving great parties. Did you see Christopher's new book?

BURROUGHS: No, I haven't seen it.

BOCKRIS: Oh, I should show you a copy. I have a copy here. It's a very beautiful book. *(Go into bedroom where book is in flight bag.)*

ISHERWOOD: People like it. I found the cover a little too elegant. The cover's a sort of pearl grey and it's got a drawing . . . well you'll see it.

BURROUGHS: Did they let you have anything to do with the cover?

ISHERWOOD: Well, yeah, in a way. They asked me.

(Re-enter from bedroom, give Burroughs a copy of Christopher Isherwood's new book which is a fascinating revisionist memoir of his early years in Berlin, collaboration with Auden, trip to China, etc, ending with his arrival in America in 1939.)

GRAUERHOLZ: I read an excerpt from this in *Christopher Street.*

ISHERWOOD: Oh that's right yes. I think we have the beginning of the book in there and there's also a bit in *Blueboy.* We did an absolute onslaught on the gay press because, after all, that's where our readers are. You must never forget that if one in every hundred gays bought a book of yours, you'd have absolutely smashing sales. You'd have about a hundred thousand copies.

BURROUGHS: I see that your South American book *The Condor and The Cow* isn't mentioned here.

ISHERWOOD: You read it?

BURROUGHS: Oh, indeed I did, because I went to all the same places.

ISHERWOOD: Oh, really? How exciting?

BURROUGHS: Yes.

ISHERWOOD: It might be over the page.

BURROUGHS: There were some great photos. Oh yes, here it is. Travel Books, yes indeed, sorry. Great photos. You knew, you knew Baron Wolfner, wasn't he a character in *Mr Norris?* (*Mr. Norris Changes Trains,* Isherwood's third novel that made him famous overnight in the early Thirties.)

ISHERWOOD: Yes, Von Pregnitz he's called.

BURROUGHS: Right, Von Pregnitz.

ISHERWOOD: Wolfner wasn't at all pleased. There was an insinuation that he thought I was attractive. This was when I was very young, of course. I did it really for purely dramatic reasons, I wasn't really . . .

GRAUERHOLZ: That's really a revelation because William has told me various tales about Baron Wolfner. You knew him, didn't you see him in Yugoslavia, is that the same period?

BURROUGHS: Knew him around Budapest.

ISHERWOOD: Well, please tell me because I heard that he was a sort of extreme sado-masochistic voyeur, that he liked to see people being beaten up. I don't really know, this may be terribly libelous. I mean by beaten up, really beaten up.

BURROUGHS: I think so yeah. But he had . . .

ISHERWOOD: Sort of gang . . .

BURROUGHS: Well, he had this sort of English public school veneer.

ISHERWOOD: He had a monocle screwed into his face, no ribbon, no security . . .

BURROUGHS: He died in London, I think . . .

ISHERWOOD: Oh really?

BURROUGHS: Yes, he escaped . . .

ISHERWOOD: Did he have a name was he sometimes called Yanchi?

BURROUGHS: Yanchi.

ISHERWOOD: Yanchi.

BOCKRIS: Sort of a nickname or something?

ISHERWOOD: Well, I suppose it was a diminutive, um . . .

BURROUGHS: It was simply his first name.

ISHERWOOD: Oh was it? I didn't know Yanchi was a first name.

BOCKRIS: The South American book of yours is the only one out of print isn't it?

ISHERWOOD: They're all out of print.

BOCKRIS: No they're not. No they're not.

ISHERWOOD: It's got to the point now where that's going to be a Spring offensive.

BURROUGHS: Very good.

BOCKRIS: But your books are all in print in England, perhaps that's what I mean.

ISHERWOOD: Oh yes, in England they are in paperback. But it got to a point here where there was almost nothing whatever except the New Directions Berlin books and they were unobtainable because New Directions has awful distribution. But now Farrar Straus are going to bring some out in their paperback series. Well, I made that rather a condition in a way, because I got tired of getting letters from people saying how can I get a copy of *A Single Man*, and I'm sure probably libraries have them stolen, so they are absolutely unobtainable. And that was one of the reasons I left Simon & Schuster.

BOCKRIS: Are you doing a second volume of this up until the present time?

ISHERWOOD: Oh, well, it would be much more than one volume. I have an awful lot of diaries. As soon as I came to this country I really started keeping diaries quite a bit and I suppose there are about three books that would come out. But actually I'm very interested at the moment in writing about our guru who just died, this Hindu monk, and I think I might write that first.

BOCKRIS: Is someone knocking?

BURROUGHS: Yes. Yes.

BOCKRIS: I'll get it.

BURROUGHS: I think it's a very beautiful . . .

ISHERWOOD: Hum?

BURROUGHS: I think it's a very well set-up book, really very well set-up.

ISHERWOOD: Oh good, I'm glad. Don did two drawings for the back and the one that they used we both feel now is too noble and the other one is just sort of a mad old man with one eye – it looks very funny at night – which we're going to have on the British edition.

BURROUGHS: Will it have a different title?

ISHERWOOD: No, no. No, no. *(Allen Ginsberg's secretary Richard Elovich arrives.)*

BURROUGHS: Ah Richard! Would you like a drink?

ELOVICH: A beer.

GRAUERHOLZ: Then we probably ought to head out.

BOCKRIS: Right. Is it very near here where we're going? *(We've been invited to dinner at a nearby loft.)*

BURROUGHS: Well, it's sort of betwixt and between, almost too near to take a cab and too far to walk. I don't mind walking really. It's about eight blocks or something.

BOCKRIS: Well Christopher enjoyed going into those bars across the street, didn't you?

ISHERWOOD: Oh, yeah, it was fantastic. I had been there ages ago. It was just so incredibly classic. I mean it was just so absolutely *The Iceman Cometh*, and then they were having fights in both bars. One fight seemed very serious, coming up in the absolutely classic fashion, very dangerous . . . But I was, I felt hardly dressed for it, if you know what I mean. I once got stuck absolutely in the midst of Harlem because the taxi driver lost the way and I was dressed up to go to The Institute of Arts and Letters, so I had a sort of something in my hand. I think it was a briefcase, and I said to myself, because I had to go into a bar to phone, I said "You're a Doctor!" and I rushed in in the way I imagine a doctor getting very quickly through to the hospital because his patient . . . and sort of *"don't bother me!"* They didn't like it at all. Oh it's a terrible feeling. At least I imagined it was a terrible feeling, but you can't possibly tell unless something happens to you . . . We've been in Morocco quite . . .

BURROUGHS: Oh, really, where?

ISHERWOOD: Well, we went to see Gavin Lambert, who was plowing cachia, and then he took us around on a bit of a tour. We went to Shawan and Fez and Marrakesh, and then out to the coast where we saw Paul Bowles.

BURROUGHS: Oh, how was Paul?

ISHERWOOD: He was in a very good mood, very sort of benign, and also Mrabet was there. And, it amuses me – I

271

don't know why it was quite so funny – but there was a young man, quite a young guy, who was sort of obviously just learning the ropes, the sort of Tangier ropes, and he had a pipe, a kif pipe, which he was very proud of and he brought this thing out with great circumstance. You know, he wanted to draw attention to it, and then he said to me – and I suddenly thought it was just like a Victorian scene in a drawing room – he said to me "Do you mind if I smoke?" And I said – just like a Victorian lady – I said "Not at all, I love the smell of it." And then, of course, the poor boy could not get the pipe to light. It was thoroughly embarrassing. And sort of he was trying to be very salty with his . . . and the damn thing simply wouldn't work.

BOCKRIS: I had no idea Sally Bowles was named after Paul Bowles until I read it in this book. I never thought of it. It's so obvious if you think of it.

ISHERWOOD: Well, I mean, it's just that I hardly knew him, I just thought he was very cute. He was twenty. I just sort of picked around for a name and it was going around in my head, you know, and what would go with Bowles, oh Sally Bowles, that's it! But Paul said in his autobiography that I was superior. I suppose I was, what, about 26 – and he was 20.

BOCKRIS: Where did you meet him?

ISHERWOOD: In Berlin.

BURROUGHS: My first visit to Berlin was not long ago, two months . . .

ISHERWOOD: *(Very intrigued)* How did it seem to you?

BURROUGHS: Well I'd never seen it before and I went there for a reading with Allen Ginsberg and Susan Sontag, and I went and saw the Wall. The area between the East and the West is populated by thousands of rabbits.

ISHERWOOD: Don't the guards shoot them?

BURROUGHS: It would be very improper.

ISHERWOOD: Does it seem menacing now?

BURROUGHS: Well you could see that it could be menacing *(chuckling)* if you did the wrong thing.

ISHERWOOD: But they don't mind tourists coming and gaping?

BURROUGHS: No, no. Tourists come and gape and they have sort of platforms where they can go up and see the Wall.

ISHERWOOD: But do people come through still or they don't?

BURROUGHS: I just don't know. I guess someone did. Allen went over to see some poet who was in bad graces with the Communist Party. And we also saw Beckett. Beckett was living in the Academy building.

ISHERWOOD: Oh, really?

BURROUGHS: Yes, in the Tiergarten. He gave us an audience for about twenty minutes.

ISHERWOOD: I always imagined Beckett was somewhere always living in France.

BURROUGHS: Well he was just there to direct his play. John Calder, my publisher, was there and he said, well, he would see us all briefly. All, by all I mean Susan Sontag, Allen Ginsberg, Fred Jordan, Professor Hollerer and your reporter. An audience.

BACHARDY: Has he been directing his plays for a long time?

BURROUGHS: Yes, yes, indeed, he always directs his plays. He feels he's the only one competent to do it. According to John Calder, he's really a brilliant director. I've never seen what he's directed.

GRAUERHOLZ: I was curious to know whether you've been doing anything in the movie business recently?

ISHERWOOD: I was commissioned to adapt Scott Fitzgerald's second novel *The Beautiful and the Damned* and it came out awfully well, we felt, and we really preserved the book. The dialogue was between 70–80% Fitzgerald, and everybody liked it, and then, suddenly, there was a change up in the higher office and they decided no more Fitzgerald. A bad bet! He's done for! Or something.

BOCKRIS: But, you know, *Gatsby* made money. They made

money before it came out, from selling rights.

BURROUGHS: I cannot *believe* that they made money on that film.

BOCKRIS: Well, I can understand your attitude, but I read in *Time Magazine* that just through selling all sorts of rights they broke even. Is *The Last Tycoon* also a flop?

ISHERWOOD: It was better than we expected.

BOCKRIS: Did you basically enjoy it?

ISHERWOOD: Well, I, I, I mean, I was a bit bored with a lot of it.

BURROUGHS: It's always been my contention that the best movies based on books are made from bad books. *Treasure of The Sierra Madre*: great film, the book . . . *Marathon Man*'s a great film and the book is . . . Because you don't have anything in the way. You just have to say (*demonstrating with his hands*) "Well, here's the idea," and you can handle it anyway you want, you don't have to defend the classics. I always thought Fitzgerald is not for the movies. That dialogue is wooden, the plot is nothing. It's all in the prose that can't be gotten onto the screen – like the last three pages of this great English prose. It's not, it's not, it's not a movie.

ISHERWOOD: Oh absolutely yes. I think it's unmakeable.

BURROUGHS: And then I can think of any number of bad or second-rate novels that would make great films.

BOCKRIS: The only book of yours that's been done as a movie is *Goodbye to Berlin*, right?

ISHERWOOD: Yes, I mean that really was, I don't know, there are other things that could have been done, I think, like *A Single Man* might . . .

BOCKRIS: But you had two movies out of that book and a couple of Broadway shows?

ISHERWOOD: Yes.

BACHARDY: All that remains is a TV series.

ISHERWOOD: Have they ever filmed any of your books?

BURROUGHS: No.

BOCKRIS: Aren't they considering *Junky?* Isn't that on the boards?

BURROUGHS: Oh no, it's not on the boards at all.

BOCKRIS: You know Penguin is re-publishing *Junky* this February. They're doing it in the original version. The version that was published in '53 was heavily censored . . .

As the conversation breaks up James Grauerholz suggests we move on to dinner: "Shall we go?" Christopher and Don go into the bathroom. We all mill around getting our coats on and generally arranging ourselves. A lot of shouting back and forth.

BOCKRIS: Are they in the urinals? *(Going into urinals with tape recorder.)* Is this an inspection of the urinals here?

ISHERWOOD: Yes.

BOCKRIS: This is an unusual bathroom isn't it? It's nice, roomy. *(Coming back into living room.)* This is a great typewriter too. What kind of typewriter do you have?

BURROUGHS: Oh it's just an old Olympia.

BOCKRIS: It's one of the best typewriters ever made. I have one of these myself . . . *(All walk downstairs and into the street. A stirring icy wind is blowing down the Bowery.)*

BURROUGHS: I'm sort of partial to walking. I think by the time we got a cab . . . it's easier this way. *(To Isherwood)* The way to walk is just lean forward like this *(Burroughs leans into the wind)*.

I knew Robert Mapplethorpe before he was famous. He was one of the most fascinating people to talk to among my generation. That's why I taped this piece on the way to the airport with him. Along with *Hell/Sontag*, *The Captain's Cocktail Party* and the *Isherwood/Burroughs*, it best evokes those far away, halcyon days in the Seventies when life still seemed infinitely rich with opportunity, creativity and joy. This whole book is about heroes. Robert was one of my biggest heroes.

24

Robert Mapplethorpe Takes Off

Saturday, October 16th 1977, 2 pm. Robert Mapplethorpe is going to California on a TWA flight. I am arriving at his fifth-floor Bond Street studio loft to join him on his trip to the airport. The elevator door opens into Robert's studio and he is hovering somewhat nervously ten feet away standing on now one now another high heel cowboy boot. He leads me into the sitting area of his beautifully appointed loft. Sam Wagstaff stands and shakes hands. As the tape goes on Robert has just given me the four photos to be used with this interview.

VICTOR BOCKRIS: It's a really beautiful day. Have you been outside today? It's so great. (Robert is walking round apartment, making last minute preparations. He is wearing tight jeans, a corduroy jacket, and tinted sunglasses.) Why are you going to California?
ROBERT MAPPLETHORPE: Just to take pictures.
BOCKRIS: Where are you going to be in California?
MAPPLETHORPE: Los Angeles for a few days and then San Francisco.
BOCKRIS: Do you like LA more than San Francisco?
MAPPLETHORPE: I've never been to San Francisco.
BOCKRIS: I used to go out there a lot, but I don't like that much anymore. (Robert walks nervously into the next room checking suitcases, looking in drawers, whispering to Sam who has followed him.) I shout: DO YOU HAVE A CAB

COMING AT TWO-THIRTY OR ARE YOU JUST GOING TO PICK ONE UP?

MAPPLETHORPE: We'll just pick one up. We have plenty of time.

BOCKRIS: Yeah, we're in no big hurry.

MAPPLETHORPE: (He comes back into room putting a cellophane bag in his coat pocket.) I was just reading the review of Patti's new album in the *New York Times*.

BOCKRIS: Oh, yeah, that John Rockwell thing. I read that yesterday. Yeah. I heard some of her new stuff on the radio this morning. It sounded real good. Is she happy with the new album?

MAPPLETHORPE: She was until this review. But she's in Europe so I don't know. It's not very nice what they say on her picture.

BOCKRIS: Oh I didn't notice that even. (Walk over, read caption under photo: "has lost some of her individuality.") Oh yeah, that's nice. You did Television's cover for their album. How's that come out?

MAPPLETHORPE: I'm quite happy with the picture. I can show it to you. But they want something less professional so they're going to use a xerox which I don't mind. I like what they're gonna do (gets portfolio to show me picture).

BOCKRIS: They're going to use a color xerox.

MAPPLETHORPE: Yeah. He's a complete dictator, Tom, and it's alright because in the end he knows what he wants. You know it's not a matter of . . . I have the xerox too.

BOCKRIS: Great. I'd love to see that.

MAPPLETHORPE: That's rough (showing me color xerox).

BOCKRIS: I like the quality. I like the skin tones.

MAPPLETHORPE: Nobody's used a xerox.

BOCKRIS: I don't understand it. These things look really great. I love it.

MAPPLETHORPE: Yeah. The thing I don't like about it is they always look the same. I mean they're always good. You can't miss. But the fact that nobody did it yet . . . I mean that, with a really elegant black border, will look great.

BOCKRIS: What's the album like?

MAPPLETHORPE: I don't know. I haven't heard. They're just in the studio now.

BOCKRIS: You shot the cover as soon as they got the contract?

MAPPLETHORPE: Yeah. They wanted it immediately 'cos he was sort of fanatical about having it come out the way he wanted it so he wanted to start from the start so that he could . . .

BOCKRIS: Begin the package first and then make the record that goes in it. That's a good idea.

MAPPLETHORPE: He doesn't want the art director to touch it. I don't really like his music. It's just too abstracted for my taste.

BOCKRIS: But he's a very interesting guy, isn't he. Tom Verlaine?

MAPPLETHORPE: I guess.

BOCKRIS: People say he's so dictatorial.

MAPPLETHORPE: I think that's a mistake though. You know, it's alright with this situation. I don't mind it for the album, and he got a very good producer to do his album, somebody who worked with The Beatles. But Tom's taken over and that's a mistake because there is a reason for a producer, especially on your first album. And if he's not willing to listen to anybody . . .

BOCKRIS: I thought it was a real pity Richard Hell left Television. I think a lot of people did. Do you know him? He was interesting because he was so sort of energetic, he had a crazy face and stuff, and I just understood that they had horrible arguments and he'd basically been forced out.

MAPPLETHORPE: I would think that was probably it, because Tom probably wants it all for himself.

BOCKRIS: Are these other people in the group interesting?

MAPPLETHORPE: Maybe the one on his left. The others are very nice but they're completely . . . when the album cover was picked out it was the other boy who came up with him and chose.

BOCKRIS: (Looks around loft.) It's a strange space. It seems so thin and long. How far does it go down? (We get up and walk to end of loft.)

MAPPLETHORPE: There's a darkroom down here. (Opens door, we lean in.)

BOCKRIS: Oh it's really nice. It's so clean. (We walk into next room.) This is where you cut everything. Bathroom.

MAPPLETHORPE: And then the studio in the front where I do pictures, but I prefer not using the studio.

BOCKRIS: Oh you have the black wall up there in the studio? (We walk up full length of loft to studio. One black high heel slipper sits on a ladder next to a champagne glass.) Ha ha ha ha ha. It's nice though. Why don't you like using it?

MAPPLETHORPE: Because it's too safe. It's too easy to take pictures here. You get the same light every day.

BOCKRIS: You just know what's going to happen basically.

MAPPLETHORPE: Yeah and you know the backgrounds. (We walk back to the lounge area.)

BOCKRIS: Do you travel constantly Robert? You always seem to be going somewhere whenever I meet you. Is that true or is it just coincidence?

MAPPLETHORPE: It's been true for the last three years I guess. I prefer (kneels down, zips up suitcase) travelling to staying in one place.

BOCKRIS: So do I. I really do a lot. I even get excited when I go to Philadelphia for the weekend.

MAPPLETHORPE: You're from England?

BOCKRIS: But I've been in the States for a long time.

MAPPLETHORPE: I think we should sort of go.

BOCKRIS: Okay. (Get up put on coats get bags etc.) This is a new idea I have. Every time somebody I know goes to the airport I go out in the cab with them and that becomes an interview. It's . . .

MAPPLETHORPE: It's a good idea.

BOCKRIS: It's a good idea, isn't it? This is the first one I've done.

MAPPLETHORPE: Good idea. I think what you should do is try to get people who have cars.

BOCKRIS: I wrote to the editor of *Chic* magazine and I said I am going to the airport with Robert Mapplethorpe in his limousine.

(Walking to the front door, standing by the elevator.)

ELEVATOR OPERATOR: Can you all get in? (Elevator is crammed with plywood etc. Elevator operator is fellow tenant, female.)

BOCKRIS: We're all going down, yeah. (Sound of buzz, sound of falling lumber etc.) What's that buzzing sound?

ELEVATOR OPERATOR: It's a saw.

BOCKRIS: Oh.

ELEVATOR OPERATOR: My aim wasn't too good.

BOCKRIS: No that's . . . I'll just hold on here for a second.

MAPPLETHORPE: When I come back I want your place to be finished.

ELEVATOR OPERATOR: Yes sir! Yes sir! Of course.

MAPPLETHORPE: It might be actually, yeah?

ELEVATOR OPERATOR: Yes. It'll be done in two weeks. Normally I would have said a week but I learn.

(Elevator arrives, door opens, squeeze out carefully.)

BOCKRIS: Right. I've got the door. OH!

MAPPLETHORPE: Okay. Thanks a lot, see you.

ELEVATOR OPERATOR: Bye bye.

(Walking out into street, bright sunlight.)

BOCKRIS: This is a wonderful day to go flying on. I really envy you. Do you like flying?

MAPPLETHORPE: Uummmm, yes.

BOCKRIS: Why'd you hesitate?

MAPPLETHORPE: Well I like getting someplace too. But I don't really get off on flying. I usually end up being critical of the people sitting around me.

BOCKRIS: I think I just like the idea I suppose. I love travelling on ships. People should travel on ships more often.

MAPPLETHORPE: I could guess that from your hat.

BOCKRIS: No. I got this at San Simeon. (I am wearing a white sailor hat with San Simeon in black letters on it purchased at William Randolph Hearst's fabulous California coastal estate.)

SAM WAGSTAFF: What are these? (We approach a series of extremely ornate ashtrays on foot high stands, bright shiny colors of cut glass and bronze covered in transparent plastic wrapping.)

BOCKRIS: Wow, really crazy . . .

MAPPLETHORPE: Strange.

BOCKRIS: Do you have a camera with you? (Robert indicates the large metal case he is carrying.) Is that your camera? It really looks like a gun case.

MAPPLETHORPE: You have the pictures, right?

BOCKRIS: I have the pictures, yeah definitely. Is that a Checker there?

MAPPLETHORPE: We do want a Checker.

WAGSTAFF: I think we better go (indicating to go across street).

BOCKRIS: Do you ever see William Burroughs round here? He walks around here a lot.

MAPPLETHORPE: I don't think I've ever seen him on the street.

BOCKRIS: I guess he doesn't go for a stroll or anything like that. (Robert giggles.) He has a nice place. He painted his floor white so he has a completely white apartment.

MAPPLETHORPE: Nothing in it?

BOCKRIS: Just a big conference table in the middle.

MAPPLETHORPE: Does he still have his orgone box?

BOCKRIS: No I don't think he has that. His places are always so clean.

MAPPLETHORPE: (Sam is waving for a cab.) Is this a Checker?

BOCKRIS: Is it a Checker, yeah? (Cab pulls up at curb.) You climb in with everything and I'll get in when you're settled. (Robert says goodbye to Sam, gets in cab with camera, tripod. Sam puts Robert's large suitcase in front next to driver.)

MAPPLETHORPE: Can I go to Kennedy airport?

BOCKRIS: Nice to meet you. (Shakes with Sam.)

WAGSTAFF: Nice to meet you too. Have a good time. (Cab drives away.)

BOCKRIS: Just want to get this open a little bit for some air (opening window).

MAPPLETHORPE: I'm so nervous that I'm going to leave something behind.

BOCKRIS: I'm terribly nervous too. I'm terribly nervous just because you're going somewhere. I feel like I'm going too. It's really exciting.

MAPPLETHORPE: But it's even more when you have a camera.

BOCKRIS: So tell me about your trip to California. Do you have appointments out there or what?

MAPPLETHORPE: No. I don't have any appointments but I'm going to LA. I was going to go straight to San Francisco instead of going to LA for a few days. I'm staying with Diane de Beauvau.

BOCKRIS: Is she living out there now?

MAPPLETHORPE: No, she's out there with Halston.

BOCKRIS: Which airline?

MAPPLETHORPE: TWA.

CAB DRIVER: Kennedy right?

MAPPLETHORPE: Kennedy. You're spilling it on your coat. Did you get some.

BOCKRIS: No. I've got to get a little bit more.

MAPPLETHORPE: So I'll go out there and see her and take some pictures and Halston will be out there, so hopefully I'll be able to photograph some of the models because he's doing a tour . . .

BOCKRIS: Sniff sniff snooooort. Ha ha ha ha, thanks very much. So, er, then you'll go down to . . .

MAPPLETHORPE: Oh then I'm going to San Francisco and I think I'll stay at a gay hotel. And take some pictures of boys for a show at The Kitchen. That's one of the reasons I'm going out there. It's a good place to take sexy pictures.

BOCKRIS: You have a very formal style. Do you feel that your photographs are very formal?

MAPPLETHORPE: If you're going to go through an ordeal you might as well be meticulous about it. I always hate it if something's off. You know, for me, if something is a straight line then it should be straight, it shouldn't be at all off.

BOCKRIS: Let's find out what this is (taking envelope out of pocket).

MAPPLETHORPE: What's that?

BOCKRIS: Speed.

MAPPLETHORPE: Speed?

BOCKRIS: Yeah. It's not very strong, it's quite weak in fact, but it's quite interesting. Don't take it if you don't want.

MAPPLETHORPE: I think I want to sleep on the plane.

BOCKRIS: Okay. This might help you sleep.

MAPPLETHORPE: It's a down?

BOCKRIS: Yeah it's not very strong. So you've got this formal camera with a tripod?

MAPPLETHORPE: I worked very closely with the people I was photographing. I'd chosen a picture and said let's do it this way. And so anyway. I never studied Polaroid and never wanted to be a photographer, but when you say it has something formal or old about it, it has an understanding of early photography. There's no better way of knowing about someone's work than buying it because you get so involved.

First of all, the idea of putting out money makes you look carefully and to hold the photograph in your hand is another thing. I got very involved in the quality that they were able to get and it's one of the reasons I use slow film. Now I use a two-and-a-quarter and I still have a tripod. I don't have to use it, but if I get back to New York and see a picture that's just crooked and I think well I really wanted it not to be crooked . . .

BOCKRIS: And if you had the tripod it wouldn't have been. God. It's interesting, but I didn't realize you took so many pictures of sex all the time. I've seen a lot of those English pictures and I've seen some of the structures, and then I've seen pictures you've taken of people, like Patti, but I haven't seen much of your sex stuff.

MAPPLETHORPE: The sex stuff is mostly Polaroids. I got away from it a little bit, but now I want to go back.

BOCKRIS: Is it okay to have the window open like this? It doesn't bother you? (Noise of wind blowing in as cab tears over big bridge.)

MAPPLETHORPE: No. (He picks up a large leather bound portfolio and we start looking at pictures.)

BOCKRIS: Oh this is a great picture. (David Hockney with Henry Geldzahler.)

MAPPLETHORPE: (Flips to sex shots.) I mean this is more of the kind of thing I'm going to show at The Kitchen. (Flips through more.)

BOCKRIS: Those are really nice.

MAPPLETHORPE: But I want to go even further. Earlier things had more to do with sex and I got out of it a little bit because it was putting too many off and I wasn't making any money out of it.

BOCKRIS: In what way was it putting people off?

MAPPLETHORPE: Well, I'd go to sell a portrait to somebody, get them interested in having a commission, and then they see that (pointing at a big cock with a ring around it) and

287

even if there's only one, it makes everything have sexual overtones.

BOCKRIS: But actually your reputation on your more straightforward portrait stuff has got you to a position where you can afford to go back and work with this again.

MAPPLETHORPE: The idea is to have a show of the straight portraits and then all of a sudden come out with the sex stuff. And it's too late. You sort of trick people (giggles). Because I think this work in dealing with sexual images is the most difficult thing and the most interesting. If I was buying one of my photographs I would buy one of those, but unless I establish myself on another level it's hard to begin.

BOCKRIS: Do you have any cigarettes?

MAPPLETHORPE: I hope so.

BOCKRIS: I'd just like one. Oh a Kool would be very nice. Thanks. Uh I see what you mean exactly.

MAPPLETHORPE: Have you seen this book here?

BOCKRIS: Which one?

MAPPLETHORPE: Did you see this at Norman's when I came over?

BOCKRIS: No.

MAPPLETHORPE: Well these are mostly London. (Opens up portfolio of formal portraits taken in London and we begin to look through it.)

BOCKRIS: When you were staying there did you have your camera on a tripod in the room all the time or did you have to set it up every time you wanted to do something?

MAPPLETHORPE: No. I just kept it on a tripod in my room.

BOCKRIS: Who's that?

MAPPLETHORPE: This is Catherine Guinness taken in London before she came to New York.

BOCKRIS: That's great. I think she's really beautiful.

MAPPLETHORPE: She's really good. This is a girl that I'd met when she was a model and I don't know too many models so I thought it'd be nice to have a model. So I went over there, I got stoned with her and talked to her for a while and showed her photographs. I always show people photographs before I take them. And then we had lunch and then took pictures, so I did get to know her by the time I got to the pictures. I think it's a big mistake that a lot of photographers make. They have people come over and snap the pictures and that's it and they don't have any relationship . . .

BOCKRIS: Well, you see someone in a different way when you know them, obviously.

MAPPLETHORPE: This is an Irish hustler that I met at The Casserole one night. He was sitting next to me at another table and I was having dinner with a girl and I just thought he was very extraordinary so I went and talked to him a bit and then he came over to visit.

BOCKRIS: This is also really extraordinary. I mean who are these people?

MAPPLETHORPE: Well this is the Bishop of Suffolk and the former Archbishop of Canterbury whose name is Ramsey. I met the Bishop of Suffolk at a dinner party and we got along and talked and he got into the idea of being photographed because the Archbishop was coming that weekend and so he arranged the whole thing.

BOCKRIS: Whose children are they?

MAPPLETHORPE: They're the children of Colin Tennant who owns the island of Mustique, and he's fantastic, this boy.

BOCKRIS: He looks fantastic. How old is he?

MAPPLETHORPE: He's mad but he's great. He's nineteen.

BOCKRIS: He looks so young.

MAPPLETHORPE: Well he's about eighteen there, seventeen . . . This is Marianne Faithfull.

BOCKRIS: Marianne Faithfull! When was that taken?

MAPPLETHORPE: At Catherine Guinness's house about a year-and-a-half ago.

BOCKRIS: That's nice, a really interesting picture of her. Do you like taking pictures of Patti?

MAPPLETHORPE: She's great to photograph. I know that I'm going to have something great out of each session that I do. I guess a lot has to do with our relationship with each other.

BOCKRIS: Yeah because you've known her for ten years. Can you get to know someone for too long to photograph them?

MAPPLETHORPE: I think you can get too involved with them to take photographs. If I was still living in the same house it might be a little hard. It seems to be better after you're not sexually involved. (Continues flipping through portfolio.)

BOCKRIS: Who's that?

MAPPLETHORPE: Virginia Dwan's daughter, Candace. That's an old boyfriend of mine, David Croland, taken out in Southampton. These were taken on my last trip to California about a year ago.

BOCKRIS: What you like doing most after you know someone for a while is going to their place . . .

MAPPLETHORPE: For them it's better as well because they're more relaxed in their own apartment and it's more about them. It's like Avedon's portfolio of pictures is sort of opposite to my approach. It's a rather cold approach to the whole thing.

BOCKRIS: It's not an interpretation of the person at all.

MAPPLETHORPE: No, no exactly it's . . .

BOCKRIS: He did a picture of William Burroughs at the same time I was writing a piece about Burroughs and his portrait was really very good. I knew Burroughs by the end of my interpretation well enough to recognize how good his picture was, but that stuff in *Rolling Stone* left me cold.

MAPPLETHORPE: They're moving to New York. I'm going to see them out in San Francisco.

BOCKRIS: I think it's really great that they're so interested in photography. I've always been more interested in photographers than writers. I've always been more influenced by

photographers, always have had some kind of a close relationship with a photographer at one time or another in my
career. I always found I learned more from that.

MAPPLETHORPE: It's very close to poetry isn't it?

BOCKRIS: Oh yeah. Hiro said something about photography
being closest to the art of conversation.

MAPPLETHORPE: (Flipping pages.) This is in Mustique.

BOCKRIS: Where's that?

MAPPLETHORPE: Off the coast of Venezuela.

BOCKRIS: When were you down there?

MAPPLETHORPE: It was about March of last year. It was the
most extraordinary vacation. This is that girl that I know really
well. Her name's Catherine Tennant. She's the half sister of
Colin who owns the island. (Going through various pictures
taken on Mustique.) That's the Vendredi Treize, a great title for
that picture (beautiful shot of yacht off island). Here's Carolina
Herrera who's as much of a jet-setter as anyone. She and her
husband are sort of the couple. They're charming and attractive, witty and all that. They travel quite a bit. Here's the whore
of the island. Here's another Venezuelan.

BOCKRIS: These are really fabulous.

MAPPLETHORPE: Yeah. I mean that's the island really, you
know, and it's about dressing up. It's about looking like that.
It's the most social . . .

BOCKRIS: It's incredible.

MAPPLETHORPE: Kind of out of the way in the middle of
nowhere . . . See I don't go up to somebody right away and
say, "Oh I want to take your picture." I find it sort of vulgar to
do that.

BOCKRIS: So you basically don't even bring your camera out
for a little while when you visit someone. (Looking at picture
of Princess Margaret.) What was taking that like?

MAPPLETHORPE: That was sort of tricky to get that picture.
She was with Roddy Llewelyn and that was at the same time
that all the story came out, the same week I was there, and she

was uptight about what her sister would think I suppose. When I took those pictures Roddy had been sitting there and we swapped seats, but I mean that was a situation where I really wanted to take Princess Margaret's picture. Unfortunately, that was the best I could do which is only a formal snapshot. I had a tripod and I was taking pictures around the table with it. But you have to be very careful, you know to get somebody's trust . . . and Colin, the owner, didn't know me very well, wasn't quite sure whether to trust me so it was a very . . .

BOCKRIS: You can almost tell from looking at the photographs how well you know the person.

MAPPLETHORPE: (Opens another portfolio.) That's taken at Fred Hughes' house in Paris. These are taken in the house I was staying in there. (A series of portraits of pieces of furniture, doorknobs, etc.)

BOCKRIS: It really is so strikingly different it's got me a little speechless.

MAPPLETHORPE: It's something I've always wanted to do and there I was in the situation where I did it. This is taken at Fred Hughes' house. They have a fantastic place in Paris. That's Versailles. (Series of shots of French countryside. Robert closes the book.) But see I want to do it all. I don't want to just concentrate on one thing. I want to know that I can do it all. (We are now arriving at airport.) You can come out, right?

BOCKRIS: Oh yeah, I'll come out and sit with you for a while. We'll have a drink.

MAPPLETHORPE: I haven't got to leave until five.

BOCKRIS: You haven't got to get on the plane until five? Oh God!

MAPPLETHORPE: How did we get here in half-an-hour?

BOCKRIS: Yeah well see I was surprised at how much time you were giving yourself, but I thought you were just very careful or something.

MAPPLETHORPE: Yes I am. (Get out of cab and wait while Robert pays fare.)

BOCKRIS: Are you going to need a skycap or shall we just carry these ourselves?

MAPPLETHORPE: No, we can carry them.

BOCKRIS: Okay I'll get, I'll get, er, yeah, fine. (We walk.) "IN". Is that us, is that where we want to be?

MAPPLETHORPE: I hope so.

BOCKRIS: This is the building that looks like a bird from the outside. We can walk around the airport or something. Is that fun?

MAPPLETHORPE: We'll find somewhere to have a snort.

BOCKRIS: Any of these places would be okay to check in. You can just check in anywhere.

MAPPLETHORPE: I haven't bought my ticket.

BOCKRIS: You have to buy a ticket? Well probably it's over the other side. (Walking around looking.) OH ROBERT! Over here, "Purchase Tickets." Just put all that stuff down right here and I'll stand by it and then you go and purchase your ticket and come back and we'll get in line.

Robert is going to purchase his ticket. Let me just describe what he's taking with him on the trip. He has here a Haliburton camera case. It's quite large. It has a combination lock and it's made of metal and it looks like the kind of case you'd carry a hunting rifle in, broken up in three little pieces. And his camera is in there. Then there's a very nice-looking black tripod which he always takes with him. And a very presentable suitcase. I don't know what kind it is, has some tags from Marseilles, J.F.K. airport, Air France, Swissair. So Robert has been travelling a lot lately. He's been to France and England, he's been . . . I'm sort of surprised Robert hasn't bought a ticket before he came out here, what if he gets here and there isn't a ticket? On the other hand that's probably the modern way to travel, just to go to the airport as if it was a bus station or something, get on the train. Have I got a ticket for the train to Philadelphia tonight? No. Just go to the station and get one. Oh, he is alright, he seems to be getting his money out, yes he actually is getting a ticket.

Now we have one-and-a-half hours of tape, that seems about right, I guess I'll stay here. The suitcase is big, its about two-and-a-half feet long, maybe one-and-a-half feet high and about a foot thick. He must be taking quite a lot of clothes with him, he's going for three weeks. I'm going to sit down on his camera case here. I hope he doesn't mind. This is so great, it's really great to be here at TWA's check-in counter at J.F.K. It's such a nice day here, it's so lovely to be here. I guess I'll have some white wine. Oh Robert's waving, I'll have to get . . .

MAPPLETHORPE: (Comes over) In fact I think we'll put one of these portfolios in the case so I don't have to carry both.

(END OF TAPE ONE/BEGIN TAPE TWO.)

BOCKRIS: What kind of suitcase is this? Any particular kind of suitcase?
MAPPLETHORPE: Oh yeah it is, but I don't know what.
BOCKRIS: It's nice.
MAPPLETHORPE: Somebody said it was the best one they could get.
TWA: Where would you like to sit?
MAPPLETHORPE: By a window.
TWA: Boarding starts at four-thirty, up the steps to the left.
MAPPLETHORPE: Thank you.
TWA: There's a snack bar around the corner and a coffee shop upstairs.
MAPPLETHORPE: Thank you. (Walking away from counter.)
BOCKRIS: The snack bar doesn't sound too good does it, let's go . . .
MAPPLETHORPE: No, let's go . . .
BOCKRIS: Upstairs I think, yeah.

MAPPLETHORPE: Paris has a fantastic place to eat in at the new airport.

BOCKRIS: Well they just pay so much attention . . .

MAPPLETHORPE: Have you seen the new airport?

BOCKRIS: No I haven't, no. They just pay attention to food in France. You can have something good to eat anywhere. I don't like these red and white colors much, do you? (Looking around building.)

MAPPLETHORPE: It's like something at the World's Fair.

BOCKRIS: Yeah I like more sort of the blue and grey airport look, the sort of British Airways. Do you have a particular airline you like best?

MAPPLETHORPE: Usually I have somebody else make a reservation.

BOCKRIS: I was really surprised you didn't buy your ticket until you got here. Look there goes Professor Einstein! Robert here yeah. Do you like this building?

MAPPLETHORPE: Oh . . . I guess not.

BOCKRIS: I don't really like it. I thought I did. I tried to. Speaking of Paris, there's the Paris Cafe. Let's sit over there, shall we at the side, this is good. (Look at menus.)

MAPPLETHORPE: You're really into those gloves. (I am pulling off a pair of tan leather gloves.)

BOCKRIS: I love these gloves.

MAPPLETHORPE: As a matter of fact, that's one of the reasons I like it to get cold because I love gloves.

BOCKRIS: I like gloves that you can do everything when you've got them on. It's very hard to get men's gloves like that. I tried to buy women's gloves, but I was very surprised, my hands don't fit into them. There must be women with big hands.

MAPPLETHORPE: Yeah. I tried women's gloves and I ripped them pulling them off.

BOCKRIS: I was going to buy one of those women's suits that look just like men's clothes except they fit me better and they're so cheap.

MAPPLETHORPE: Have you spent much time in San Francisco?

BOCKRIS: Yeah. Quite a lot.

MAPPLETHORPE: Because I never did. I went there . . . do you know what you want?

BOCKRIS: Would you like some white wine?

MAPPLETHORPE: I'd prefer not.

BOCKRIS: Okay. So I'm just going to have a drink. A glass of white wine please.

MAPPLETHORPE: Could I have a cheeseburger and a Coca-Cola. No ice. Is it cold without ice?

WAITRESS: Uuuummmm.

MAPPLETHORPE: If it's warm put a little ice.

WAITRESS: Okay.

MAPPLETHORPE: That really irritates me that . . . you know beer they never serve with ice.

BOCKRIS: San Francisco is exactly what you read it was in the newspapers in the Sixties.

MAPPLETHORPE: I'm sorry I sort of missed that, but I did go out there once. The first fight I had with Patti, I went to California. I left school and just went out there for about four weeks.

BOCKRIS: You just had a fight and left?

MAPPLETHORPE: Well it was more than that, I guess it went on for a while and we sort of split up for a little but . . . and we ended up going back and during that time I went to California. I flew out to San Francisco not knowing anyone and met some boy on the plane who was sort of a hippie and he was going to stay in a commune so I just went with him. It was in the middle of a suburban area where all these young kids had taken over this house and it was amazing. They were all very sweet and made food for everybody and if some didn't have money you know . . . it worked at that time.

BOCKRIS: Oh it did, it worked for about two or three years.

MAPPLETHORPE: And you know everybody took all kinds of

drugs. I wonder what happened to them all? Probably half of them are dead. They were so young. I mean, fourteen, and, you know, that's pretty young.

BOCKRIS: But it would be strange to go back now. I just find it a little dull, but maybe that's because I have relatives there which is a bad thing to have anywhere.

MAPPLETHORPE: My attraction out there is to go out there to go to leather bars and meet some people to photograph.

BOCKRIS: What a great way to live, just to travel and portray the situation.

MAPPLETHORPE: Oh there's nothing greater than having just a camera with you and some clothes and not having to worry about things I worry about in New York, like just having the printer come in . . .

BOCKRIS: You have printers who come and print your work?

MAPPLETHORPE: One boy who does.

BOCKRIS: You take the pictures and just give him the film?

MAPPLETHORPE: He does the negatives and then I go through. It takes me a good week really to decide what negatives and that's half taking pictures, is the selection. I get quite obsessive about which ones are the right ones to do. Doing a commissioned portrait say, really takes a long time for me because the actual picture taking is sometimes only fifteen minutes for a role of film but that isn't what it's about. Once you have the contacts figuring out which one . . . Then I make pieces with the pictures. And the framing is very important. At my show at Holly's (which opens Feb 5), that would be what the show will be about, triples and doubles and a couple of singles and sometimes a sequence.

BOCKRIS: Is that a new thing photographers are doing right now or is that, has that been done for a long time?

MAPPLETHORPE: I have the greatest picture of Queen Victoria which is a sequential photograph taken by Princess Alexandra. It's four photographs put on one page. But the thing about sequential photographs, it's easier for people to read it as art, so it's a gimmick. And it comes out of the conceptual ideas, relationship of one to the next, you know. I had an argument for about three weeks with Sam. You know he has this fantastic collection, and I had the argument with him about the idea after having done a lot of sequential photographs. I was saying that it's really a wrong thing to do because it's so often that you see one photograph out of the three that's really the best picture and why have three when there's one that's better. I think if each picture holds up equally well then you can get away with it. But the whole conceptual attitude about photography is rather annoying. They think they can get away with bad quality just because ???? idea. "My idea is so important that I don't have ???? photograph." And I think it's an excuse, because I used to almost use it myself, because I didn't know that much about printing and stuff. But there's no reason why, if you're going to work with an idea, that the idea can't be there as well as a beautiful image to go with it. I think that's what it should be about and not just the idea.

BOCKRIS: What kind of life do you lead in New York?

MAPPLETHORPE: It goes from being very social to going to leather bars to working. Those are the three things I do.

BOCKRIS: Tell me what you do what percent of the time.

MAPPLETHORPE: It depends on the week.

BOCKRIS: One week you spend the whole time in a leather bar and then the next . . .

MAPPLETHORPE: It does almost work that way. I really get off on being social, but I don't like to only do that. It's a great advantage to be able to move from one world to another.

BOCKRIS: Why did you enjoy Andy's party so much the other night?

MAPPLETHORPE: Because of the person I was with. A combination of being on the right drugs and being with the right people. And it seemed glamorous. There were a few stars, the cameras were clicking, everybody seemed in a good . . . I don't know. I had a good time. You are walking through the door and having four people say hi, hi. I get off on it (giggles). In fact I think what we should do is go to the bathroom and . . .

BOCKRIS: Yeah. I guess so. Just leave all our stuff here do you think?

MAPPLETHORPE: We'll go one at a time.

BOCKRIS: Okay right. Want to take this with you (offering tape recorder)? No I guess not.

(GO TO THE BATHROOM INDIVIDUALLY. COME BACK.)

BOCKRIS: Sorry I was so long. I was having so much fun. Do you find the amount of sex you're having relates to the amount of work you are doing? I don't know whether that's true or not.

MAPPLETHORPE: Do you mean having more sex doing more work?

BOCKRIS: A lot of people think . . .

MAPPLETHORPE: No. I mean if anything could be my downfall it could be that. I could just let myself get into sex considering it's the most exciting thing in the world to do.

BOCKRIS: So you have to discipline yourself?

MAPPLETHORPE: I have to a little bit. I was a nymphomaniac when I was in Paris. Well there's coke there for one thing and it makes me think of sex a lot more than I would otherwise. Some people don't, you know, are just obsessed with what they're doing, their work.

BOCKRIS: I go through periods with sex having a lot of sex and then having no sex. It does relate to my work somehow, but I can't figure out exactly how. Do you work pretty constantly? 'Cos those periods where you don't work are pretty horrible.

MAPPLETHORPE: Yeah. I think few people would admit but one way of disciplining oneself is by imposing a guilt thing and I feel really nervous and neurotic if I haven't actually accomplished anything and I think it's more a self-imposed guilt. I mean I get neurotic if I haven't done something. Like when I do the social thing that really is work because it's about looking for people to photograph. So when I do the sexual thing it's work as well. You know I do take pictures of people and stuff so I mean . . . Well, to what extent are your photographs an autobiography?

BOCKRIS: Quite. You're photographing your life.

MAPPLETHORPE: Exactly. I mean I guess it is pretty close.

BOCKRIS: I always think that's the most interesting art when someone describes whatever is right under their nose.

MAPPLETHORPE: Isn't all great art that though?

BOCKRIS: I think so. Did you get paid well for doing Patti's cover?

MAPPLETHORPE: Not really. I exam, for the first album you don't get paid the same as if you did the Stones' album cover. Then you get $5,000. It certainly wasn't that. And Television is less.

BOCKRIS: How do you relate to money?

MAPPLETHORPE: I like it because it means that you can do so much more. If you can make it work for you. I've lost money for the last few years, enormous amounts, so it'll take me years before I catch up, but the timing is right. Up until this point I've been able to do it. It'll probably take another two years before I really see clear.

BOCKRIS: If *Vogue* asks you to do fashion spreads is that the kind of thing you will just do?

MAPPLETHORPE: If I can control it. I want to do something more than studio photography. I just think it's too boring to do. But I want very much to do a spread in *Vogue*. But I don't want to be a fashion photographer because I know fashion photographers and they might as well be brick layers. It's nine-to-five and it's not very creative and it can't be 'cos everything has to come out and you can't take risks so you end up repeating yourself. You know what you can do without taking risks. And in the end they start resenting the fact that they are commercial photographers and end up having a chip on their shoulder because they want more than that and in fact I think most of them should be doing exactly what they're doing. Everybody's sort of getting grand ideas about photography. "I too am an artist," is what it comes to and you know, not every photographer is an artist. It's one of the things that I think drugs had something to do with, people getting egos that went beyond their capabilities.

BOCKRIS: Well I think the mistake a lot of people make is they think you have to have a big ego in order to be an artist. I'm not sure if that's really true or not. I don't think it is really true.

MAPPLETHORPE: Well I suppose every artist I know has a big ego.

BOCKRIS: Well maybe it depends on how . . .

MAPPLETHORPE: No, not the ego. It's the outfrontness of . . .

BOCKRIS: I find that very offputting in a lot of people.

MAPPLETHORPE: But I think a lot of people that have that outfront ego are in fact not artists, you know it's a sort of neurotic . . .

BOCKRIS: And they get a long way on that ego . . .

MAPPLETHORPE: It's a funny thing that's happening to photography because it's obviously going to become very important in the art world. It's happening I think partly because painting hasn't been interesting. I think photography is a perfect medium for this era. It's so quick. The idea of belaboring a painting, working for a month at one image is just not conducive to this period of time.

BOCKRIS: I just moved into a new apartment and the only art work I'm going to have in the apartment is going to be photographs. It's so nice to live with photographs.

MAPPLETHORPE: When I get back to New York I'll show you a row of good pictures that I have. I got very much into the framing and presenting of them and they look fantastic.

Even in galleries they don't know how to display and one of the great problems of the show I'm having is figure out which way I want to show them you know. I think the way to do it is to not make it look like a photography show.

BOCKRIS: I'll buy a packet of cigarettes before we go, okay? (Taking another.) I think I'll have another glass of wine. Did you always think Patti was going to make it when you were living with her?

MAPPLETHORPE: She had something that nobody else I've ever met had.

BOCKRIS: What's that? It's alright I'm just waving at the waitress. Can I have another glass of white wine please?

WAITRESS: Would you like some more coffee?

BOCKRIS: Maybe that's a crazy question to say, "What's that?"

MAPPLETHORPE: Well she's a genius in one sense or another. In a certain way she's brilliant. In other ways she isn't but everybody has certain . . .

BOCKRIS: Are you into music or not?

MAPPLETHORPE: No. But I know when something's right. I mean I'm always looking at photographs and paintings and trying to find something that I think would be great and I have a terrible problem with painting and sculpture right now. Photographs as well. I don't think it's good enough. In a way we've had a low point.

BOCKRIS: Yes, we have had a low point. But when did it start?

MAPPLETHORPE: Post Pop. Pop was great.

BOCKRIS: Do you like to live alone or with someone in the best of all states.

MAPPLETHORPE: Alone.

BOCKRIS: You don't ever get lonely?

MAPPLETHORPE: Well I go out a lot. No I can't stand having people around in the same environment. I mean, I usually have a lover of one sort or another. Patti's the only person I ever lived with. We lived together for seven years.

BOCKRIS: How old are you now?

MAPPLETHORPE: 29.

WAITRESS: Can I take this away from you, are you finished?

MAPPLETHORPE: Umhum. You know Sam, whom I've known very well for the last four years, had a great painting collection and decided he wasn't getting off on painting and he was selling it off when I met him and he was into something called Arica at the time and he diced he wasn't going to collect anything, but he's an obsessive collector and he's a great collector, one of the best. And I knew him for about a year and I was just getting more and more involved in photography at the time and I suggested to him that he collect photographs. And he started looking a little and anyway he became obsessed about it and put together the best collection in America, but the reason I suggested it was half because if you have that money you have to think of it. If you're putting over a million dollars into something you can't just do it for fun. Although people hate the term 'investment' when it comes up in relation to art. It really annoys me, they think they're beyond it. I mean bullshit, anybody that buys something for more than a hundred dollars is not just . . . Anyway that worked perfectly because the things are worth three times what Sam paid for them.

BOCKRIS: What do you think a collector is? It seems to me a collector is an artist in the sense of being an audience.

MAPPLETHORPE: The great ones are. I mean Sam's an artist. I've met people like that guy Colin Tennant who owns the island. I mean I may not think the island is the way I'd make it, but he's an artist. He's created something that no artist has ever done. Smithson's Spiral Jetty is nothing compared to creating a whole excitement and glamour about a little island called 'mosquito' in French. It's like great businessmen are too. I sold a couple of photographs to Steve Ross, the President of Warner Communications. Talk about high-powered executives. It was so impressive. First of all, he's quite attractive. And he has a very attractive office and he's the boyfriend of Amanda Burden and you know with a conference room on one side and a private secretary. He only had ten minutes for me and I went up there with the pictures and he had bought something from Holly before and the secretary sat there and sort of helped, but the whole thing he had it really down. He was trying to eat his lunch because he had another conference.

BOCKRIS: You must have a lot of confidence basically.

MAPPLETHORPE: I certainly do have that. I mean I have confidence about my work.

BOCKRIS: That's confidence about your life.

MAPPLETHORPE: I mean I don't think of anybody as being competitive with me. I don't worry about that. I don't see anything that is about what I'm doing.

BOCKRIS: It's unusual not to have any competition with particular people. Most people do I think.

MAPPLETHORPE: I'd almost like that in a way.

BOCKRIS: It gets you out of bed in the morning.

MAPPLETHORPE: I've always wanted to find some sort of school I could attach myself to.

BOCKRIS: That always helps so much. A school provides instant publicity.

(I get up to get a fresh pack of cigarettes. When I come back Robert is staring across the airport at the runway. Jets are floating in and out. The tape has ended.)